John's Gospel

from

THE LEARNING BIBLE

New International Version

John's Gospel

from
THE
LEARNING
BIBLE

New International Version

AMERICAN BIBLE SOCIETY
NEW YORK

John's Gospel from THE LEARNING BIBLE
New International Version

Consulting editors: Howard Clark Kee, David G. Burke, Steven W. Berneking,
and Erroll F. Rhodes.
Development editors: Charles Houser and Scott Tunseth.
Art development editor: Carol Sailors.
Contributing editors: Mark A. Throntveit, Carol Throntveit, Celia Brewer Marshall,
David A. Renwick, and J. Clinton McCann Jr.
Cover design by Bill Smith Studio.
Text design by A Good Thing, Inc.
Composition and page make-up by The Livingstone Corporation, www.livingstonecorp.com.

ISBN 1-58516-649-9

Printed in the United States of America
Eng. Portion NIV560P-112670
ABS-7/02-10,000—RRD1

New International Version ®
Copyright © 1993, 1978, 1984 by
International Bible Society.

FOREWORD

THE NEW INTERNATIONAL VERSION (NIV) is a completely new translation of the Holy Bible made by over a hundred scholars working directly from the best available Hebrew, Aramaic, and Greek texts. From the beginning of the project, the Committee on Bible Translation, a self-governing body of fifteen biblical scholars, held to certain goals for the *New International Version*: that it would be an accurate translation and one that would have clarity and literary quality and so prove suitable for public and private reading, teaching, preaching, memorizing, and liturgical use. The Committee also sought to preserve some measure of continuity with the long tradition of translating the Scriptures into English.

In working toward these goals, the translators were united in their commitment to the authority and infallibility of the Bible as God's Word in written form. They believe that it contains the divine answer to the deepest needs of humanity, that it sheds unique light on our path in a dark world, and that it sets forth the way to our eternal well-being. (For more about the NIV translation of the Bible, see the article called "About the *New International Version*" on page 69.)

CONTENTS

Alphabetical Listing with Abbreviations

Book	Abbrev.	Test.	Book	Abbrev.	Test.
Acts	Acts	NT	Judges	Judg	OT
Amos	Amos	OT	1 Kings	1 Kgs	OT
1 Chronicles	1 Chr	OT	2 Kings	2 Kgs	OT
2 Chronicles	2 Chr	OT	Lamentations	Lam	OT
Colossians	Col	NT	Leviticus	Lev	OT
1 Corinthians	1 Cor	NT	Luke	Luke	NT
2 Corinthians	2 Cor	NT	Malachi	Mal	OT
Daniel	Dan	OT	Mark	Mark	NT
Deuteronomy	Deut	OT	Matthew	Matt	NT
Ecclesiastes	Eccl	OT	Micah	Mic	OT
Ephesians	Eph	NT	Nahum	Nah	OT
Esther	Esth	OT	Nehemiah	Neh	OT
Exodus	Exod	OT	Numbers	Num	OT
Ezekiel	Ezek	OT	Obadiah	Obad	OT
Ezra	Ezra	OT	1 Peter	1 Pet	NT
Galatians	Gal	NT	2 Peter	2 Pet	NT
Genesis	Gen	OT	Philemon	Phlm	NT
Habakkuk	Hab	OT	Philippians	Phil	NT
Haggai	Hag	OT	Proverbs	Prov	OT
Hebrews	Heb	NT	Psalms	Ps	OT
Hosea	Hos	OT	Revelation	Rev	NT
Isaiah	Isa	OT	Romans	Rom	NT
James	Jas	NT	Ruth	Ruth	OT
Jeremiah	Jer	OT	1 Samuel	1 Sam	OT
Job	Job	OT	2 Samuel	2 Sam	OT
Joel	Joel	OT	Song of Songs	Song	OT
John	John	NT	1 Thessalonians	1 Thes	NT
1 John	1 John	NT	2 Thessalonians	2 Thes	NT
2 John	2 John	NT	1 Timothy	1 Tim	NT
3 John	3 John	NT	2 Timothy	2 Tim	NT
Jonah	Jonah	OT	Titus	Titus	NT
Joshua	Josh	OT	Zechariah	Zech	OT
Jude	Jude	NT	Zephaniah	Zeph	OT

HOW TO USE THE LEARNING BIBLE

The *Learning Bible* is an easy and colorful way to discover God's Word. Whether you began reading the Bible as a child or whether you are taking on this challenge now for the first time, the *Learning Bible* will help you get the most out of the time you set aside for this important educational and spiritual experience. This short article will introduce you to the many features and tools that are built into the *Learning Bible*. Take a moment to locate them in the text and become familiar with how they work. Each feature is designed to help you in one of three ways: (1) Point you in the right direction; (2) Get you the information you need; and (3) Help you connect with the Bible's message.

Getting You Pointed in the Right Direction

When church members have been surveyed and asked why they don't read the Bible on their own more often, the most frequent replies are "I don't know where to begin" and "I began at the beginning with GENESIS, but couldn't get through LEVITICUS." The Bible is a difficult book to read and even a modern translation can be hard to understand, because the events and customs it describes happened "long ago and far away" (some of them thousands of years ago). Because the Bible is a collection of many books, it doesn't matter which book of the Bible you read first. Some people like to begin with GENESIS. Others want to learn about Jesus right away, and select one of the Gospels. Wherever you begin, the *Learning Bible* has a number of tools to help you find your footing and head you in the right direction on the path of discovery.

Introductions and Outlines

Each book of the Bible starts with an Introduction, which gives information about who may have written the book and when it may have been written. It also introduces the book's important themes and provides you with clues to understanding its structure, including an outline of the book's contents.

In addition, the *Learning Bible* has Introductions to the Old and New Testaments and to groups of books within each Testament. These Introductions will give you a quick overview of the books contained in these sections and can help you decide which ones you'll want to read first.

Section Headings and Summary Introductions

The Bible text, which runs in the wide columns on either side of the book's "gutter," is divided by headings that have been added to make it easy for the reader to follow the action or the framework of a book. The large purple Section Headings are followed by short summaries of key events or teachings that will be covered in the Scripture text to follow. Some of these large sections may be further divided by blue-green headings that are printed in all capital letters. Note that both types of headings are taken directly from the outlines in the book Introductions. Then there are smaller, black headings that divide the Bible text even further. Bible references are usually noted by Bible book name, then the number of the chapter followed by the verse number or numbers. For guidance on how to look up these parallel text references, see the explanation in "How To Look Up a Scripture Reference" (shaded box below).

Getting You the Information You Need

The *Learning Bible* is designed so that you won't have to leave your chair in order to get the information you need to understand what's going on in the Bible. Definitions of words and explanations of concepts and customs that may be unfamiliar are on the page near the Scripture text they refer to. Or, you can find them in clearly identified sections positioned throughout the *Learning Bible*.

The New International Version

The *New International Version (NIV)* is a best-selling translation that is clear and easy to understand. Over a hundred scholars worked directly from the best available Hebrew, Aramaic, and Greek texts to produce a translation that is accurate and has literary quality suitable for public and private reading. For more about the translation, see "About the NIV" on page 69.

Notes

The *Learning Bible* provides six different categories of notes, which appear in the narrow outside columns on each page. Each of these categories is marked with its own colored symbol:

- Geography
- People and Nations
- Objects, Plants, and Animals
- History and Culture
- Ideas and Concepts
- Cross references

Mini-Articles and Background Articles

Some important topics call for more information than can be given in a simple note in the margin. The *Learning Bible* has over

HOW TO LOOK UP A SCRIPTURE REFERENCE

Here's a helpful hint for those who are unfamiliar with looking up Bible passages. Like many books, the Bible is divided into units (here called "books" of the Bible); and each book is divided into chapters. However, unlike most books, chapters are divided into much smaller units called "verses" (usually consisting of a sentence or two). Both chapters and verses are numbered. This provides a very convenient and useful system for identifying specific verses in the Bible. References to Bible passages will be listed in the following way.

BOOK TITLE ABBREVIATION

Matt 6:10

CHAPTER NUMBER

VERSE NUMBER

Matt 6:10-14 — INDICATES VERSES 10 THROUGH 14 WITHIN CHAPTER 6

Matt 6:10—7:21 — INDICATES ALL VERSES FROM CHAPTER 6, VERSE 10 THROUGH CHAPTER 7, VERSE 21

The more you look up Scripture references, the sooner you will become familiar with the abbreviations used and this system of notation. In the meantime, the "Alphabetical Listing with Abbreviations" will help you become familiar with any abbreviations you don't recognize.

one hundred mini-articles on such topics positioned at various places in the text. Like the marginal notes, they are keyed with one of the five color symbols to let you know if it is an article about Geography, People, an Object, History and Culture, or an Idea and Concept. The *Learning Bible* also includes fifteen longer background articles that give an overview of important topics. These are collected in three separate sections: (1) Articles on the Bible and how it came to be, (2) Articles on the ancient world and the religion of Israel, and (3) Articles on the world in the time of Jesus.

Cross References

Sometimes the author of one book of the Bible quotes another book of the Bible or makes a statement that is very similar to what another biblical author has written. Where this has happened, the *Learning Bible* lists a cross reference. Cross references are shown in one of two ways: (1) Listed within a note, footnote, or article; or (2) listed without text or comment after the orange symbol at the bottom of the narrow column on any page.

Footnotes

The *NIV* Bible was translated into English from ancient Greek and Hebrew manuscripts. These manuscripts are very old and were copied out by hand. Consequently, they do not always agree with one another word for word. When these differences occur, translators need to decide which manuscript to use in the translation. After making their decision, they often list other possible renderings in a footnote. They also use footnotes to identify when the original language text is unclear and to explain other decisions they had to make.

Charts and Bible Timeline

The *Learning Bible* provides throughout the book a number of charts that summarize detailed information and display it in a way that is easy for the reader to look up. At the back of the *Learning Bible* is a Bible Timeline that provides an easy-to-follow overview of the history of the Ancient World from the earliest times through the time of the apostles.

Maps

The events described in the Bible occurred over a period of thousands of years and in places as far apart as Mesopotamia, Egypt, Greece, and Rome. To help the reader keep track of the way the "Bible Lands" changed from one era to the next, the *Learning Bible* provides a number of reference maps. Large, full-color, topographical maps keyed to specific periods of history are gathered together in the Mini-Atlas at the back of the Bible. These provide a good overview of the Holy Land and include most of the place names you will encounter when reading the Bible. From time to time, one of the articles or marginal notes will direct you to one of these maps. In addition, there are a number of small spot maps positioned at various points within the text for quick reference.

Illustrations and Photographs

The *Learning Bible* also provides illustrations, diagrams, and photographs to help you understand life in Bible times and to get a view of the way the Holy Land looks today.

Helping You Connect with the Bible's Message

Most people who read the Bible are looking for more than information about ancient people and customs. They believe (or hope) it contains truth, comfort, and spiritual insight that will provide them with guidance for their daily lives. The *Learning Bible* has a number of features that will help you understand and appreciate the impact God's Word has had and continues to have.

Art from Around the World

The events and stories in the Bible have touched people's hearts and lives throughout the world for many centuries. The

Learning Bible includes reproductions of paintings, drawings, sculpture, and other powerful works of art from many cultures.

Questions about Each Book of the Bible

Sections of "Reflection Questions" are provided at various points within the Scripture books. These questions are intended to help you review the content of the book, discover what it means, and see how it relates to your life today. You can answer these questions silently to yourself, keep a "devotional journal" of your responses, or use the questions as a discussion guide for group Bible study.

Memory Verses

Many people find comfort and strength from memorizing Scripture verses. A number of important and inspirational verses have been highlighted in the top outside corners of the pages. These are by no means the *only* verses worth memorizing, but they do represent the kinds of messages that you'll discover each time you read the Bible.

> *Your statutes are wonderful;*
> *therefore I obey them.*
> *The unfolding of your words gives light;*
> *it gives understanding to the simple.*
> *I open my mouth and pant,*
> *longing for your commands.*
> Psalm 119:129-131

JOHN'S GOSPEL

JOHN

Signs point us in the right direction.
As you read JOHN, watch for the signs (miracles)
that point out how Jesus is God's powerful Son.

WHAT MAKES JOHN SPECIAL?

JOHN tells about the life and words of Jesus in a way that is different from the Gospels of MATTHEW, MARK, and LUKE. The key events in Jesus' life are mentioned, but JOHN pays a lot of attention to three questions:

1. *Who is Jesus?* In the first chapter, the author calls Jesus the "Word," who was present with God from the beginning and participated with God in creating everything. This Word became a human being (1:14), so people could see what God is really like. John the Baptist calls Jesus the "Lamb of God, who takes away the sin of the world" (1:29). Philip soon believed Jesus to be "the one Moses wrote about in the Law, and about whom the prophets also wrote" (1:45). Nathanael says to Jesus, "You are the Son of God; you are the King of Israel" (1:49). In this Gospel, Jesus describes himself as: the Messiah (4:25, 26); the bread of life (6:35); the source of living water (7:37-39); the good shepherd (10:14); the resurrection and the life (11:25); the way, the truth, and the life (14:6); and the true vine (15:1). JOHN also reports that when Jesus explains who he is and what God is doing through him, he uses the words "I am." These are the same words God told Moses to use when referring to God (Exod 3:13-15).

2. *What did Jesus do that proves that he is God's Son?* JOHN describes many miracles ("signs") that point to the deeper meaning of Jesus' actions and words. When Jesus changes water into wine, calms the storm on the lake, feeds the hungry crowd, heals the sick, and brings the dead to life, he shows that he is God's Son and that he is doing what God sent him to do: bring new life to all people.

3. *What was the relationship between Jesus and his followers and those who were against him?* This Gospel helps us to better understand the struggle between Jesus and those who followed his new teachings and those who felt they could not do that and still remain loyal to the teachings of the Law of Moses.

WHY WAS JOHN WRITTEN?

John 20:31 clearly states why the Gospel was written: "These are written that you may believe that Jesus is the Christ, the Son of God, and that by believing you may have life in his name."

light and darkness: Light and darkness are important images in JOHN. The first thing God created was light (Gen 1:3). In the Bible, light is used to describe God or God's word (1 John 1:5; Ps 119:105), and those people or things that reveal God's truth (Isa 49:6). Darkness refers to places of pain and suffering (Ps 107:10) or confusion (Eccl 2:14). God's opponents are called the rulers of darkness (Eph 6:12), and those who do not do what God expects may be thrown "into the darkness" (Matt 22:13). John uses the opposites "light" and "darkness" to refer to the struggle between those who accept Jesus and those who refuse to believe (see, for example, 1:4-9; 8:12-20).

son of Joseph from Nazareth: Both MATTHEW and LUKE report that Mary was a virgin when she became pregnant with Jesus (Matt 1:18; Luke 1:30-35). Mary's husband, Joseph, was a carpenter or builder from Nazareth (Matt 1:18—2:23). MATTHEW gives a list of his ancestors (Matt 1:1-17) and explains that everyone thought Joseph was Jesus' father.

Nazareth was a small village in the hills of Galilee overlooking caravan routes through Palestine. Since the Messiah was expected to come from David's family, whose home was in Bethlehem in Judea, some people wondered if Jesus from Nazareth could be the one the Jewish people expected (see, for example, 1:46).

Lamb of God: John the Baptist said that Jesus was like the lamb that would be silently led to be slaughtered (1:29; see also Isa 53:4-12) in order to restore God's people. "The Lamb" also refers to the lambs that were killed at the Passover Feast (Exod 12), which was celebrated each year to remind the people how God had set Israel free from slavery in Egypt. The apostle Paul also refers to Jesus as "our Passover lamb [who] has been sacrificed" (1 Cor 5:7). See also Rom 3:24, 25; Rev 5:6-13.

1:1-3 *In the beginning . . . the Word:* This same phrase is used in Genesis 1, which describes how God created all things. The Greek word translated here as "Word" also means "reason" or "purpose." In the Jewish Scriptures (Old Testament), God used Wisdom to create the world (Prov 8:12, 22, 23). The Word also shows God's power, a power that was able to create simply by speaking (see "God said" in Gen 1). The Word refers to Jesus Christ, who brings God's message to all people and reveals God's power and purpose. These verses show that even though Jesus is God's Son born as a human being, he is also truly God, because he has existed with God from the beginning of time.

1:4, 5 *light . . . darkness:* See the note on p. 7.

1:6 *John:* See the mini-article called "John the Baptist," p. 118.

1:7 *that light:* Here, "light" refers to Jesus. See also verse 9.

1:11 *that which was his own:* Jesus was Jewish. He came to his own people as Messiah, but many people from his own country did not believe in him or accept his message.

1:12 *children of God:* This phrase is used to describe those who trust Jesus as God's true light.

1:14 *The Word became flesh:* Jesus lived as a human being in order to show God's glory. Sometimes this is referred to as the "incarnation."

The Gospel seems to have been written down a number of years after Jesus died and was raised from death, and probably after the Romans destroyed the temple and ended a Jewish uprising in A.D. 70.

The action in JOHN shifts back and forth quickly between Galilee and the area in and around Jerusalem. Time is also marked by certain Jewish festivals. The basic outline of JOHN can be described in the following way:

> **Who Jesus is (1:1-51)**
>
> **Jesus' seven miracles (2:1—11:44)**
>> These miracles caused people to see Jesus as either the Messiah or an enemy.
>> *Miracle one—Jesus at a wedding in Cana (2:1-11)*
>> Jesus in Judea and Samaria (2:12—4:42)
>>> *Miracle two—Jesus heals a royal official's son (4:43-54)*
>>> *Miracle three—Jesus heals an invalid (5:1-47)*
>>> *Miracle four—Jesus feeds five thousand (6:1-15)*
>>> *Miracle five—Jesus walks on the water (6:16-24)*
>> Jesus teaches in Galilee and Judea (6:25—8:59)
>>> *Miracle six—Jesus heals a man born blind (9:1-41)*
>> The good shepherd and the true flock (10:1-42)
>>> *Miracle seven—Jesus brings Lazarus to life (11:1-44)*
>
> **Jesus' final days (11:45—19:42)**
>> Preparations for Jesus' death (11:45—12:50)
>> Jesus prepares his followers (13:1—17:26)
>> Jesus' arrest, trial, and death on a cross (18:1—19:42)
>
> **Jesus appears to his followers (20:1—21:25)**

Who Jesus Is

The first chapter of JOHN makes it clear from the start just who Jesus is. An opening hymn (1:1-14) identifies Jesus as the Word in human form. John the Baptist and some of Jesus' first disciples recognize that Jesus is the Lamb of God, Messiah, Rabbi, and the Son of God.

The Word Became Flesh

1 In the beginning was the Word, and the Word was with God, and the Word was God. ²He was with God in the beginning.

³Through him all things were made; without him nothing was made that has been made. ⁴In him was life, and that life was the light of men. ⁵The light shines in the darkness, but the darkness has not understood[a] it.

⁶There came a man who was sent from God; his name was John. ⁷He came as a witness to testify concerning that light, so that

---

[a] 5 Or *darkness, and the darkness has not overcome*

through him all men might believe. ⁸He himself was not the light; he came only as a witness to the light. ⁹The true light that gives light to every man was coming into the world.ᵃ

¹⁰He was in the world, and though the world was made through him, the world did not recognize him. ¹¹He came to that which was his own, but his own did not receive him. ¹²Yet to all who received him, to those who believed in his name, he gave the right to become children of God— ¹³children born not of natural descent,ᵇ nor of human decision or a husband's will, but born of God.

¹⁴The Word became flesh and made his dwelling among us. We have seen his glory, the glory of the One and Only,ᶜ who came from the Father, full of grace and truth.

¹⁵John testifies concerning him. He cries out, saying, "This was he of whom I said, 'He who comes after me has surpassed me because he was before me.'" ¹⁶From the fullness of his grace we have all received one blessing after another. ¹⁷For the law was given through Moses; grace and truth came through Jesus Christ. ¹⁸No one has ever seen God, but God the One and Only,ᶜ ᵈ who is at the Father's side, has made him known.

John the Baptist Denies Being the Christ

¹⁹Now this was John's testimony when the Jews of Jerusalem sent priests and Levites to ask him who he was. ²⁰He did not fail to confess, but confessed freely, "I am not the Christ.ᵉ"

²¹They asked him, "Then who are you? Are you Elijah?"

He said, "I am not."

"Are you the Prophet?"

He answered, "No."

²²Finally they said, "Who are you? Give us an answer to take back to those who sent us. What do you say about yourself?"

²³John replied in the words of Isaiah the prophet, "I am the voice of one calling in the desert, 'Make straight the way for the Lord.'"ᶠ

²⁴Now some Pharisees who had been sent ²⁵questioned him, "Why then do you baptize if you are not the Christ, nor Elijah, nor the Prophet?"

²⁶"I baptize withᵍ water," John replied, "but among you stands one you do not know. ²⁷He is the one who comes after me, the thongs of whose sandals I am not worthy to untie."

²⁸This all happened at Bethany on the other side of the Jordan, where John was baptizing.

ᵃ9 Or *This was the true light that gives light to every man who comes into the world* ᵇ13 Greek *of bloods* ᶜ14,18 Or *the Only Begotten* ᵈ18 Some manuscripts *but the only* (or *only begotten*) *Son* ᵉ20 Or *Messiah*. "The Christ" (Greek) and "the Messiah" (Hebrew) both mean "the Anointed One"; also in verse 25.
ᶠ23 Isaiah 40:3 ᵍ26 Or *in*; also in verses 31 and 33

1:15 *John:* See the note at 1:6. See also 1:29, 30.

1:16 *the fullness of his grace:* Refers to Jesus. See the mini-article called "Son of God," p. 10.

1:17 *the law was given through Moses:* The Law of Moses contained instructions that told the Israelite people how they should live and worship. Jesus did not intend to throw out the law, but he wanted to show how people can fill their lives with "grace and truth." See also the mini-article called "Law," p. 119.

1:19, 20 *priests:* The "priests" may refer to the high priest, who was in charge of the temple in Jerusalem, influential Jewish teachers such as the Pharisees, and other community leaders. The Roman authorities allowed these leaders to make decisions about things that affected the Jewish people, especially their religion. See also the mini-article called "Israel's Priests," p. 116.

1:19, 20 *the Christ:* See the mini-article called "Messiah (Chosen One)," p. 120.

1:21 *Elijah . . . the Prophet:* See the mini-article called "Elijah," p. 114. See also Mal 4:5. The "Prophet" had been spoken of by Moses (Deut 18:15).

1:23 *Isaiah:* A prophet in Judah from about 740 to 701 B.C.

1:24 *Pharisees:* These religious Jews believed in following God's law as closely as possible. See also the article called "The World of Jesus: Peoples, Powers, and Politics," p. 103.

1:26 *I baptize with water:* See the mini-article called "Baptism," p. 109.

1:27 *thongs of whose sandals I am not worthy to untie:* One of the duties of a servant or slave.

1:6 Matt 3:1; Mark 1:4; Luke 3:1, 2. **1:23** Isa 40:3 (Septuagint).

1:29 *Lamb of God:* See the note on p. 7.

1:32 *Spirit:* See the mini-article called "Holy Spirit," p. 48.

1:33 *baptize with the Holy Spirit:* Just as God poured the Spirit on Jesus (1:32), Jesus will pour out the Spirit on those who follow him.

1:34 *Son of God:* John is claiming that Jesus is the one God has chosen to rule over Israel. See also the mini-article called "Son of God," below.

1:36 *Look, the Lamb of God:* See the note p. 7.

1:40 *Andrew:* Andrew was a fisherman who came from Bethsaida, but he lived in Capernaum (Mark 1:21, 29) with his brother Simon Peter.

Jesus the Lamb of God

[29]The next day John saw Jesus coming toward him and said, "Look, the Lamb of God, who takes away the sin of the world! [30]This is the one I meant when I said, 'A man who comes after me has surpassed me because he was before me.' [31]I myself did not know him, but the reason I came baptizing with water was that he might be revealed to Israel."

[32]Then John gave this testimony: "I saw the Spirit come down from heaven as a dove and remain on him. [33]I would not have known him, except that the one who sent me to baptize with water told me, 'The man on whom you see the Spirit come down and remain is he who will baptize with the Holy Spirit.' [34]I have seen and I testify that this is the Son of God."

Jesus' First Disciples

[35]The next day John was there again with two of his disciples. [36]When he saw Jesus passing by, he said, "Look, the Lamb of God!"

[37]When the two disciples heard him say this, they followed Jesus. [38]Turning around, Jesus saw them following and asked, "What do you want?"

SON OF GOD

Many passages in the Jewish Scriptures, which Christians call the Old Testament, describe the people of Israel as God's son or child (Exod 4:22, 23; Jer 31:19, 20; Hos 11:1), but the title "Son of God" is given to an unnamed king of Israel (Ps 2:7). God said that King David is "my firstborn, the most exalted of the kings of the earth" (Ps 89:27). David is also told that one of his children would be God's son (2 Sam 7:14). The later prophets spoke of the faithful members of the people of Israel as God's children (Isa 43:6; Hos 1:10).

Only in later Jewish writings is the Messiah spoken of as Son of God (*Enoch* 105:2; *2 Esdras* 7:28, 29).

In the Gospels, Jesus is the only true Son of God, as is declared by the voice from heaven at his baptism (Mark 1:11). The religious leaders who wanted to have him put to death asked him if he was the Son of God, and he said that he was (Mark 14:61, 62). The devil recognizes Jesus as the Son of God (Luke 4:1-12), and the demons that he brought under control do so as well (Mark 3:11; 5:7).

Most important is the direct claim of Jesus in Luke 10:21, 22 to be the Son of God who has been given God's wisdom, which he shares with those who trust him as one sent by God. Before Jesus was born, he was identified by the angel as the Son of God (Luke 1:32-35). Matthew 2:15 quotes Hosea 11:1, which speaks of God bringing his Son back from Egypt. Paul wrote that Jesus is by human birth the son of David, but he is now the Son of God, because God raised him from the dead (Rom 1:3, 4). John wrote that Jesus is the Son of God (1:12-14) who was sent by God into the world to save his people from their sins (3:16, 17). He does God's work in the world (10:34-36) and is one with God (17:1, 22).

John begins his Gospel by claiming that Jesus is truly God and has existed from the beginning. As John concludes his Gospel, he states his purpose for writing in 20:31.

They said, "Rabbi" (which means Teacher), "where are you staying?"

[39]"Come," he replied, "and you will see."

So they went and saw where he was staying, and spent that day with him. It was about the tenth hour.

[40]Andrew, Simon Peter's brother, was one of the two who heard what John had said and who had followed Jesus. [41]The first thing Andrew did was to find his brother Simon and tell him, "We have found the Messiah" (that is, the Christ). [42]And he brought him to Jesus.

Jesus looked at him and said, "You are Simon son of John. You will be called Cephas" (which, when translated, is Peter[a]).

Jesus Calls Philip and Nathanael

[43]The next day Jesus decided to leave for Galilee. Finding Philip, he said to him, "Follow me."

[44]Philip, like Andrew and Peter, was from the town of Bethsaida. [45]Philip found Nathanael and told him, "We have found the one Moses wrote about in the Law, and about whom the prophets also wrote—Jesus of Nazareth, the son of Joseph."

[46]"Nazareth! Can anything good come from there?" Nathanael asked.

"Come and see," said Philip.

[47]When Jesus saw Nathanael approaching, he said of him, "Here is a true Israelite, in whom there is nothing false."

[48]"How do you know me?" Nathanael asked.

Jesus answered, "I saw you while you were still under the fig tree before Philip called you."

[49]Then Nathanael declared, "Rabbi, you are the Son of God; you are the King of Israel."

[50]Jesus said, "You believe[b] because I told you I saw you under the fig tree. You shall see greater things than that." [51]He then added, "I tell you[c] the truth, you[c] shall see heaven open, and the angels of God ascending and descending on the Son of Man."

---

[a]42 Both *Cephas* (Aramaic) and *Peter* (Greek) mean *rock*.   [b]50 Or *Do you believe ...?*
[c]51 The Greek is plural.

1:41 *Messiah . . . Christ:* Both *Messiah* (Hebrew; see the note at 1:19, 20) and *Christos* (Greek) mean "anointed one," or one chosen by God to lead God's people.

1:42 *Simon . . . Cephas . . . Peter:* Both the Aramaic name "Cephas" and the Greek name "Peter" mean "rock."

1:43, 44 *Galilee . . . Bethsaida:* Galilee was the area west of the upper Jordan River and the Sea of Galilee. Bethsaida was a fishing village on the northeast shore of the Sea of Galilee. See the map on p. 138.

1:45 *Philip . . . Nathanael . . . Joseph:* Philip was from Bethsaida and probably knew Andrew and Simon.

Nathanael's name means "God has given." He recognizes Jesus as God's Son and the King of Israel (1:49).

See also the note on p. 7 (Son of Joseph from Nazareth).

1:45 *Moses . . . the prophets:* The Jewish Scriptures, which Christians call the Old Testament.

1:47 *Israel:* The name that the Lord gave to Jacob (Gen 27:36; 32:22-32) See also the mini-article called "Israel," p. 116.

1:51 *the angels of God ascending and descending on the Son of Man:* Jacob had a dream about angels going up and down on a ladder from earth to heaven (Gen 28:10-17). See also the mini-article called "Son of Man," p. 130.

QUESTIONS ABOUT JOHN 1:1-51

1. Who is the "Word" of God, and what did this Word do? What might this Word offer to people living today?
2. What other titles for Jesus are suggested in the first chapter of John's Gospel?

What makes each of these titles important?
3. What do you think is the main purpose of this chapter? Why? Which verses support your point of view?

2:1 *Jesus' mother:* This was Mary. See Luke 1:26-56; 2:1-52. Mary lived in Nazareth, which was about ten miles south of Cana.

2:1 *Cana in Galilee:* See the map on p. 138.

2:4 *My time has not yet come:* Jesus was referring to the time of his death and being raised back to life, when his true glory as God's Son would be recognized.

Jesus' Seven Miracles

This lengthy section of John *(2:1—11:44) includes seven key miracles that Jesus performed. Each of these miracles (signs) point to Jesus as the true Messiah, the Son of God. This section also includes people Jesus met and things that Jesus taught about himself.*

MIRACLE ONE—
JESUS AT A WEDDING IN CANA

Jesus Changes Water to Wine

2 On the third day a wedding took place at Cana in Galilee. Jesus' mother was there, [2]and Jesus and his disciples had also been invited to the wedding. [3]When the wine was gone, Jesus' mother said to him, "They have no more wine."

[4]"Dear woman, why do you involve me?" Jesus replied. "My time has not yet come."

Making Wine. Vineyards required much care and intensive labor, especially during harvest time when extra workers were needed to gather the ripened grapes and to make wine. After grapes were picked, they were crushed under foot in stone pits, which were often built into the ground. Sometimes, the workers held onto straps for balance. As they trampled the grapes, they danced and gave expression to their belief that wine was one of life's blessings.

[5]His mother said to the servants, "Do whatever he tells you." [6]Nearby stood six stone water jars, the kind used by the Jews for ceremonial washing, each holding from twenty to thirty gallons.[a]

[7]Jesus said to the servants, "Fill the jars with water"; so they filled them to the brim.

[8]Then he told them, "Now draw some out and take it to the master of the banquet."

They did so, [9]and the master of the banquet tasted the water that had been turned into wine. He did not realize where it had come from, though the servants who had drawn the water knew. Then he called the bridegroom aside [10]and said, "Everyone brings out the choice wine first and then the cheaper wine after the guests have had too much to drink; but you have saved the best till now."

[a] 6 Greek *two to three metretes* (probably about 75 to 115 liters)

2:6 *jars . . . for ceremonial washing:* According to the Law of Moses, if people touched something unclean before they ate, any food they touched would also be made unclean. See also the mini-article called "Purity (Clean and Unclean)," p. 125.

2:10 *Everyone brings out the choice wine first:* The best wine was served early in the celebration, because people would be more aware of the wine's quality and taste. As they drank more wine, their senses would become dull, making it difficult to appreciate good wine. See the mini-article called "Wine" below.

WINE

In the Middle East wine is made from grapes that are picked late in the summer and then spread out on the ground for a while before they are pressed to get out the juice. The annual Feast of Tabernacles, which celebrated Israel's journey through the desert on their way to the promised land, took place in the early fall. It was at this time that grapes were gathered (Deut 16:13-15). Pits or vats were dug out of the rock or out of rocky ground. The pits were joined together in pairs, so that when the grapes were pressed in the upper pit, the juice would flow down into the lower pit. Workers squeezed the juice out of the grapes by walking back and forth on them in the pit (Isa 16:10). The juice was collected from the lower pit in clay jars or in bags made from animal skins. These containers had to have an opening to let out the gas that was created as the wine fermented (Job 32:19). Skins that had become old and stiff would often burst when new wine was stored in them (Matt 9:17).

Palestine and Syria produced large quantities of excellent wine. Even before the people of Israel settled in Canaan they knew the land was fertile. When Moses sent spies to inspect the land, they brought back a cluster of grapes so large it had to be carried on a pole (Num 13:21-27). Other reports of the things produced in Canaan often mention grain, olive oil, and wine (Gen 27:28; Deut 7:13; 18:4; 2 Kgs 18:32; Jer 31:12).

Since water was scarce in Palestine, people drank wine at both ordinary meals and banquets, and especially at wedding feasts (John 2:1-12). Wine was also used as medicine (Luke 10:34; 1 Tim 5:23). Jewish people visiting the temple brought wine with them (1 Sam 1:24) and drank it when they celebrated Passover.

Because wine and winemaking were so familiar to people in Israel and Judah, the prophets could refer to them when trying to explain God's attitude toward the people. Joel, for instance, compares God's coming judgment of the wicked with the trampling of grapes (Joel 3:13). He also says wine is one of the good things God will give the people to bless them (Joel 3:18).

In the New Testament, wine is the symbol of Jesus' blood, which was poured out when he died in order to save people from their sins (Mark 14:23-25). Jesus compared the new life he brings to new wine put in fresh wineskins (Matt 9:17). And the Book of REVELATION uses the image of grapes being trampled in a winepress to describe how God will judge the wicked (Rev 14:19, 20).

2:11 *the first of his miraculous signs:* In JOHN the Greek word *semeia* ("sign") is used for "miracle." In this way the author points to Jesus as the Son of God.

2:11 *Cana in Galilee:* See the note at 2:1.

2:12 *Capernaum:* Capernaum was a base for Roman soldiers who enforced the collection of taxes. Jesus moved there from Nazareth when he was an adult. See the map on p. 138.

2:13 *Passover:* See the mini-article called "Passover and the Feast of Unleavened Bread," p. 124.

2:14 *men selling . . . exchanging money:* In the Court of the Gentiles at the temple, priests made lots of money buying and selling animals for the sacrifices that were required by the Law of Moses. See also the mini-article called "Money Changing in the Temple," p. 120.

2:18 *the Jews:* See the note at 1:19, 20.

2:19 *I will raise it again in three days:* Jesus was claiming that his body—not the actual temple—would be destroyed and that God would raise him from death in three days (2:21).

2:22 *the Scripture:* Referring to the Old Testament.

2:23 *Jerusalem:* The capital city of Judea in southern Palestine. See also the mini-article called "Jerusalem," p. 117.

3:1 *a man of the Pharisees named Nicodemus, a member of the Jewish ruling council:* The fact that Nicodemus came to Jesus at night suggests that he didn't want to be seen. Nicodemus is only mentioned in JOHN (7:50; 19:39).

3:3 *kingdom of God:* God's kingdom is not simply a place. It is what happens when God rules and God's people do what God wants them to do, like serving others and telling the good news about Jesus.

[11]This, the first of his miraculous signs, Jesus performed at Cana in Galilee. He thus revealed his glory, and his disciples put their faith in him.

JESUS IN JUDEA AND SAMARIA

The scene now quickly shifts from Galilee to the southern and middle parts of Palestine known as Judea and Samaria. Jesus throws the money changers out of the temple in Jerusalem and talks to Nicodemus and the Samaritan woman.

Jesus Clears the Temple

[12]After this he went down to Capernaum with his mother and brothers and his disciples. There they stayed for a few days. [13]When it was almost time for the Jewish Passover, Jesus went up to Jerusalem. [14]In the temple courts he found men selling cattle, sheep and doves, and others sitting at tables exchanging money. [15]So he made a whip out of cords, and drove all from the temple area, both sheep and cattle; he scattered the coins of the money changers and overturned their tables. [16]To those who sold doves he said, "Get these out of here! How dare you turn my Father's house into a market!" [17]His disciples remembered that it is written: "Zeal for your house will consume me."[a]

[18]Then the Jews demanded of him, "What miraculous sign can you show us to prove your authority to do all this?"

[19]Jesus answered them, "Destroy this temple, and I will raise it again in three days."

[20]The Jews replied, "It has taken forty-six years to build this temple, and you are going to raise it in three days?" [21]But the temple he had spoken of was his body. [22]After he was raised from the dead, his disciples recalled what he had said. Then they believed the Scripture and the words that Jesus had spoken.

[23]Now while he was in Jerusalem at the Passover Feast, many people saw the miraculous signs he was doing and believed in his name.[b] [24]But Jesus would not entrust himself to them, for he knew all men. [25]He did not need man's testimony about man, for he knew what was in a man.

Jesus Teaches Nicodemus

3 Now there was a man of the Pharisees named Nicodemus, a member of the Jewish ruling council. [2]He came to Jesus at night and said,

---

[a] **17** Psalm 69:9 [b] **23** Or *and believed in him*

"Rabbi, we know you are a teacher who has come from God. For no one could perform the miraculous signs you are doing if God were not with him."

[3]In reply Jesus declared, "I tell you the truth, no one can see the kingdom of God unless he is born again.[a]"

[4]"How can a man be born when he is old?" Nicodemus asked. "Surely he cannot enter a second time into his mother's womb to be born!"

[5]Jesus answered, "I tell you the truth, no one can enter the kingdom of God unless he is born of water and the Spirit. [6]Flesh gives birth to flesh, but the Spirit[b] gives birth to spirit. [7]You should not be surprised at my saying, 'You must be born again.' [8]The wind blows wherever it pleases. You hear its sound, but you cannot tell where it comes from or where it is going. So it is with everyone born of the Spirit."

[9]"How can this be?" Nicodemus asked.

[10]"You are Israel's teacher," said Jesus, "and do you not understand these things? [11]I tell you the truth, we speak of what we know, and we testify to what we have seen, but still you people do not accept our testimony. [12]I have spoken to you of earthly things and you do not believe; how then will you believe if I speak of heavenly things? [13]No one has ever gone into heaven except the one who came from heaven—the Son of Man.[d] [14]Just as Moses lifted up the snake in the desert, so the Son of Man must be lifted up, [15]that everyone who believes in him may have eternal life.[e]

[16]"For God so loved the world that he gave his one and only Son,[f] that whoever believes in him shall not perish but have eternal life. [17]For God did not send his Son into the world to condemn the world, but to save the world through him. [18]Whoever believes in him is not condemned, but whoever does not believe stands condemned already because he has not believed in the name of God's one and only Son.[g] [19]This is the verdict: Light has come into the world, but men loved darkness instead of light because their deeds were evil. [20]Everyone who does evil hates the light, and will not come into the light for fear that his deeds will be exposed. [21]But whoever lives by the truth comes into the light, so that it may be seen plainly that what he has done has been done through God."[h]

John the Baptist's Testimony About Jesus

[22]After this, Jesus and his disciples went out into the Judean countryside, where he spent some time with them, and baptized.

3:5 *born of water and the Spirit:* See the notes at 1:26 and 1:33 (baptism) and 1:32 (Spirit).

3:6 *the Spirit gives birth to spirit:* That the Spirit gives birth to spirit means that the spirit gives birth to spiritual children—God's children. The Jewish people believed that they were God's children because they were descendants of Abraham. Jesus is saying that being a child of God no longer has to do simply with being born into a Jewish family or following the Law of Moses. See also Gal 3:1-5, 26-29.

3:10 *Israel's teacher:* As a Pharisee, Nicodemus was also a teacher of the Jewish Scriptures.

3:12 *heaven:* See the mini-article called "Heaven," p. 115.

3:13 *Son of Man:* See the note at 1:51.

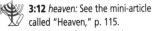

3:14 *Moses lifted up the snake in the desert:* Jesus is saying that he would be lifted up like the snake Moses lifted up to cure the people of snake bites in the desert (Num 21:4-9). Jesus would be nailed to a cross, and whoever believed in him would be saved from death.

3:15 *eternal life:* See the mini-article called "Eternal Life," p. 38.

3:19 *Light . . . darkness:* See the note on p. 7.

3:22 *Judea:* "Judea" is the Latin name that was used for the territory that once had been called "Judah." In the time of Jesus, Judea was under Roman rule. See the map on p. 138.

3:22 *baptized:* See the notes at 1:26 and 1:33.

2:12 Matt 4:13. **2:17** Ps 69:9. **2:19** Matt 26:61; 27:40; Mark 14:58; 15:29. **2:22** John 20:1-23. **3:17** John 5:36, 38; 12:47; Matt 1:21.

---

[a] 3 Or *born from above*; also in verse 7   [b] 6 Or *but spirit*   [c] 7 The Greek is plural.
[d] 13 Some manuscripts *Man, who is in heaven*   [e] 15 Or *believes may have eternal life in him*   [f] 16 Or *his only begotten Son*   [g] 18 Or *God's only begotten Son*
[h] 21 Some interpreters end the quotation after verse 15.

3:23, 24 *Aenon near Salim:* The exact location of this place is not known, though it probably was west of the Jordan River at a place where there were springs.

3:25 *ceremonial washing:* The Jewish people had rules about washing themselves and their dishes, in order to make themselves fit to worship God. See also the mini-article called "Purity (Clean and Unclean)," p. 125.

3:28 *the Christ:* See the note at 1:19, 20.

3:31 *The one who comes from above . . . heaven:* See the notes at 1:34 (Son of God) and 3:12 (heaven).

3:34 *the one whom God . . . God gives the Spirit:* See the notes at 1:34 (Son of God) and 1:32 (Spirit).

4:1 *Pharisees:* See the note at 1:24.

4:3, 4 *Judea . . . Galilee . . . Samaria:* See the notes at 3:22 (Judea) and 1:43, 44 (Galilee). Samaria was an area in central Palestine between Judea and Galilee (see the map on p. 138). In 722 B.C. the Assyrians attacked the Israelite people living in the northern kingdom (Israel) and took many of them away (2 Kgs 17:5-23). Some of the Israelites who were left behind married people from Assyria or Canaan. They eventually set up their own temple, chose their own priests, and followed their own version of the Law of Moses. Because they lived in the area around their capital city, Samaria, they became known as Samaritans. The Jews living in Judea in Jesus' day did not like Samaritans, because they thought the Samaritans were not faithful to the God of Israel.

4:5 *Sychar:* This refers to Shechem, the place where Abraham stayed when he first came to Palestine (Gen 12:6) and where Jacob bought land and built an altar (Gen 33:18-20). Before he died, Jacob gave the hillside near Shechem to his son Joseph (Gen 48:22). See also Josh 24:32.

[23]Now John also was baptizing at Aenon near Salim, because there was plenty of water, and people were constantly coming to be baptized. [24](This was before John was put in prison.) [25]An argument developed between some of John's disciples and a certain Jew[a] over the matter of ceremonial washing. [26]They came to John and said to him, "Rabbi, that man who was with you on the other side of the Jordan—the one you testified about—well, he is baptizing, and everyone is going to him."

[27]To this John replied, "A man can receive only what is given him from heaven. [28]You yourselves can testify that I said, 'I am not the Christ[b] but am sent ahead of him.' [29]The bride belongs to the bridegroom. The friend who attends the bridegroom waits and listens for him, and is full of joy when he hears the bridegroom's voice. That joy is mine, and it is now complete. [30]He must become greater; I must become less.

[31]"The one who comes from above is above all; the one who is from the earth belongs to the earth, and speaks as one from the earth. The one who comes from heaven is above all. [32]He testifies to what he has seen and heard, but no one accepts his testimony. [33]The man who has accepted it has certified that God is truthful. [34]For the one whom God has sent speaks the words of God, for God[c] gives the Spirit without limit. [35]The Father loves the Son and has placed everything in his hands. [36]Whoever believes in the Son has eternal life, but whoever rejects the Son will not see life, for God's wrath remains on him."[d]

Jesus Talks With a Samaritan Woman

4 The Pharisees heard that Jesus was gaining and baptizing more disciples than John, [2]although in fact it was not Jesus who baptized, but his disciples. [3]When the Lord learned of this, he left Judea and went back once more to Galilee.

[4]Now he had to go through Samaria. [5]So he came to a town in Samaria called Sychar, near the plot of ground Jacob had given to his son Joseph. [6]Jacob's well was there, and Jesus, tired as he was from the journey, sat down by the well. It was about the sixth hour.

[7]When a Samaritan woman came to draw water, Jesus said to her, "Will you give me a drink?" [8](His disciples had gone into the town to buy food.)

[9]The Samaritan woman said to him, "You are a Jew and I am a Samaritan woman. How can you ask me for a drink?" (For Jews do not associate with Samaritans.[e])

[10]Jesus answered her, "If you knew the gift of God and who it is that asks you for a drink, you would have asked him and he would have given you living water."

---

[a] **25** Some manuscripts *and certain Jews*   [b] **28** Or *Messiah*   [c] **34** Greek *he*   [d] **36** Some interpreters end the quotation after verse 30.   [e] **9** Or *do not use dishes Samaritans have used*

¹¹"Sir," the woman said, "you have nothing to draw with and the well is deep. Where can you get this living water? ¹²Are you greater than our father Jacob, who gave us the well and drank from it himself, as did also his sons and his flocks and herds?"

¹³Jesus answered, "Everyone who drinks this water will be thirsty again, ¹⁴but whoever drinks the water I give him will never thirst. Indeed, the water I give him will become in him a spring of water welling up to eternal life."

¹⁵The woman said to him, "Sir, give me this water so that I won't get thirsty and have to keep coming here to draw water."

¹⁶He told her, "Go, call your husband and come back."

¹⁷"I have no husband," she replied.

4:6-8 *Jacob's well:* This well, which was cut into the rock, can still be seen near the ruins of ancient Shechem. The woman mentioned here went to the well during the hottest part of the day when few other people would do so.

4:9 *Jews do not associate with Samaritans:* See the note at 4:3, 4. Jewish people who were strict about following certain purity laws were not supposed to come in contact with Samaritans, and certainly were not supposed to drink from a Samaritan's cup or bucket.

4:12 *our father Jacob:* See the note at 4:5. Like the Jews living in Judea, the Samaritans were descendants of the earliest ancestors of Israel. The woman wonders if Jesus is claiming to be greater than Jacob, one of the most important of all these ancestors.

4:14 *eternal life:* See the note at 3:15.

4:15 *give me this water:* The woman thinks Jesus is going to give her a private supply of water that will never run out. Then she wouldn't have to go to the well each day in the hot sun.

4:16 *call your husband:* Jesus knew that the woman had lived with many men and that she had no husband (either because she was divorced or her last husband had died).

3:23, 24 Matt 14:3; Mark 6:17, 18; Luke 3:19, 20. **3:35** Matt 11:27; Luke 10:22. **3:36** John 3:16-18. **4:9** Ezra 4:1-5; Neh 4:1, 2.

Woman at the Well by Hatigammana Uttarananda. The writer of JOHN understood the tensions that existed between Jews and Samaritans. When Jesus was resting at Jacob's well he asked a Samaritan woman for water. She was surprised because she knew he was Jewish. But Jesus showed her that God cares for all people by telling her about the water that gives life. "The water I give him will become in him a spring of water welling up to eternal life." (See 4:3-27.)

4:19 *a prophet:* Prophets sometimes had visions about things that would happen in the future. More often prophets were faithful people who observed what was happening around them and brought a message from God that fit the situation. See the article called "Prophets and Prophecy," p. 99.

4:20 *Our fathers worshiped on this mountain:* The Samaritans worshiped God in a temple they built on Mount Gerizim near the city of Shechem, while Jews worshiped only in the temple in Jerusalem. See the map on p. 139.

4:23 *true worshipers will worship the Father in spirit and truth:* See the note at 1:32 (Spirit). Jesus is saying that true worship does not depend on being at a certain place. Rather, true worship happens when people are led by God's Spirit.

4:25 *Messiah . . . Christ:* See the note at 1:41.

4:34 *My food . . . is to do the will of him who sent me:* In JOHN, Jesus often talks about doing the work that God sent him to do. Here he calls this work his "food." See also 3:16, 17, 34; 5:26; 6:27, 33-35; 17:1, 2. Later, Jesus describes doing what God wants him to do as drinking from the cup (18:11), an image that is often used in the Bible as a symbol of suffering (Isa 51:17, 22; Jer 25:15, 17).

4:35 *Four months more and then the harvest . . . ripe for harvest:* The grain harvest for the area was still months away, but Jesus is saying that the harvest (gathering) of many new followers is ready right away.

4:37 *One sows and another reaps:* Those who sow the seed are those who tell God's message to others; those who reap are those who help others trust in Jesus.

4:39 *Samaritans:* See the note at 4:3, 4. They believed that Jesus was the Savior of the world (verse 42) because of what the woman told them she learned at the well.

Jesus said to her, "You are right when you say you have no husband. ¹⁸The fact is, you have had five husbands, and the man you now have is not your husband. What you have just said is quite true."

¹⁹"Sir," the woman said, "I can see that you are a prophet. ²⁰Our fathers worshiped on this mountain, but you Jews claim that the place where we must worship is in Jerusalem."

²¹Jesus declared, "Believe me, woman, a time is coming when you will worship the Father neither on this mountain nor in Jerusalem. ²²You Samaritans worship what you do not know; we worship what we do know, for salvation is from the Jews. ²³Yet a time is coming and has now come when the true worshipers will worship the Father in spirit and truth, for they are the kind of worshipers the Father seeks. ²⁴God is spirit, and his worshipers must worship in spirit and in truth."

²⁵The woman said, "I know that Messiah" (called Christ) "is coming. When he comes, he will explain everything to us."

²⁶Then Jesus declared, "I who speak to you am he."

The Disciples Rejoin Jesus

²⁷Just then his disciples returned and were surprised to find him talking with a woman. But no one asked, "What do you want?" or "Why are you talking with her?"

²⁸Then, leaving her water jar, the woman went back to the town and said to the people, ²⁹"Come, see a man who told me everything I ever did. Could this be the Christ[a]?" ³⁰They came out of the town and made their way toward him.

³¹Meanwhile his disciples urged him, "Rabbi, eat something."

³²But he said to them, "I have food to eat that you know nothing about."

³³Then his disciples said to each other, "Could someone have brought him food?"

³⁴"My food," said Jesus, "is to do the will of him who sent me and to finish his work. ³⁵Do you not say, 'Four months more and then the harvest'? I tell you, open your eyes and look at the fields! They are ripe for harvest. ³⁶Even now the reaper draws his wages, even now he harvests the crop for eternal life, so that the sower and the reaper may be glad together. ³⁷Thus the saying 'One sows and another reaps' is true. ³⁸I sent you to reap what you have not worked for. Others have done the hard work, and you have reaped the benefits of their labor."

Many Samaritans Believe

³⁹Many of the Samaritans from that town believed in him because of the woman's testimony, "He told me everything I ever did." ⁴⁰So when the Samaritans came to him, they urged him to

---

[a] **29** Or *Messiah*

stay with them, and he stayed two days. [41]And because of his words many more became believers.

[42]They said to the woman, "We no longer believe just because of what you said; now we have heard for ourselves, and we know that this man really is the Savior of the world."

MIRACLE TWO—
JESUS HEALS A ROYAL OFFICIAL'S SON

Jesus Heals the Official's Son

[43]After the two days he left for Galilee. [44](Now Jesus himself had pointed out that a prophet has no honor in his own country.) [45]When he arrived in Galilee, the Galileans welcomed him. They had seen all that he had done in Jerusalem at the Passover Feast, for they also had been there.

[46]Once more he visited Cana in Galilee, where he had turned the water into wine. And there was a certain royal official whose son lay sick at Capernaum. [47]When this man heard that Jesus had arrived in Galilee from Judea, he went to him and begged him to come and heal his son, who was close to death.

[48]"Unless you people see miraculous signs and wonders," Jesus told him, "you will never believe."

[49]The royal official said, "Sir, come down before my child dies."

[50]Jesus replied, "You may go. Your son will live."

The man took Jesus at his word and departed. [51]While he was still on the way, his servants met him with the news that his boy was living. [52]When he inquired as to the time when his son got better, they said to him, "The fever left him yesterday at the seventh hour."

[53]Then the father realized that this was the exact time at which Jesus had said to him, "Your son will live." So he and all his household believed.

[54]This was the second miraculous sign that Jesus performed, having come from Judea to Galilee.

MIRACLE THREE—
JESUS HEALS AN INVALID

The Healing at the Pool

5 Some time later, Jesus went up to Jerusalem for a feast of the Jews. [2]Now there is in Jerusalem near the Sheep Gate a pool, which in Aramaic is called Bethesda[a] and which is surrounded by five covered colonnades. [3]Here a great number of disabled people used

---

[a] 2 Some manuscripts Bethzatha; other manuscripts Bethsaida

---

4:43, 44 *a prophet:* See the note at 4:19 (a prophet). Many Samaritans in the area around Sychar believed Jesus was God's chosen Messiah, but Jesus knew that many people in his own home area of Nazareth in Galilee would not accept him as the Messiah.

4:45 *Galilee:* See the note at 1:43, 44 (Galilee).
4:46 *Cana in Galilee:* See 2:1-11 and the note at 2:1 (Cana).

4:46 *royal official whose son lay sick at Capernaum:* The Greek word describing this "official" suggests that he was a royal officer who served the king (Herod Antipas). See the note at 2:12 (Capernaum). Because Jesus healed the boy at the very moment he said he would, the official and his whole family put their faith in Jesus (4:53).

5:1 *Jerusalem . . . feast of the Jews:* See the note at 2:23 (Jerusalem). The feast was either the Feast of Tabernacles or Passover. The Feast of Tabernacles takes place at the end of the fall harvest (Lev 23:33-36; Deut 16:13-17). To celebrate this feast the people built temporary shelters to remind themselves of how God provided for the people of Israel when they wandered in the desert after leaving Egypt. See also the note at 2:13 (Passover) and the chart called "Jewish Calendar and Festivals," p. 84.

5:2 *near the Sheep Gate a pool . . . called Bethesda . . . surrounded by five covered colonnades:* This pool was just north of the temple area. A pool that fits this description has been found. See the map on p. 139 for its possible location at the time of Jesus.

4:43,44 Matt 13:57; Mark 6:4; Luke 4:24. **4:45** John 2:23. **5:3, 4** Isa 35:5, 6; Luke 4:16-20.

5:7 *when the water is stirred:* The water may have been stirred once in a while by a spring. Some believed an angel of God stirred the waters.

5:9 *Sabbath:* This Jewish day of rest begins at sunset on Friday. It ends with a blessing at sunset on Saturday. The Sabbath is the seventh day of the week, the day that God rested after the work of creation (Gen 2:2, 3). Jewish law forbade Jews and their servants from working on the Sabbath (Exod 20:8-11; Deut 5:12-15). For more, see the chart called "Jewish Calendar and Festivals," p. 84. Carrying bedding was considered work, so it was not allowed on the Sabbath.

5:10 *the Jews:* See the notes at 1:19, 20 (priests) and 1:24 (Pharisees).

5:14 *Stop sinning:* People sin when they turn away from God and disobey God's Law. Jesus' warning to the man he healed does not mean that the man's illness was caused by sin. See also the note at 9:2 and the article called "Miracles, Magic, and Medicine," p. 95.

5:16 *doing these things on the Sabbath:* Doing any kind of work on the Sabbath was a serious offense according to the Law of Moses (Exod 31:14, 15; 35:2). However, during Jesus' day when the Roman Empire controlled Judea, Jewish leaders did not have the authority to execute people for this crime. It is not clear exactly how the Jewish leaders "persecuted" Jesus.

5:17 *My Father:* In this Gospel, Jesus often refers to God as his Father (3:35; 5:20-30; 15:1, 16; 17). For Jesus to call God his Father was to claim a special relationship with God and authority in relation to God's people (Ps 2:6, 7). Since the Jewish leaders believed no human being could be equal with God, they thought Jesus was dishonoring the Law of Moses by saying God was his Father (5:18).

5:10 Neh 13:19; Jer 17:21-24.

to lie—the blind, the lame, the paralyzed.[a] [5]One who was there had been an invalid for thirty-eight years. [6]When Jesus saw him lying there and learned that he had been in this condition for a long time, he asked him, "Do you want to get well?"

[7]"Sir," the invalid replied, "I have no one to help me into the pool when the water is stirred. While I am trying to get in, someone else goes down ahead of me."

[8]Then Jesus said to him, "Get up! Pick up your mat and walk." [9]At once the man was cured; he picked up his mat and walked.

The day on which this took place was a Sabbath, [10]and so the Jews said to the man who had been healed, "It is the Sabbath; the law forbids you to carry your mat."

[11]But he replied, "The man who made me well said to me, 'Pick up your mat and walk.'"

[12]So they asked him, "Who is this fellow who told you to pick it up and walk?"

[13]The man who was healed had no idea who it was, for Jesus had slipped away into the crowd that was there.

[14]Later Jesus found him at the temple and said to him, "See, you are well again. Stop sinning or something worse may happen to you." [15]The man went away and told the Jews that it was Jesus who had made him well.

Life Through the Son

[16]So, because Jesus was doing these things on the Sabbath, the Jews persecuted him. [17]Jesus said to them, "My Father is always at his work to this very day, and I, too, am working." [18]For this reason the Jews tried all the harder to kill him; not only was he breaking the Sabbath, but he was even calling God his own Father, making himself equal with God.

[19]Jesus gave them this answer: "I tell you the truth, the Son can do nothing by himself; he can do only what he sees his Father doing, because whatever the Father does the Son also does. [20]For the Father loves the Son and shows him all he does. Yes, to your amazement he will show him even greater things than these. [21]For just as the Father raises the dead and gives them life, even so the Son gives life to whom he is pleased to give it. [22]Moreover, the Father judges no one, but has entrusted all judgment to the Son, [23]that all may honor the Son just as they honor the Father. He who does not honor the Son does not honor the Father, who sent him.

[24]"I tell you the truth, whoever hears my word and believes him who sent me has eternal life and will not be condemned; he has crossed over from death to life. [25]I tell you the truth, a time is

---

[a] **3** Some less important manuscripts *paralyzed—and they waited for the moving of the waters.* [4]*From time to time an angel of the Lord would come down and stir up the waters. The first one into the pool after each such disturbance would be cured of whatever disease he had.*

coming and has now come when the dead will hear the voice of the Son of God and those who hear will live. [26]For as the Father has life in himself, so he has granted the Son to have life in himself. [27]And he has given him authority to judge because he is the Son of Man.

[28]"Do not be amazed at this, for a time is coming when all who are in their graves will hear his voice [29]and come out—those who have done good will rise to live, and those who have done evil will rise to be condemned. [30]By myself I can do nothing; I judge only as I hear, and my judgment is just, for I seek not to please myself but him who sent me.

Testimonies About Jesus

[31]"If I testify about myself, my testimony is not valid. [32]There is another who testifies in my favor, and I know that his testimony about me is valid.

[33]"You have sent to John and he has testified to the truth. [34]Not that I accept human testimony; but I mention it that you may be saved. [35]John was a lamp that burned and gave light, and you chose for a time to enjoy his light.

[36]"I have testimony weightier than that of John. For the very work that the Father has given me to finish, and which I am doing, testifies that the Father has sent me. [37]And the Father who sent me has himself testified concerning me. You have never heard his voice nor seen his form, [38]nor does his word dwell in you, for you do not believe the one he sent. [39]You diligently study[a] the Scriptures because you think that by them you possess eternal life. These are the Scriptures that testify about me, [40]yet you refuse to come to me to have life.

[41]"I do not accept praise from men, [42]but I know you. I know that you do not have the love of God in your hearts. [43]I have come in my Father's name, and you do not accept me; but if someone else comes in his own name, you will accept him. [44]How can you believe if you accept praise from one another, yet make no effort to obtain the praise that comes from the only God[b]?

[45]"But do not think I will accuse you before the Father. Your accuser is Moses, on whom your hopes are set. [46]If you believed Moses, you would believe me, for he wrote about me. [47]But since you do not believe what he wrote, how are you going to believe what I say?"

MIRACLE FOUR—
JESUS FEEDS FIVE THOUSAND

Jesus Feeds the Five Thousand

6 Some time after this, Jesus crossed to the far shore of the Sea of Galilee (that is, the Sea of Tiberias), [2]and a great crowd of people

---

[a] **39** Or *Study diligently* (the imperative)   [b] **44** Some early manuscripts *the Only One*

5:19 *Son ... Father:* Jesus calls himself God's Son (1:1-3, 18).

5:21 *the Father raises the dead and gives them life:* Jesus was referring here to eternal life (see the note at 3:15).

5:25 *a time is coming and has now come:* Jesus is saying that those who hear his message of forgiveness and new life have life that will never end. This includes those who have already died as faithful people. See also 1 Cor 15:12-57; 1 Thes 4:13-18.

5:27 *Son of Man:* See the note at 1:51.

5:35 *John was a lamp that burned and gave light:* See the note at 1:6 (John) and on p. 1944XX (light and darkness).

5:39, 40 *You diligently study the Scriptures . . . possess eternal life:* The Scriptures are the Jewish Scriptures, which Christians call the Old Testament. The teachers followed the teachings of Scripture as a guide to living as God expected. Jesus is saying that those same Scriptures point to him as the way to eternal life (14:6). See also the note at 3:15.

5:45-47 *Moses, on whom your hopes are set:* Jesus was referring to the Law of Moses (see the note at 1:17), which was an important part of the Jewish Scriptures. Moses was the great leader who led the Israelite people out of slavery in Egypt and received from God the laws that the Israelite people were to live by. When Jesus says that Moses "wrote about me," he is referring to the overall message of the first five books of the Jewish Scriptures, traditionally called the Books of Moses.

6:1 *Sea of Galilee (that is, the Sea of Tiberias):* Jesus apparently crossed the lake from west to east. The Sea of Galilee is also known as the Lake of Gennesaret (Luke 5:1); and the Romans called it the Sea of Tiberias (also 21:1), after the Roman Emperor Tiberius.

5:24 John 3:16, 17. **5:29** Dan 12:2. **5:33** John 1:19-27; 3:27-30.

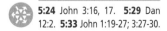

6:3, 4 *Jewish Passover Feast:* See the note at 2:13.

6:3, 4 *sat down:* Possibly to teach. Teachers in the ancient world usually sat down to teach. This was a sign of their authority.

6:5 *Philip:* See the note at 1:45 (Philip).

6:7 *Eight months' wages:* The amount paid was two hundred silver coins. Each coin was worth the average day's wages for a worker.

6:8 *Andrew, Simon Peter's brother:* See the notes at 1:40 (Andrew) and 1:42 (Simon).

6:9 *five small barley loaves:* Barley was a very cheap source of food in Palestine. It was mainly used to feed cattle, but it was also used for making bread in times of emergency. See also the mini-article called "Bread," p. 24.

6:11 *Jesus then took the loaves:* Over a thousand years earlier, God miraculously fed the Israelite people in the desert with bread (manna) that came down from heaven (Exod 16:1-35; Num 11:7-9). Those who saw Jesus' miracle of feeding five thousand may have been reminded of God's earlier miracle.

6:13 *twelve baskets:* Twelve is a very significant number to the Jewish people because Israel was made up of twelve tribes. See the chart called "Numbers in the Bible," p. 123.

6:14 *the Prophet:* See the note at 1:21.

6:16 *lake:* Meaning the Sea of Galilee. See the note at 6:1. Storms often sweep across the lake because it is surrounded on nearly every side by mountains.

6:17 *Capernaum:* See the note at 2:12. The disciples and Jesus had been on the east side of the lake.

followed him because they saw the miraculous signs he had performed on the sick. [3]Then Jesus went up on a mountainside and sat down with his disciples. [4]The Jewish Passover Feast was near.

[5]When Jesus looked up and saw a great crowd coming toward him, he said to Philip, "Where shall we buy bread for these people to eat?" [6]He asked this only to test him, for he already had in mind what he was going to do.

[7]Philip answered him, "Eight months' wages[a] would not buy enough bread for each one to have a bite!"

[8]Another of his disciples, Andrew, Simon Peter's brother, spoke up, [9]"Here is a boy with five small barley loaves and two small fish, but how far will they go among so many?"

[10]Jesus said, "Have the people sit down." There was plenty of grass in that place, and the men sat down, about five thousand of them. [11]Jesus then took the loaves, gave thanks, and distributed to those who were seated as much as they wanted. He did the same with the fish.

[12]When they had all had enough to eat, he said to his disciples, "Gather the pieces that are left over. Let nothing be wasted." [13]So they gathered them and filled twelve baskets with the pieces of the five barley loaves left over by those who had eaten.

[14]After the people saw the miraculous sign that Jesus did, they began to say, "Surely this is the Prophet who is to come into the world." [15]Jesus, knowing that they intended to come and make him king by force, withdrew again to a mountain by himself.

MIRACLE FIVE— JESUS WALKS ON THE WATER

Jesus Walks on the Water

[16]When evening came, his disciples went down to the lake, [17]where they got into a boat and set off across the lake for Capernaum. By now it was dark, and Jesus had not yet joined them. [18]A strong wind was blowing and the waters grew rough. [19]When they had rowed three or three and a half miles,[b] they saw Jesus approaching the boat, walking on the water; and they were terrified. [20]But he said to them, "It is I; don't be afraid." [21]Then they were willing to take him into the boat, and immediately the boat reached the shore where they were heading.

[22]The next day the crowd that had stayed on the opposite shore of the lake realized that only one boat had been there, and that Jesus had not entered it with his disciples, but that they had gone away alone. [23]Then some boats from Tiberias landed near the place where the people had eaten the bread after the Lord had

---

[a] **7** Greek *two hundred denarii* [b] **19** Greek *rowed twenty-five or thirty stadia* (about 5 or 6 kilometers)

Christ at the Sea of Galilee by Jacopo Tintoretto, painted around 1575-1580. The evening after Jesus had fed over five thousand people with only five loaves of bread and two fish, Jesus' disciples got a boat on the east side of the Sea of Galilee and began sailing for Capernaum on the west side. While they were out on the lake the water began to get rough. In the storm they saw Jesus coming toward them, walking on the water. Jesus said to them, "It is I; don't be afraid." (See 6:16-21.)

given thanks. ²⁴Once the crowd realized that neither Jesus nor his disciples were there, they got into the boats and went to Capernaum in search of Jesus.

JESUS TEACHES IN GALILEE AND JUDEA

In this section (6:25—8:59), Jesus teaches many important things. He describes himself as the bread that gives life, the source of living water, and the light for the world. His words and his actions continue to cause conflicts with the Jewish leaders.

Jesus the Bread of Life

²⁵When they found him on the other side of the lake, they asked him, "Rabbi, when did you get here?"

²⁶Jesus answered, "I tell you the truth, you are looking for me, not because you saw miraculous signs but because you ate the loaves and had your fill. ²⁷Do not work for food that spoils, but for food that endures to eternal life, which the Son of Man will give you. On him God the Father has placed his seal of approval."

6:19 *Jesus . . . walking on the water:* Jesus' miracle of walking on the water may have reminded the disciples of two miracles God had done earlier: controlling the waters of creation (Gen 1:1-13) and saving the Israelite people when Moses parted the waters of the Red Sea (Exod 14:21-31).

6:23, 24 *Tiberias ... Capernaum:* Tiberias was a city on the west coast of the Sea of Galilee, built around 25 A.D. by Herod Antipas to honor the emperor, Tiberius Caesar. See the map on p. 138. When the people didn't find Jesus on the east side of the lake, they sailed back to Capernaum (see the note at 2:12).

6:27 *eternal life ... Son of Man:* See the notes at 3:15 (eternal life) and 1:51 (Son of Man).

6:31 *manna:* See the note at 6:11.

6:35 *I am the bread of life:* Jesus compares himself to the miraculous gift of manna that God sent from heaven. Just as God sent the manna, God sends Jesus to bring life. See also the mini-article called "Bread," below.

6:39 *the last day:* Jesus is referring to the time when God will judge all people. Those who have faith in Jesus, the Son, will be raised up to life (6:40), that is, have eternal life. See also the mini-articles called "Eternal Life," p. 38 and "Day of the LORD," p. 113.

6:31 Exod 16:4, 15; Ps 78:24.

[28]Then they asked him, "What must we do to do the works God requires?"

[29]Jesus answered, "The work of God is this: to believe in the one he has sent."

[30]So they asked him, "What miraculous sign then will you give that we may see it and believe you? What will you do? [31]Our forefathers ate the manna in the desert; as it is written: 'He gave them bread from heaven to eat.'[a] "

[32]Jesus said to them, "I tell you the truth, it is not Moses who has given you the bread from heaven, but it is my Father who gives you the true bread from heaven. [33]For the bread of God is he who comes down from heaven and gives life to the world."

[34]"Sir," they said, "from now on give us this bread."

[35]Then Jesus declared, "I am the bread of life. He who comes to me will never go hungry, and he who believes in me will never be thirsty. [36]But as I told you, you have seen me and still you do not believe. [37]All that the Father gives me will come to me, and whoever comes to me I will never drive away. [38]For I have come down from heaven not to do my will but to do the will of him who

---

[a] **31** Exodus 16:4; Neh. 9:15; Psalm 78:24,25

BREAD

Bread has always been an important and basic food for people. Bread was made at home by wives (Gen 18:6) and daughters (2 Sam 13:7, 8). It was usually made fresh each day, but because it could last for several days without going bad, it could also be given to those setting out on a long journey (Gen 45:23). Bread was offered to strangers who passed through the land (Gen 14:18), and when God's people were disobedient, God warned them that their supply of daily bread would be taken away as punishment (Lev 26:23-26).

Most bread was made in flat cakes on flat stones or in pans. Some was baked into larger, thicker loaves that were placed on a special table in the temple and offered to God as "the bread of the Presence" (Exod 25:23-30). Only priests could eat this bread, but David and his supporters were once given some by priests when they were hungry (1 Sam 21:1-6). God provided bread for the Israelite people as they were wandering through the desert of Sinai on the way from Egypt to the promised land. They called this bread *manna*, which in Hebrew means, "What is it?" This bread is also referred to as the "bread from heaven" (Exod 16:4).

Ancient documents discovered in the twentieth century known as the Dead Sea Scrolls reveal that Jews in the community at Qumran shared meals of bread and wine. These meals were both a celebration of good times in the present and a celebration of the day when God would defeat their enemies and send the Messiah. Jesus' followers believed that he was God's chosen Messiah and the true bread from heaven that gives life (John 6:32-35). Jesus told his followers to ask God to give them the basic food (bread) they needed to live from day to day (Luke 11:3). After Jesus was taken to heaven, they continued to celebrate their new life together as God's people by "breaking bread" in ordinary meals (Acts 2:42-46), and by sharing in the bread of communion, which Jesus said was his body (Mark 14:22-25; 1 Cor 11:23-26).

Making Bread in Jesus' Day. Bread-baking, a daily chore, was almost always done by women and girls. Wheat or barley grain was ground into a coarse flour in hand-mills. The flour was then mixed with water, salt, and unbaked dough from the day before. This left-over dough contained the yeast needed to make the new batch of dough rise. The yeast was massaged into the dough (a process called "kneading") to distribute it throughout the batch, and the batches were set aside until the gasses produced by the yeast made the dough rise. The dough was then shaped into round, flat loaves that baked quickly in outdoor ovens.

sent me. ³⁹And this is the will of him who sent me, that I shall lose none of all that he has given me, but raise them up at the last day. ⁴⁰For my Father's will is that everyone who looks to the Son and believes in him shall have eternal life, and I will raise him up at the last day."

⁴¹At this the Jews began to grumble about him because he said, "I am the bread that came down from heaven." ⁴²They said, "Is this not Jesus, the son of Joseph, whose father and mother we know? How can he now say, 'I came down from heaven'?"

⁴³"Stop grumbling among yourselves," Jesus answered. ⁴⁴"No one can come to me unless the Father who sent me draws him, and I will raise him up at the last day. ⁴⁵It is written in the Prophets: 'They will all be taught by God.'^a Everyone who listens to the Father and learns from him comes to me. ⁴⁶No one has seen the Father except the one who is from God; only he has seen the Father. ⁴⁷I tell you the truth, he who believes has everlasting life. ⁴⁸I am the bread

 6:42 *the son of Joseph:* See the note on p. 7 (son of Joseph).

6:44 *raise him up at the last day:* See the note at 6:39.

6:45 Isa 54:13; Jer 31:33, 34.

^a **45** Isaiah 54:13

6:53 *eat the flesh of the Son of Man and drink his blood:* This is probably a reference to the Lord's Supper, which Jesus' followers share in response to his command (Matt 26:26-30; Mark 14:22-26; Luke 22:14-23; 1 Cor 11:23-29). See also the mini-article called "Son of Man," p. 130.

6:58 *bread that came down from heaven:* See the notes at 6:11 and 6:35.

6:59 *the synagogue in Capernaum:* The Greek word that is translated here as *synagogue* means "gathering." See also the mini-article called "Synagogues," p. 130.

See the note at 2:12 (Capernaum). A Roman army officer built a meeting place for the Jewish people in Capernaum (Luke 7:5).

6:63 *Spirit:* See the note at 1:32.

6:67 *the Twelve:* These are the ones whom Jesus called to be his special apostles (Matt 10:1-4).

6:68 *Simon Peter:* See the note at 1:42.

6:68 *eternal life:* See the note at 3:15.

6:70, 71 *a devil . . . Judas . . . Iscariot:* Demons were understood to be the helpers of Satan and God's enemies. Jesus is saying that Judas, one of Jesus' twelve special disciples, would betray him. "Iscariot" may mean "a man from Kerioth" (a place in Judea). Or, "a man who was a liar" or "a man who was a betrayer" (Matt 10:4).

7:1 *Galilee . . . Judea:* See the notes at 1:43, 44 (Galilee) and 3:22 (Judea). In chapter 6, Jesus is reported as being in Capernaum, which is in Galilee (6:59). JOHN does not explain when Jesus returned to Judea (7:1).

7:1 *the Jews:* See the notes at 1:19, 20 (priests) and 1:24 (Pharisees).

7:2 *Feast of Tabernacles:* See the note at 5:1.

of life. [49]Your forefathers ate the manna in the desert, yet they died. [50]But here is the bread that comes down from heaven, which a man may eat and not die. [51]I am the living bread that came down from heaven. If anyone eats of this bread, he will live forever. This bread is my flesh, which I will give for the life of the world."

[52]Then the Jews began to argue sharply among themselves, "How can this man give us his flesh to eat?"

[53]Jesus said to them, "I tell you the truth, unless you eat the flesh of the Son of Man and drink his blood, you have no life in you. [54]Whoever eats my flesh and drinks my blood has eternal life, and I will raise him up at the last day. [55]For my flesh is real food and my blood is real drink. [56]Whoever eats my flesh and drinks my blood remains in me, and I in him. [57]Just as the living Father sent me and I live because of the Father, so the one who feeds on me will live because of me. [58]This is the bread that came down from heaven. Your forefathers ate manna and died, but he who feeds on this bread will live forever." [59]He said this while teaching in the synagogue in Capernaum.

Many Disciples Desert Jesus

[60]On hearing it, many of his disciples said, "This is a hard teaching. Who can accept it?"

[61]Aware that his disciples were grumbling about this, Jesus said to them, "Does this offend you? [62]What if you see the Son of Man ascend to where he was before! [63]The Spirit gives life; the flesh counts for nothing. The words I have spoken to you are spirit[a] and they are life. [64]Yet there are some of you who do not believe." For Jesus had known from the beginning which of them did not believe and who would betray him. [65]He went on to say, "This is why I told you that no one can come to me unless the Father has enabled him."

[66]From this time many of his disciples turned back and no longer followed him.

[67]"You do not want to leave too, do you?" Jesus asked the Twelve.

[68]Simon Peter answered him, "Lord, to whom shall we go? You have the words of eternal life. [69]We believe and know that you are the Holy One of God."

[70]Then Jesus replied, "Have I not chosen you, the Twelve? Yet one of you is a devil!" [71](He meant Judas, the son of Simon Iscariot, who, though one of the Twelve, was later to betray him.)

Jesus Goes to the Feast of Tabernacles

7 After this, Jesus went around in Galilee, purposely staying away from Judea because the Jews there were waiting to take his life. [2]But when the Jewish Feast of Tabernacles was near, [3]Jesus' broth-

---

[a] 63 Or *Spirit*

ers said to him, "You ought to leave here and go to Judea, so that your disciples may see the miracles you do. [4]No one who wants to become a public figure acts in secret. Since you are doing these things, show yourself to the world." [5]For even his own brothers did not believe in him.

[6]Therefore Jesus told them, "The right time for me has not yet come; for you any time is right. [7]The world cannot hate you, but it hates me because I testify that what it does is evil. [8]You go to the Feast. I am not yet[a] going up to this Feast, because for me the right time has not yet come." [9]Having said this, he stayed in Galilee.

[10]However, after his brothers had left for the Feast, he went also, not publicly, but in secret. [11]Now at the Feast the Jews were watching for him and asking, "Where is that man?"

[12]Among the crowds there was widespread whispering about him. Some said, "He is a good man."

Others replied, "No, he deceives the people." [13]But no one would say anything publicly about him for fear of the Jews.

Jesus Teaches at the Feast

[14]Not until halfway through the Feast did Jesus go up to the temple courts and begin to teach. [15]The Jews were amazed and asked, "How did this man get such learning without having studied?"

[16]Jesus answered, "My teaching is not my own. It comes from him who sent me. [17]If anyone chooses to do God's will, he will find out whether my teaching comes from God or whether I speak on my own. [18]He who speaks on his own does so to gain honor for himself, but he who works for the honor of the one who sent him is a man of truth; there is nothing false about him. [19]Has not Moses given you the law? Yet not one of you keeps the law. Why are you trying to kill me?"

[20]"You are demon-possessed," the crowd answered. "Who is trying to kill you?"

[21]Jesus said to them, "I did one miracle, and you are all astonished. [22]Yet, because Moses gave you circumcision (though actually it did not come from Moses, but from the patriarchs), you circumcise a child on the Sabbath. [23]Now if a child can be circumcised on the Sabbath so that the law of Moses may not be broken, why are you angry with me for healing the whole man on the Sabbath? [24]Stop judging by mere appearances, and make a right judgment."

Is Jesus the Christ?

[25]At that point some of the people of Jerusalem began to ask, "Isn't this the man they are trying to kill? [26]Here he is, speaking publicly, and they are not saying a word to him. Have the authorities

---

[a]**8** Some early manuscripts do not have *yet*.

7:3 *Jesus' brothers:* These were most likely Jesus' half-brothers—other children of Mary and Joseph after Jesus was born.

7:6 *The right time for me has not yet come:* See the note at 2:4.

7:10 *he went also, not publicly, but in secret:* Jesus goes in secret rather than attracting attention to himself. He knows that there is danger in having people believe in him just because of his miracles.

7:14 *temple:* The center of Jewish worship in Jerusalem. Herod greatly expanded this important building as a way of trying to win the favor of the Jewish people. During the time of the festivals, many visitors came to Jerusalem to offer sacrifices at the temple and Jesus would have been able to speak to large crowds of people. See also the article called "People of the Law: The Religion of Israel," p. 80.

7:16 *him who sent me:* Jesus was referring to God, the Father. See the notes at 5:17 and 5:19.

7:19 *Has not Moses given you the law?:* See the note at 1:17. Jesus tells his listeners that they have not really understood what God was saying in the law.

7:21 *I did one miracle:* Jesus is talking about his healing of the man who was crippled (5:1-16).

7:22 *Moses gave you circumcision . . . you circumcise a child on the Sabbath:* See the mini-article called "Circumcision," p. 111. Jesus is arguing that if it is acceptable to circumcise on the Sabbath, then it should be acceptable to treat the whole body, as he did when he healed the man who was crippled (5:1-16).

6:68, 69 Matt 16:16; Mark 8:29; Luke 9:20. **7:2** Lev 23:34; Deut 16:13-15.

7:26 *the Christ:* See the note at 1:19, 20.

7:30 *his time had not yet come:* See the note at 2:4.

7:31 *the Christ:* See the note at 1:19, 20.

7:32 *Pharisees . . . chief priests . . . temple guards:* See the note at 1:24 (Pharisees). Chief priests were members of a group in charge of the temple in Jerusalem. The temple guards guarded the temple area and helped the council of Jewish leaders in Jerusalem keep order among the Jewish people.

7:35 *The Jews . . . the Greeks:* The "Jews" refers to the Jewish leaders; see the note at 1:19, 20 (priests) and 1:24 (Pharisees). "Greeks" may refer to Gentiles (non-Jews) or to Jews who followed Greek customs.

7:37 *On the last and greatest day:* On each of the seven days of the festival, a group of priests would go to the Pool of Siloam (see the note at 9:7) to fill a container of water to bring back to the temple. People would follow the priests to the pool and back up the steps to the temple. It may have been at the Pool of Siloam or somewhere along the ceremonial route to the temple that Jesus stood up and shouted that he was the source of living water (7:38). See also Ezek 47:1-12; Zech 14:16, 17; and the mini-article called "Water," p. 131.

7:39 *the Spirit:* See the note at 1:32.

7:39 *Jesus had not yet been glorified:* John speaks of Jesus being given his full glory, both when he is nailed to the cross and when he is raised from death.

7:40 *the Prophet:* See the note at 1:21.

7:41, 42 *the Christ . . . Bethlehem:* See the notes at 1:19, 20 (the Christ) and the note on page 7 (son of Joseph from Nazareth). Bethlehem was known as King David's hometown (Luke 2:4).

really concluded that he is the Christ[a] ? [27]But we know where this man is from; when the Christ comes, no one will know where he is from."

[28]Then Jesus, still teaching in the temple courts, cried out, "Yes, you know me, and you know where I am from. I am not here on my own, but he who sent me is true. You do not know him, [29]but I know him because I am from him and he sent me."

[30]At this they tried to seize him, but no one laid a hand on him, because his time had not yet come. [31]Still, many in the crowd put their faith in him. They said, "When the Christ comes, will he do more miraculous signs than this man?"

[32]The Pharisees heard the crowd whispering such things about him. Then the chief priests and the Pharisees sent temple guards to arrest him.

[33]Jesus said, "I am with you for only a short time, and then I go to the one who sent me. [34]You will look for me, but you will not find me; and where I am, you cannot come."

[35]The Jews said to one another, "Where does this man intend to go that we cannot find him? Will he go where our people live scattered among the Greeks, and teach the Greeks? [36]What did he mean when he said, 'You will look for me, but you will not find me,' and 'Where I am, you cannot come'?"

[37]On the last and greatest day of the Feast, Jesus stood and said in a loud voice, "If anyone is thirsty, let him come to me and drink. [38]Whoever believes in me, as[b] the Scripture has said, streams of living water will flow from within him." [39]By this he meant the Spirit, whom those who believed in him were later to receive. Up to that time the Spirit had not been given, since Jesus had not yet been glorified.

[40]On hearing his words, some of the people said, "Surely this man is the Prophet."

[41]Others said, "He is the Christ."

Still others asked, "How can the Christ come from Galilee? [42]Does not the Scripture say that the Christ will come from David's family[c] and from Bethlehem, the town where David lived?" [43]Thus the people were divided because of Jesus. [44]Some wanted to seize him, but no one laid a hand on him.

Unbelief of the Jewish Leaders

[45]Finally the temple guards went back to the chief priests and Pharisees, who asked them, "Why didn't you bring him in?"

[46]"No one ever spoke the way this man does," the guards declared.

[47]"You mean he has deceived you also?" the Pharisees retorted. [48]"Has any of the rulers or of the Pharisees believed in him? [49]No! But

---

[a] **26** Or *Messiah;* also in verses 27, 31, 41 and 42   [b] **37, 38** Or / *If anyone is thirsty, let him come to me. / And let him drink,* [38]*who believes in me. / As*   [c] **42** Greek *seed*

this mob that knows nothing of the law—there is a curse on them."

[50]Nicodemus, who had gone to Jesus earlier and who was one of their own number, asked, [51]"Does our law condemn anyone without first hearing him to find out what he is doing?"

[52]They replied, "Are you from Galilee, too? Look into it, and you will find that a prophet[a] does not come out of Galilee."

[The earliest manuscripts and many other ancient witnesses do not have John 7:53-8:11.]

[53]Then each went to his own home.

8 But Jesus went to the Mount of Olives. [2]At dawn he appeared again in the temple courts, where all the people gathered around

---

[a] 52 Two early manuscripts *the Prophet*

Christ and the Woman Taken in Adultery by Max Beckmann, 1917. When Jesus was teaching in the temple courtyard, some Pharisees and teachers of the Law of Moses brought in a woman who had been caught in bed with a man who wasn't her husband. The Pharisees and teachers, testing Jesus, said she should be put to death, a punishment commanded by the Law (Lev 20:10). But Jesus challenged their narrow understanding of sin and told the woman, "Neither do I condemn you ... Go now and leave your life of sin." (See 8:1-11.)

7:50 *Nicodemus . . . one of their own number:* See the note at 3:1 (Nicodemus). "Their own number" refers to the Jewish ruling council (also called the Sanhedrin), which was made up of religious and civic leaders, including the chief priests, Pharisees, and Sadducees. The Romans, who ruled Palestine, allowed the local leaders in each part of their empire to decide cases against those who broke religious laws and to make people obey local laws.

7:51 *our law:* The Law of Moses taught that two witnesses were needed before a person could be convicted of a crime (Deut 17:6; 19:15) and put to death (Num 35:30).

7:52 *a prophet does not come out of Galilee:* Since Jesus is from Nazareth in Galilee, they don't believe he could be the Messiah. What the leaders didn't realize was that Jesus was born in Bethlehem in Judea, the hometown of King David, and that he was a descendant of David. It was from the family of King David that a Messiah was to come (2 Sam 7:16, 17; Isa 11:1).

8:1 *Mount of Olives:* The Mount of Olives is a ridge about two and a half miles long that is located about one-half mile east of the temple area in Jerusalem, across the Kidron Valley. It got its name because of all the olive trees that grew on its slopes. See the map on p. 139.

8:2 *temple:* See the note at 7:14.

 7:23 John 5:9 **7:34** John 14:1-6. **7:37** Lev 23:36. **7:38** Ezek 47:1; Zech 14:8. **7:42** 1 Sam 16:1; Mic 5:2.

8:3 *The teachers of the law and the Pharisees:* The teachers of the law were Jewish scholars who studied the Law of Moses (1:17) and explained to others how to live by what the law taught. See the note at 1:24 (Pharisees).

8:5 *the Law . . . stone such women:* According to the Law of Moses, a woman caught sleeping with a man who is not her husband, and the man she slept with, are both to be killed by stoning (Lev 20:10; Deut 22:22-24). The witnesses are supposed to be the first ones to throw the stones. Only the woman is mentioned in this passage.

8:12 *I am the light of the world:* Jesus is defending his message as true. He has come into the world to help people see who God really is and to show them that God wants to give new life to all people. See also the note at 1:7 and the note on p. 7 (light and darkness). See also Matt 5:14; John 9:5.

8:16 *Father:* See the note at 5:17. Jesus has come from the Father and will go back to rule beside the Father (8:14).

8:17 *your own Law . . . testimony of two men:* See the note at 7:51.

8:20 *in the temple area near the place where the offerings were put:* It is not likely that Jesus spoke with the Pharisees inside the temple storage rooms, since only the priests were allowed to go into them. This verse could refer to the part of the temple known as "the court of the women," where offering boxes for the temple treasury were located (Luke 21:1). See also the mini-article called "Temple Offerings," p. 131.

8:20 *his time had not yet come:* See the note at 2:4.

8:23 *You are from below; I am from above:* Jesus is referring to the fact that he was sent from God in heaven (above). When he uses the word "below" he is referring to "the world," which is often described in the Scriptures as being opposed to God (15:18, 19; Gal 6:14).

him, and he sat down to teach them. ³The teachers of the law and the Pharisees brought in a woman caught in adultery. They made her stand before the group ⁴and said to Jesus, "Teacher, this woman was caught in the act of adultery. ⁵In the Law Moses commanded us to stone such women. Now what do you say?" ⁶They were using this question as a trap, in order to have a basis for accusing him.

But Jesus bent down and started to write on the ground with his finger. ⁷When they kept on questioning him, he straightened up and said to them, "If any one of you is without sin, let him be the first to throw a stone at her." ⁸Again he stooped down and wrote on the ground.

⁹At this, those who heard began to go away one at a time, the older ones first, until only Jesus was left, with the woman still standing there. ¹⁰Jesus straightened up and asked her, "Woman, where are they? Has no one condemned you?"

¹¹"No one, sir," she said.

"Then neither do I condemn you," Jesus declared. "Go now and leave your life of sin."

The Validity of Jesus' Testimony

¹²When Jesus spoke again to the people, he said, "I am the light of the world. Whoever follows me will never walk in darkness, but will have the light of life."

¹³The Pharisees challenged him, "Here you are, appearing as your own witness; your testimony is not valid."

¹⁴Jesus answered, "Even if I testify on my own behalf, my testimony is valid, for I know where I came from and where I am going. But you have no idea where I come from or where I am going. ¹⁵You judge by human standards; I pass judgment on no one. ¹⁶But if I do judge, my decisions are right, because I am not alone. I stand with the Father, who sent me. ¹⁷In your own Law it is written that the testimony of two men is valid. ¹⁸I am one who testifies for myself; my other witness is the Father, who sent me."

¹⁹Then they asked him, "Where is your father?"

"You do not know me or my Father," Jesus replied. "If you knew me, you would know my Father also." ²⁰He spoke these words while teaching in the temple area near the place where the offerings were put. Yet no one seized him, because his time had not yet come.

²¹Once more Jesus said to them, "I am going away, and you will look for me, and you will die in your sin. Where I go, you cannot come."

²²This made the Jews ask, "Will he kill himself? Is that why he says, 'Where I go, you cannot come'?"

²³But he continued, "You are from below; I am from above. You are of this world; I am not of this world. ²⁴I told you that you

would die in your sins; if you do not believe that I am ⌊the one I claim to be⌋,[a] you will indeed die in your sins."

25"Who are you?" they asked.

"Just what I have been claiming all along," Jesus replied. 26"I have much to say in judgment of you. But he who sent me is reliable, and what I have heard from him I tell the world."

27They did not understand that he was telling them about his Father. 28So Jesus said, "When you have lifted up the Son of Man, then you will know that I am ⌊the one I claim to be⌋ and that I do nothing on my own but speak just what the Father has taught me. 29The one who sent me is with me; he has not left me alone, for I always do what pleases him." 30Even as he spoke, many put their faith in him.

The Children of Abraham

31To the Jews who had believed him, Jesus said, "If you hold to my teaching, you are really my disciples. 32Then you will know the truth, and the truth will set you free."

33They answered him, "We are Abraham's descendants[b] and have never been slaves of anyone. How can you say that we shall be set free?"

34Jesus replied, "I tell you the truth, everyone who sins is a slave to sin. 35Now a slave has no permanent place in the family, but a son belongs to it forever. 36So if the Son sets you free, you will be free indeed. 37I know you are Abraham's descendants. Yet you are ready to kill me, because you have no room for my word. 38I am telling you what I have seen in the Father's presence, and you do what you have heard from your father.[c] "

39"Abraham is our father," they answered.

"If you were Abraham's children," said Jesus, "then you would[d] do the things Abraham did. 40As it is, you are determined to kill me, a man who has told you the truth that I heard from God. Abraham did not do such things. 41You are doing the things your own father does."

"We are not illegitimate children," they protested. "The only Father we have is God himself."

The Children of the Devil

42Jesus said to them, "If God were your Father, you would love me, for I came from God and now am here. I have not come on my own; but he sent me. 43Why is my language not clear to you? Because you are unable to hear what I say. 44You belong to your father, the devil, and you want to carry out your father's

---

Jesus said,
"You will know the truth, and the truth will set you free."
John 8:32

8:24 *if you do not believe that I am the one I claim to be:* Jesus refers to himself as "I Am." See the mini-article called "I Am," p. 47. Those who don't have faith in him as God's Son will be cutting themselves off from the forgiveness that God offers.

8:27 *his Father:* See the note at 5:17.

8:28 *lifted up the Son of Man:* See the note at 7:39 (not yet been glorified).

8:33 *Abraham's descendants . . . never been slaves of anyone:* See the mini-article called "Abraham," p. 108. God chose Abraham (Gen 12:1-3; 15:1-6; 17:1-8), and so it was believed that anyone who was a descendant of Abraham was also a child of God. The people of Israel had once been slaves in Egypt (Exod 1—14), and they were presently ruled by the Romans. Still, they believed that because they were descendants of Abraham, they would never be enslaved by anyone.

8:34, 35 *a slave to sin:* See also the mini-articles called "Sin," p. 127 and "God's Saving Love (Salvation)," p. 115.

8:44 *devil:* The devil, sometimes called Satan, is the leader of all the forces that are against God and God's people. One of the reasons God sent Jesus was to defeat the devil and all the devil has done (1 John 3:7, 8). See also the mini-article called "Satan," p. 126.

8:13 John 5:31. **8:33** Matt 3:9; Luke 3:8.

---

[a] 24 Or *I am he*; also in verse 28   [b] 33 Greek *seed*; also in verse 37   [c] 38 Or *presence. Therefore do what you have heard from the Father.*   [d] 39 Some early manuscripts *"If you are Abraham's children," said Jesus, "then*

8:48 *you are a Samaritan:* See the notes at 4:3, 4 and 4:9.

8:49 *demon:* See the note at 6:70, 71 (a devil).

8:52 *Abraham died and so did the prophets:* The people don't understand what Jesus means when he tells them that they will never die if they obey him (8:51). At this time, there were differing opinions about eternal life (see the note at 3:15).

8:56 *Abraham rejoiced at the thought of seeing my day:* Jesus is saying that Abraham was able to see how the promises God made to Abraham would be fulfilled.

8:58 *before Abraham was born, I am!:* See the note at 1:1-3 and the mini-article called "I Am," p. 47.

9:2 *who sinned, this man or his parents:* At the time of Jesus, some believed that a person who was blind was being punished by God for sinning, or for the sin of his or her parents (Exod 20:5).

9:4 *Night is coming:* Night is a place of darkness, or symbolizes a lack of understanding (see the note on p. 7, light and darkness). Jesus may also be referring to a time of judgment.

desire. He was a murderer from the beginning, not holding to the truth, for there is no truth in him. When he lies, he speaks his native language, for he is a liar and the father of lies. [45]Yet because I tell the truth, you do not believe me! [46]Can any of you prove me guilty of sin? If I am telling the truth, why don't you believe me? [47]He who belongs to God hears what God says. The reason you do not hear is that you do not belong to God."

The Claims of Jesus About Himself

[48]The Jews answered him, "Aren't we right in saying that you are a Samaritan and demon-possessed?"

[49]"I am not possessed by a demon," said Jesus, "but I honor my Father and you dishonor me. [50]I am not seeking glory for myself; but there is one who seeks it, and he is the judge. [51]I tell you the truth, if anyone keeps my word, he will never see death."

[52]At this the Jews exclaimed, "Now we know that you are demon-possessed! Abraham died and so did the prophets, yet you say that if anyone keeps your word, he will never taste death. [53]Are you greater than our father Abraham? He died, and so did the prophets. Who do you think you are?"

[54]Jesus replied, "If I glorify myself, my glory means nothing. My Father, whom you claim as your God, is the one who glorifies me. [55]Though you do not know him, I know him. If I said I did not, I would be a liar like you, but I do know him and keep his word. [56]Your father Abraham rejoiced at the thought of seeing my day; he saw it and was glad."

[57]"You are not yet fifty years old," the Jews said to him, "and you have seen Abraham!"

[58]"I tell you the truth," Jesus answered, "before Abraham was born, I am!" [59]At this, they picked up stones to stone him, but Jesus hid himself, slipping away from the temple grounds.

MIRACLE SIX—
JESUS HEALS A MAN BORN BLIND

Jesus heals a man born with physical blindness, but the central message behind this event is that Jesus is the light that has power over the darkness of the world.

Jesus Heals a Man Born Blind

9 As he went along, he saw a man blind from birth. [2]His disciples asked him, "Rabbi, who sinned, this man or his parents, that he was born blind?"

[3]"Neither this man nor his parents sinned," said Jesus, "but this happened so that the work of God might be displayed in his

life. [4]As long as it is day, we must do the work of him who sent me. Night is coming, when no one can work. [5]While I am in the world, I am the light of the world."

[6]Having said this, he spit on the ground, made some mud with the saliva, and put it on the man's eyes. [7]"Go," he told him, "wash in the Pool of Siloam" (this word means Sent). So the man went and washed, and came home seeing.

[8]His neighbors and those who had formerly seen him begging asked, "Isn't this the same man who used to sit and beg?" [9]Some claimed that he was.

Others said, "No, he only looks like him."

But he himself insisted, "I am the man."

[10]"How then were your eyes opened?" they demanded.

[11]He replied, "The man they call Jesus made some mud and put it on my eyes. He told me to go to Siloam and wash. So I went and washed, and then I could see."

[12]"Where is this man?" they asked him.

"I don't know," he said.

The Pharisees Investigate the Healing

[13]They brought to the Pharisees the man who had been blind. [14]Now the day on which Jesus had made the mud and opened the man's eyes was a Sabbath. [15]Therefore the Pharisees also asked him how he had received his sight. "He put mud on my eyes," the man replied, "and I washed, and now I see."

[16]Some of the Pharisees said, "This man is not from God, for he does not keep the Sabbath."

But others asked, "How can a sinner do such miraculous signs?" So they were divided.

[17]Finally they turned again to the blind man, "What have you to say about him? It was your eyes he opened."

The man replied, "He is a prophet."

[18]The Jews still did not believe that he had been blind and had received his sight until they sent for the man's parents. [19]"Is this your son?" they asked. "Is this the one you say was born blind? How is it that now he can see?"

[20]"We know he is our son," the parents answered, "and we know he was born blind. [21]But how he can see now, or who opened his eyes, we don't know. Ask him. He is of age; he will speak for himself." [22]His parents said this because they were afraid of the Jews, for already the Jews had decided that anyone who acknowledged that Jesus was the Christ[a] would be put out of the synagogue. [23]That was why his parents said, "He is of age; ask him."

[24]A second time they summoned the man who had been blind. "Give glory to God,[b]" they said. "We know this man is a sinner."

---

[a] **22** Or *Messiah*   [b] **24** A solemn charge to tell the truth (see Joshua 7:19)

9:7 *Pool of Siloam:* This pool is actually a reservoir that was constructed inside the walls of Jerusalem at the time of King Hezekiah (715-687 B.C.). It was located in the valley below and south of the Jerusalem temple. See the map on p. 138. Those who knew the Jewish Scriptures would have been reminded of the time when the prophet Elisha told Naaman, the man with leprosy, to go wash in the Jordan River (2 Kgs 5:1-14). Like the man born blind, Naaman was healed.

9:13, 14 *Sabbath:* See the note at 5:9. When Jesus healed the blind man, he was accused of violating the Sabbath law (9:16).

9:13, 14 *Pharisees:* See the note at 1:24.

9:17 *He is a prophet:* See the note at 4:19. Prophets like Elijah and Elisha had worked miracles, so those who heard Jesus and saw him do miracles would have been reminded of what the Jewish Scriptures said about the prophets.

9:18 *The Jews:* See the note at 7:35.

9:22, 23 *put out of the synagogue:* The Jewish leaders were going to put out of the Jewish community and Jewish meeting places (9:34) anyone who became a follower of Jesus. See also the Introduction to JOHN, p. 7.

9:22, 23 *the Christ:* See the note at 1:19, 20 (the Christ) and the mini-article called "Messiah (Chosen One)," p. 120.

9:24 *this man is a sinner:* The leaders thought Jesus was a sinner because he did not follow the Law of Moses.

9:5 Matt 5:14; John 1:4, 5; 8:12.

9:28 *disciples of Moses:* Those who followed the Law of Moses.

9:34 *You were steeped in sin at birth:* See the note at 9:2.

9:34 *they threw him out:* See the note at 9:22, 23 (put out of the synagogue). See also the note at 6:59 (synagogue).

9:35 *Son of Man:* See the note at 1:51.

9:41 *If you were blind:* Jesus is saying that those who are blind spiritually but open to the truth are not guilty. But those who claim they understand the truth (based on the Law of Moses) but will not trust Jesus continue to be guilty.

10:1 *sheep pen . . . thief and a robber:* A sheep pen was an enclosed area for keeping sheep safe at night.

10:2, 3 *gate . . . shepherd . . . watchman:* The watchman decided who or what got into the sheep pen. Often the watchman was the shepherd himself, who counted the sheep as they entered the pen for the night. The gate was the only way to go into or out of the pen.

9:39 Matt 13:11; Luke 4:16-19.

The Good Shepherd, unknown Nigerian artist, 1978. Shepherds were a familiar sight in Palestine in Jesus' day. The crowds that gathered to hear Jesus speak knew that looking after sheep was difficult, and sometimes dangerous, work. Even so, it probably surprised some of them to hear Jesus say, "I am the good shepherd; I know my sheep, and my sheep know me . . . and I lay down my life for the sheep." (See 10:7-21.)

²⁵He replied, "Whether he is a sinner or not, I don't know. One thing I do know. I was blind but now I see!"

²⁶Then they asked him, "What did he do to you? How did he open your eyes?"

²⁷He answered, "I have told you already and you did not listen. Why do you want to hear it again? Do you want to become his disciples, too?"

²⁸Then they hurled insults at him and said, "You are this fellow's disciple! We are disciples of Moses! ²⁹We know that God spoke to Moses, but as for this fellow, we don't even know where he comes from."

³⁰The man answered, "Now that is remarkable! You don't know where he comes from, yet he opened my eyes. ³¹We know that God does not listen to sinners. He listens to the godly man who does his will. ³²Nobody has ever heard of opening the eyes of a man born blind. ³³If this man were not from God, he could do nothing."

³⁴To this they replied, "You were steeped in sin at birth; how dare you lecture us!" And they threw him out.

Spiritual Blindness

³⁵Jesus heard that they had thrown him out, and when he found him, he said, "Do you believe in the Son of Man?"

³⁶"Who is he, sir?" the man asked. "Tell me so that I may believe in him."

³⁷Jesus said, "You have now seen him; in fact, he is the one speaking with you."

³⁸Then the man said, "Lord, I believe," and he worshiped him. ³⁹Jesus said, "For judgment I have come into this world, so that the blind will see and those who see will become blind."

⁴⁰Some Pharisees who were with him heard him say this and asked, "What? Are we blind too?"

⁴¹Jesus said, "If you were blind, you would not be guilty of sin; but now that you claim you can see, your guilt remains.

THE GOOD SHEPHERD AND THE TRUE FLOCK

In chapter 10, Jesus uses the images of the shepherd, flock, and thieves to describe the relationship between himself, his true followers, and those who want to come between God and God's people.

The Shepherd and His Flock

10 "I tell you the truth, the man who does not enter the sheep pen by the gate, but climbs in by some other way, is a thief and a robber. ²The man who enters by the gate is the shepherd of his sheep. ³The watchman opens the gate for him, and the sheep listen to his voice. He calls his own sheep by name and leads them out. ⁴When he has brought out all his own, he goes on ahead of them, and his sheep follow him because they know his voice. ⁵But they will never follow a stranger; in fact, they will run away from him because they do not recognize a stranger's voice." ⁶Jesus used this figure of speech, but they did not understand what he was telling them.

⁷Therefore Jesus said again, "I tell you the truth, I am the gate for the sheep. ⁸All who ever came before me were thieves and robbers, but the sheep did not listen to them. ⁹I am the gate; whoever enters through me will be saved.ᵃ He will come in and go out, and find pasture. ¹⁰The thief comes only to steal and kill and destroy; I have come that they may have life, and have it to the full.

¹¹"I am the good shepherd. The good shepherd lays down his life for the sheep. ¹²The hired hand is not the shepherd who owns the sheep. So when he sees the wolf coming, he abandons the sheep and runs away. Then the wolf attacks the flock and scatters it. ¹³The man runs away because he is a hired hand and cares nothing for the sheep.

¹⁴"I am the good shepherd; I know my sheep and my sheep know me— ¹⁵just as the Father knows me and I know the Father— and I lay down my life for the sheep. ¹⁶I have other sheep that are not of this sheep pen. I must bring them also. They too will listen to my voice, and there shall be one flock and one shepherd. ¹⁷The reason my Father loves me is that I lay down my life—only to take

---

ᵃ**9** Or *kept safe*

10:2, 3 *the sheep listen to his voice:* In the Scriptures, sheep and flocks of sheep are symbols for God's people (Ps 23:1; 77:20; Isa 53:6; Ezek 34:11-16). See also the mini-article called "Shepherds," p. 126. A "Good Shepherd" was an early Christian symbol for Christ, as in this stone carving from a catacomb in Rome (third century).

10:7 *I am the gate for the sheep:* See the note at 10:2, 3. As the gate for the sheep (his followers), Jesus stands guard and protects them. He also determines who will go through the gate.

10:8 *thieves and robbers:* Jesus is talking about those who have been teaching the people (God's sheep or flock) the Law of Moses in a way that led them away from the truth about what God wants.

10:11 *good shepherd lays down his life for the sheep:* See 10:15; 13:37; 15:13; and the note on p. 1945XX.

10:13 *a hired hand:* This may be a reference to Israel's leaders, but the key point is that the real shepherd (Jesus) who "owns" the sheep would never run away when danger threatened.

10:16 *one flock ... and one shepherd:* Jesus will help his followers become "one" in spite of their differences (see also Gal 3:26-29).

 10:15 Matt 11:27; Luke 10:22.

10:20 *demon:* See the note at 6:70, 71.

10:22 *Feast of Dedication:* This was a celebration of how God freed the Jewish people from Antiochus IV Epiphanes, the Syrian king who had set up a statue of himself as a god in the Jerusalem temple in 168 B.C. This feast is also known as Hanukkah.

10:23 *Solomon's Colonnade:* This was a public place made from huge stone columns on the east and south sides of the temple area. See the map on p. 139.

10:24 *the Christ:* See the note at 1:19, 20 (the Christ).

10:28 *eternal life:* See the note at 3:15.

10:31 *the Jews picked up stones:* See the note at 1:19, 20 (priests) and 1:24 (Pharisees). Anyone who disobeyed the Law of Moses in a way that threatened the purity of the community was to be killed by the joint action of the group (Lev 24:15, 16; Deut 21:18-21; 22:20-22). The group would throw big stones to crush and bury the one who was accused of being a threat to all of God's people.

10:33 *you, a mere man, claim to be God:* The Jewish leaders accused Jesus of claiming he was God. Since they believed he was only a man, and not God, they said that Jesus was guilty of one of the most horrible offenses against God (blasphemy), which was punishable by death.

10:34, 35 *in your Law . . . Scripture cannot be broken:* The Law refers to the Jewish Scriptures, which Christians call the Old Testament. By saying that "Scripture cannot be broken," Jesus asserts the total reliability and authority of the Jewish Scriptures, which Christians call the Old Testament.

10:40 *across the Jordan:* Jesus escaped and traveled east, crossing the Jordan River near where John had been baptizing (see 1:28).

it up again. [18]No one takes it from me, but I lay it down of my own accord. I have authority to lay it down and authority to take it up again. This command I received from my Father."

[19]At these words the Jews were again divided. [20]Many of them said, "He is demon-possessed and raving mad. Why listen to him?"

[21]But others said, "These are not the sayings of a man possessed by a demon. Can a demon open the eyes of the blind?"

The Unbelief of the Jews

[22]Then came the Feast of Dedication[a] at Jerusalem. It was winter, [23]and Jesus was in the temple area walking in Solomon's Colonnade. [24]The Jews gathered around him, saying, "How long will you keep us in suspense? If you are the Christ,[b] tell us plainly."

[25]Jesus answered, "I did tell you, but you do not believe. The miracles I do in my Father's name speak for me, [26]but you do not believe because you are not my sheep. [27]My sheep listen to my voice; I know them, and they follow me. [28]I give them eternal life, and they shall never perish; no one can snatch them out of my hand. [29]My Father, who has given them to me, is greater than all[c] ; no one can snatch them out of my Father's hand. [30]I and the Father are one."

[31]Again the Jews picked up stones to stone him, [32]but Jesus said to them, "I have shown you many great miracles from the Father. For which of these do you stone me?"

[33]"We are not stoning you for any of these," replied the Jews, "but for blasphemy, because you, a mere man, claim to be God."

[34]Jesus answered them, "Is it not written in your Law, 'I have said you are gods'[d] ? [35]If he called them 'gods,' to whom the word of God came—and the Scripture cannot be broken— [36]what about the one whom the Father set apart as his very own and sent into the world? Why then do you accuse me of blasphemy because I said, 'I am God's Son'? [37]Do not believe me unless I do what my Father does. [38]But if I do it, even though you do not believe me, believe the miracles, that you may know and understand that the Father is in me, and I in the Father." [39]Again they tried to seize him, but he escaped their grasp.

[40]Then Jesus went back across the Jordan to the place where John had been baptizing in the early days. Here he stayed [41]and many people came to him. They said, "Though John never performed a miraculous sign, all that John said about this man was true." [42]And in that place many believed in Jesus.

---

[a] **22** That is, Hanukkah   [b] **24** Or *Messiah*   [c] **29** Many early manuscripts *What my Father has given me is greater than all*   [d] **34** Psalm 82:6

MIRACLE SEVEN—
JESUS BRINGS LAZARUS TO LIFE

The Death of Lazarus

11 Now a man named Lazarus was sick. He was from Bethany, the village of Mary and her sister Martha. [2]This Mary, whose brother Lazarus now lay sick, was the same one who poured perfume on the Lord and wiped his feet with her hair. [3]So the sisters sent word to Jesus, "Lord, the one you love is sick."

[4]When he heard this, Jesus said, "This sickness will not end in death. No, it is for God's glory so that God's Son may be glorified through it." [5]Jesus loved Martha and her sister and Lazarus. [6]Yet when he heard that Lazarus was sick, he stayed where he was two more days.

[7]Then he said to his disciples, "Let us go back to Judea."

[8]"But Rabbi," they said, "a short while ago the Jews tried to stone you, and yet you are going back there?"

[9]Jesus answered, "Are there not twelve hours of daylight? A man who walks by day will not stumble, for he sees by this world's light. [10]It is when he walks by night that he stumbles, for he has no light."

[11]After he had said this, he went on to tell them, "Our friend Lazarus has fallen asleep; but I am going there to wake him up."

[12]His disciples replied, "Lord, if he sleeps, he will get better." [13]Jesus had been speaking of his death, but his disciples thought he meant natural sleep.

[14]So then he told them plainly, "Lazarus is dead, [15]and for your sake I am glad I was not there, so that you may believe. But let us go to him."

[16]Then Thomas (called Didymus) said to the rest of the disciples, "Let us also go, that we may die with him."

Jesus Comforts the Sisters

[17]On his arrival, Jesus found that Lazarus had already been in the tomb for four days. [18]Bethany was less than two miles[a] from Jerusalem, [19]and many Jews had come to Martha and Mary to comfort them in the loss of their brother. [20]When Martha heard that Jesus was coming, she went out to meet him, but Mary stayed at home.

[21]"Lord," Martha said to Jesus, "if you had been here, my brother would not have died. [22]But I know that even now God will give you whatever you ask."

[23]Jesus said to her, "Your brother will rise again."

11:1, 2 *Lazarus . . . Mary and her sister Martha:* The name Lazarus in Hebrew means "God helps." Martha and Mary are mentioned in Luke 10:38-42. Mary is also the one who pours perfume on Jesus' feet in 12:3.

11:1, 2 *Bethany:* A small village about two miles east of Jerusalem, on the slopes of the Mount of Olives. It is known as El-'Azariyeh, named after Lazarus (11:1), whose tomb is still said to be in Bethany where he lived. See also the map on p. 138.

11:7 *go back to Judea:* Jesus apparently got the message about Lazarus while on the east side of the Jordan River (10:40).

11:11 *Lazarus has fallen asleep:* Jesus meant that Lazarus was dead (11:13). Jesus would "wake him up" by bringing him back to life from the dead.

11:16 *Thomas:* Thomas was one of Jesus' twelve close apostles (disciples). His Aramaic name means "Twin." Thomas is mentioned in the lists of the twelve apostles (Matt 10:3; Mark 3:18; and Luke 6:15). He is sometimes known as doubting Thomas, because he refused at first to believe that Jesus had been raised from death (20:24-29).

11:17 *tomb:* Tombs were usually carved out of the soft limestone hillsides in Palestine. Most tombs had more than one room and more than one burial chamber. Each chamber held one body. The door to a burial chamber was a stone slab that could be moved. A large circular stone was sometimes used to seal the entrance to the tomb.

10:33 Lev 24:16. **10:34** Ps 82:6. **11:1** Luke 10:38, 39.

---

[a] **18** Greek *fifteen stadia* (about 3 kilometers)

11:24 *rise again in the resurrection at the last day:* Martha apparently believed in the hope of life after death. See the mini-article called "Eternal Life," below. See also the note at 6:39.

11:27 *Christ, the Son of God:* See the notes at 1:41 (Christ) and 1:34 (Son of God), and the mini-article called "Son of God," p. 10.

[24]Martha answered, "I know he will rise again in the resurrection at the last day."

[25]Jesus said to her, "I am the resurrection and the life. He who believes in me will live, even though he dies; [26]and whoever lives and believes in me will never die. Do you believe this?"

[27]"Yes, Lord," she told him, "I believe that you are the Christ,[a] the Son of God, who was to come into the world."

<hr>

[a] 27 Or *Messiah*

ETERNAL LIFE

In ancient times, the people of Israel based their hope for life beyond death on the lives of their descendants. It was considered a tragedy when a man died without having a son to carry on the family line. Most people expected that their bodies would rot and turn to dust after they died (Eccl 12:7; Ps 104:29; Job 7:9, 10). Some believed that the souls of the dead went to a special place, but these souls had no thoughts or feelings there (Eccl 9:10; Isa 38:10). The Bible reports that a few people did not die but were taken up to be with God (Gen 5:21-24; 2 Kgs 2:1-14).

The idea of people being raised from death appears in the book of the prophet Daniel, who said that both good and bad people would be raised from death to new life. The good would experience eternal life, while the bad would have eternal shame (Dan 12:1-3). Other passages express confidence that God would not send faithful people to the world of the dead, but would save them from death (Ps 16:10, 11; 49:13-15; Isa 26:19).

The people of Israel were taken into exile in Babylon around 586 B.C. Later, the Persians defeated Babylon and let the people of Israel begin to return home (538 B.C.). Some Israelites were influenced by Persians who believed that God's enemy, Satan, would be defeated and that the souls and bodies of faithful people who had died would be brought back to life. During the four centuries before the birth of Christ, the Jewish people were also influenced by some Greek thinkers who believed that the physical human body had no lasting value and would rot away, but the invisible soul or spirit would live forever. The apostle Paul told the church in Corinth that the physical bodies of Christ's followers will die, but when God raises them to new life, their bodies will change into "spiritual bodies" (1 Cor 15:35-54). This is different from the belief that only the soul would live on after the body decayed. Paul says that the whole person—both soul and body—will be new and experience life after death (eternal life).

Jesus called himself "the resurrection and the life" (John 11:25, 26) and promises that all who believe in him will have eternal life (John 3:16). One group of religious Jews called Sadducees questioned Jesus' teachings about life after death (Luke 20:27). Jesus told them that when God's people rise from death they will not marry but their new lives will be like those of the angels in heaven (Mark 12:18-27). Jesus also gave a surprising parable in Luke 14:15-24: about which people would be part of God's future kingdom.

Early Christians believed that God's people would be raised to new life because God raised Jesus from death to new life (Acts 2:22-24, 29-32; 1 Cor 15:20-28; 1 Thes 4:13-17). Revelation 21 describes the new Jerusalem, where God will live among people on earth and where God will feed and protect his followers forever. (See also Ezek 37:26, 27; Matt 1:23; 2 Cor 4:16—5:5.)

²⁸And after she had said this, she went back and called her sister Mary aside. "The Teacher is here," she said, "and is asking for you." ²⁹When Mary heard this, she got up quickly and went to him. ³⁰Now Jesus had not yet entered the village, but was still at the place where Martha had met him. ³¹When the Jews who had been with Mary in the house, comforting her, noticed how quickly she got up and went out, they followed her, supposing she was going to the tomb to mourn there.

³²When Mary reached the place where Jesus was and saw him, she fell at his feet and said, "Lord, if you had been here, my brother would not have died."

³³When Jesus saw her weeping, and the Jews who had come along with her also weeping, he was deeply moved in spirit and troubled. ³⁴"Where have you laid him?" he asked.

"Come and see, Lord," they replied.

³⁵Jesus wept.

³⁶Then the Jews said, "See how he loved him!"

³⁷But some of them said, "Could not he who opened the eyes of the blind man have kept this man from dying?"

Jesus Raises Lazarus From the Dead

³⁸Jesus, once more deeply moved, came to the tomb. It was a cave with a stone laid across the entrance. ³⁹"Take away the stone," he said.

"But, Lord," said Martha, the sister of the dead man, "by this time there is a bad odor, for he has been there four days."

⁴⁰Then Jesus said, "Did I not tell you that if you believed, you would see the glory of God?"

⁴¹So they took away the stone. Then Jesus looked up and said, "Father, I thank you that you have heard me. ⁴²I knew that you always hear me, but I said this for the benefit of the people standing here, that they may believe that you sent me."

Jesus said, "Did I not tell you that if you believed, you would see the glory of God?"
John 11:40

11:39 *a bad odor:* A body that had been dead for four days would have begun to decay, causing a bad odor to come from the tomb. Martha was concerned with the practical fact that the body would smell when Jesus goes in to look at it.

QUESTIONS ABOUT JOHN 2:1—11:44

1. What do the many miracles in chapters 2–11 say about Jesus? What effect did Jesus' miracles have on people?
2. What did Jesus mean when he described himself as "the bread of life" (6:35)? As "living water" (7:38, 39)? As "the light of the world" (8:12)? As "the good shepherd" (10:14)?
3. What was remarkable about Jesus' meeting with the Samaritan woman at the well (4:3-42)? What point did Jesus make about worship (4:21-24)?
4. What did Jesus do that made the leaders angry enough to kill him (5:17, 18)? Why did they want to get rid of Jesus?
5. What did Jesus mean when he said, "If the Son sets you free, you will be free indeed" (8:36)? In what areas of your life do you feel you are not "free"?
6. When Jesus says he has come to give sight to the blind and make blind everyone who can see, what does he mean (9:39)? In your life, what would you like to "see" more clearly? Why?

11:44 *grave clothes:* In Jesus' day, dead bodies were usually wrapped in strips of linen cloth. Sometimes sweet-smelling spices and ointments were also put on the body. A single piece of cloth was used to cover the face of the person who had died. See also the mini-article called "Burial," p. 109.

11:46, 47 *chief priests and the Pharisees . . . Sanhedrin:* See the notes at 1:24 (Pharisees), 7:32 (chief priests), and 7:50 (Sanhedrin).

11:48 *the Romans will come and take away both our place and our nation:* The Jewish leaders were afraid that Jesus would lead his followers to rebel against Rome and that the Roman army would then destroy their nation and the temple. They were also afraid that if many people started to follow Jesus and his teachings, their own power would be lessened.

11:49 *Caiaphas:* Caiaphas was the high priest in Jerusalem from A.D. 18-37. He was in charge of the priests who served in the temple. He had great power among the religious and political leaders of Israel.

11:52 *the scattered children of God, to bring them together:* Though God had chosen Israel (the Jewish nation), people of all nations are invited to be part of God's new family.

The Resurrection of Lazarus by Henry Ossawa Tanner, 1896. All of the Gospels tell of Jesus' raising to life someone who had died, but only JOHN tells about Jesus raising his good friend, Lazarus, back to life. Lazarus had been dead and buried for four days when Jesus came to Lazarus's tomb, prayed to God, and shouted, "Lazarus, come out!" (See 11:1-44.) This miracle, the last one reported in JOHN, upset the chief priests so much that they began to make plans to kill Lazarus. (See 12:9-11.)

⁴³When he had said this, Jesus called in a loud voice, "Lazarus, come out!" ⁴⁴The dead man came out, his hands and feet wrapped with strips of linen, and a cloth around his face.

Jesus said to them, "Take off the grave clothes and let him go."

Jesus' Final Days

This section (11:45—19:42) describes the final days before Jesus' death on the cross, which in JOHN is the time when his full glory is to be revealed (7:39). First, the plot to arrest and kill Jesus is revealed. Then Jesus visits Bethany where Mary pours expensive oil on him in preparation for his upcoming burial (12:7). Later, Jesus prepares his own disciples for his death and prays for them just before he is arrested, put on trial, and put to death.

PREPARATIONS FOR JESUS' DEATH

The Plot to Kill Jesus

⁴⁵Therefore many of the Jews who had come to visit Mary, and had seen what Jesus did, put their faith in him. ⁴⁶But some of them went to the Pharisees and told them what Jesus had done.

⁴⁷Then the chief priests and the Pharisees called a meeting of the Sanhedrin.

"What are we accomplishing?" they asked. "Here is this man performing many miraculous signs. ⁴⁸If we let him go on like this, everyone will believe in him, and then the Romans will come and take away both our place[a] and our nation."

⁴⁹Then one of them, named Caiaphas, who was high priest that year, spoke up, "You know nothing at all! ⁵⁰You do not realize that it is better for you that one man die for the people than that the whole nation perish."

⁵¹He did not say this on his own, but as high priest that year he prophesied that Jesus would die for the Jewish nation, ⁵²and not only for that nation but also for the scattered children of God, to bring them together and make them one. ⁵³So from that day on they plotted to take his life.

⁵⁴Therefore Jesus no longer moved about publicly among the Jews. Instead he withdrew to a region near the desert, to a village called Ephraim, where he stayed with his disciples.

⁵⁵When it was almost time for the Jewish Passover, many went up from the country to Jerusalem for their ceremonial cleansing before the Passover. ⁵⁶They kept looking for Jesus, and as they stood in the temple area they asked one another, "What do you think? Isn't he coming to the Feast at all?" ⁵⁷But the chief priests and Pharisees had given orders that if anyone found out where Jesus was, he should report it so that they might arrest him.

Jesus Anointed at Bethany

12 Six days before the Passover, Jesus arrived at Bethany, where Lazarus lived, whom Jesus had raised from the dead. ²Here a dinner was given in Jesus' honor. Martha served, while Lazarus was among those reclining at the table with him. ³Then Mary took about a pint[b] of pure nard, an expensive perfume; she poured it on Jesus' feet and wiped his feet with her hair. And the house was filled with the fragrance of the perfume.

⁴But one of his disciples, Judas Iscariot, who was later to betray him, objected, ⁵"Why wasn't this perfume sold and the money given to the poor? It was worth a year's wages.[c]" ⁶He did not say this because he cared about the poor but because he was a thief; as keeper of the money bag, he used to help himself to what was put into it.

⁷"Leave her alone," Jesus replied. "[It was intended] that she should save this perfume for the day of my burial. ⁸You will always have the poor among you, but you will not always have me."

⁹Meanwhile a large crowd of Jews found out that Jesus was there and came, not only because of him but also to see Lazarus,

11:53 *plotted to take his life:* They probably hoped to arrest and kill Jesus during the time of the upcoming Passover Feast.

 11:54 *Ephraim:* This village was probably north of Jerusalem on the border of the Judean desert toward the Jordan River.

11:55 *Passover:* See the note at 2:13.

11:55 *ceremonial cleansing:* The Jewish people had to purify themselves with certain cleansing rituals in order to prepare to worship God and to celebrate the feast.

11:57 *chief priests and Pharisees:* See the notes at 1:24 (Pharisees), and 7:32 (chief priests).

12:1 *Passover:* See the note at 2:13.

 12:1, 2 *Bethany ... Lazarus ... Martha:* See the notes at 11:1, 2.

12:3 *a pint of pure nard, an expensive perfume:* The Greek text has "perfume made of pure spikenard," a plant used to make perfume. In ancient times perfumed ointment and oil were kept in sealed jars, which could be opened only by breaking the jar's neck. The perfume made from the nard plant had to be imported from India, so it was very expensive.

12:4 *Judas Iscariot:* Judas was the disciple in charge of the money bag that was used to support Jesus and the disciples and to give to the poor. See also the note at 6:70, 71.

12:7 *for the day of my burial:* Without knowing, Mary was preparing Jesus ahead of time for his burial. See also the mini-article called "Burial," p. 109.

 **12:8** Deut 15:11.

---
[a] **48** Or *temple*   [b] **3** Greek *a litra* (probably about 0.5 liter)   [c] **5** Greek *three hundred denarii*

12:10 *chief priests made plans to kill Lazarus:* See the note at 7:32 (chief priests). They wanted to kill Lazarus because he was living proof of Jesus' power (12:11).

12:12 *the Feast . . . Jerusalem:* See the notes at 2:23 (Jerusalem) and the note at 2:13 (Passover).

12:13 *palm branches:* Palm branches were regularly used to welcome visiting rulers or famous people.

12:15 *donkey:* See Zech 9.9, which predicts the coming of Israel's king on a donkey. Roman leaders usually rode large horses when they entered a city in a parade.

12:16 *after Jesus was glorified:* See the note at 7:39 (glorified).

12:16 *these things had been written:* In the Jewish Scriptures, which Christians call the Old Testament.

12:19 *Pharisees:* See the note at 1:24.

12:20 *Greeks:* Perhaps Gentiles who worshiped with Jews. See the note at 7:35.

12:21, 22 *Philip ... Andrew:* See the notes at 1:45 (Philip) and 1:40 (Andrew).

12:23 *the Son of Man to be glorified:* See the notes at 1:51 and 7:39 (glorified).

12:25 *eternal life:* See the note at 3:15.

12:27 *my heart is troubled . . . for this very reason I came:* Jesus knows that he will fulfill God's purposes by suffering death on a cross. His death would also bring glory to God the Father.

12:28, 29 *voice came from heaven . . . thundered . . . an angel had spoken:* The voice is from God, but some think the voice is thunder and others think it is an angel. Thunder is linked with God's voice in the Bible (Exod 20:18; 1 Sam 7:9, Ps 29:3; 10; Rev 14:2).

whom he had raised from the dead. [10]So the chief priests made plans to kill Lazarus as well, [11]for on account of him many of the Jews were going over to Jesus and putting their faith in him.

The Triumphal Entry

[12]The next day the great crowd that had come for the Feast heard that Jesus was on his way to Jerusalem. [13]They took palm branches and went out to meet him, shouting,

> "Hosanna![a]"
>
> "Blessed is he who comes in the name of the Lord!"[b]
>
> "Blessed is the King of Israel!"

[14]Jesus found a young donkey and sat upon it, as it is written,

> [15]"Do not be afraid, O Daughter of Zion;
>   see, your king is coming,
>   seated on a donkey's colt."[c]

[16]At first his disciples did not understand all this. Only after Jesus was glorified did they realize that these things had been written about him and that they had done these things to him.

[17]Now the crowd that was with him when he called Lazarus from the tomb and raised him from the dead continued to spread the word. [18]Many people, because they had heard that he had given this miraculous sign, went out to meet him. [19]So the Pharisees said to one another, "See, this is getting us nowhere. Look how the whole world has gone after him!"

Jesus Predicts His Death

[20]Now there were some Greeks among those who went up to worship at the Feast. [21]They came to Philip, who was from Bethsaida in Galilee, with a request. "Sir," they said, "we would like to see Jesus." [22]Philip went to tell Andrew; Andrew and Philip in turn told Jesus.

[23]Jesus replied, "The hour has come for the Son of Man to be glorified. [24]I tell you the truth, unless a kernel of wheat falls to the ground and dies, it remains only a single seed. But if it dies, it produces many seeds. [25]The man who loves his life will lose it, while the man who hates his life in this world will keep it for eternal life. [26]Whoever serves me must follow me; and where I am, my servant also will be. My Father will honor the one who serves me.

[27]"Now my heart is troubled, and what shall I say? 'Father, save me from this hour'? No, it was for this very reason I came to this hour. [28]Father, glorify your name!"

---

[a] **13** A Hebrew expression meaning "Save!" which became an exclamation of praise
[b] **13** Psalm 118:25,26   [c] **15** Zech. 9:9

Then a voice came from heaven, "I have glorified it, and will glorify it again." [29]The crowd that was there and heard it said it had thundered; others said an angel had spoken to him.

[30]Jesus said, "This voice was for your benefit, not mine. [31]Now is the time for judgment on this world; now the prince of this world will be driven out. [32]But I, when I am lifted up from the earth, will draw all men to myself." [33]He said this to show the kind of death he was going to die.

[34]The crowd spoke up, "We have heard from the Law that the Christ[a] will remain forever, so how can you say, 'The Son of Man must be lifted up'? Who is this 'Son of Man'?"

[35]Then Jesus told them, "You are going to have the light just a little while longer. Walk while you have the light, before darkness overtakes you. The man who walks in the dark does not know where he is going. [36]Put your trust in the light while you have it, so that you may become sons of light." When he had finished speaking, Jesus left and hid himself from them.

The Jews Continue in Their Unbelief

[37]Even after Jesus had done all these miraculous signs in their presence, they still would not believe in him. [38]This was to fulfill the word of Isaiah the prophet:

> "Lord, who has believed our message
> > and to whom has the arm of the Lord been revealed?"[b]

[39]For this reason they could not believe, because, as Isaiah says elsewhere:

> [40] "He has blinded their eyes
> > and deadened their hearts,
> > so they can neither see with their eyes,
> > nor understand with their hearts,
> > nor turn—and I would heal them."[c]

[41]Isaiah said this because he saw Jesus' glory and spoke about him.

[42]Yet at the same time many even among the leaders believed in him. But because of the Pharisees they would not confess their faith for fear they would be put out of the synagogue; [43]for they loved praise from men more than praise from God.

[44]Then Jesus cried out, "When a man believes in me, he does not believe in me only, but in the one who sent me. [45]When he looks at me, he sees the one who sent me. [46]I have come into the world as a light, so that no one who believes in me should stay in darkness.

12:31 *prince of this world:* This is one of John's names for the devil, sometimes called Satan, who is the leader of the forces in the world that are against God and God's people (8:44; 14:30; 16:11). In JOHN "world" sometimes refers to the people who live in this world and to the evil forces that seek to control their lives (see the note at 8:23).

12:32 *lifted up from the earth:* Jesus used these words to refer both to the time when he will be nailed to a cross (12:33) and when he will be raised from death to live with God in heaven.

12:34 *the Christ will remain forever:* No specific passage in the Jewish Scriptures says this, but the people may be referring to the promise that the family of King David would rule forever (2 Chron 21:7; Ps 89:36; Isa 9:7). See the note 1:19, 20 (the Christ). If Jesus was the Christ, the people didn't understand why he, the Son of Man, would have to be "lifted up," which here means put to death on a cross.

12:35 *light:* See the note on p. 7.

12:42 *Pharisees . . . put out of the synagogue:* The Pharisees (see the note at 1:24) were in charge of many of the Jewish meeting places. Some Jewish leaders had secretly put their faith in Jesus, but they were afraid to be open about this, for fear that they would be thrown out of the Jewish synagogues by the Pharisees. See the notes at 9:22, 23 (put out of the synagogue) and 6:59 (synagogue).

12:44 *When a man believes in me . . . in the one who sent me:* Jesus is saying that when people put their trust in him it is the same as putting their trust in God. See also the mini-article called "Faith," p. 114.

12:46 *light . . . darkness:* See the note on p. 7.

12:13 Ps 118:25, 26. **12:25** Matt 10:39; 16:25; Mark 8:35; Luke 9:24; 17:33. **12:34** Ps 110:4; Isa 9:7; Ezek 37:25; Dan 7:14. **12:38** Isa 53:1 (Septuagint). **12:40** Isa 6:9, 10 (Septuagint).

---

[a] **34** Or *Messiah*   [b] **38** Isaiah 53:1   [c] **40** Isaiah 6:10

12:48 *condemn him at the last day:* See the note at 6:39.

12:50 *eternal life:* See the note at 3:15.

13:1 *before the Passover Feast:* See the note at 2:13 (Passover). It is not clear just how long before the Passover this is. In the other Gospels, Jesus' last supper with the disciples is the Passover meal (see Mark 14:12, for example).

13:2 *devil had already prompted Judas Iscariot:* See the note at 8:44 (devil); the mini-article called "Satan," p. 126; and the notes at 6:70, 71, and 12:4 (Judas). For more about Judas, see Mark 14:10, 11 and Luke 22:3-6.

13:5 *began to wash his disciples' feet:* In ancient Jewish society, it was the duty of the servant to wash his or her master's feet. Jesus takes the job of a servant and washes his disciples' feet. The foot washing is a symbol of his great servant act to come, dying on the cross for the sins of the world.

13:6 *Simon Peter:* See the note at 1:42. Peter's argument (13:8) is understandable, since Jesus was the master.

13:11 *not every one was clean:* Jesus was talking about Judas (13:2).

13:12 *returned to his place:* This means that Jesus returned to his place at the meal. On special occasions the Jewish people followed the Greek and Roman custom of lying down on their side and leaning on their left elbow, while eating with their right hand.

13:13 *Lord:* The Greek word for "Lord" is *kyrios,* which may mean master or may be used to address someone as "sir." When it is used for Jesus, it emphasizes his authority and power. See also the note at 20:28 and the mini-article called "Lord," p. 119.

13:12-15 Luke 22:27. **13:16** Matt 10:24; Luke 6:40; John 15:20.

[47]"As for the person who hears my words but does not keep them, I do not judge him. For I did not come to judge the world, but to save it. [48]There is a judge for the one who rejects me and does not accept my words; that very word which I spoke will condemn him at the last day. [49]For I did not speak of my own accord, but the Father who sent me commanded me what to say and how to say it. [50]I know that his command leads to eternal life. So whatever I say is just what the Father has told me to say."

JESUS PREPARES HIS FOLLOWERS

Jesus Washes His Disciples' Feet

13 It was just before the Passover Feast. Jesus knew that the time had come for him to leave this world and go to the Father. Having loved his own who were in the world, he now showed them the full extent of his love.[a]

[2]The evening meal was being served, and the devil had already prompted Judas Iscariot, son of Simon, to betray Jesus. [3]Jesus knew that the Father had put all things under his power, and that he had come from God and was returning to God; [4]so he got up from the meal, took off his outer clothing, and wrapped a towel around his waist. [5]After that, he poured water into a basin and began to wash his disciples' feet, drying them with the towel that was wrapped around him.

[6]He came to Simon Peter, who said to him, "Lord, are you going to wash my feet?"

[7]Jesus replied, "You do not realize now what I am doing, but later you will understand."

[8]"No," said Peter, "you shall never wash my feet."

Jesus answered, "Unless I wash you, you have no part with me."

[9]"Then, Lord," Simon Peter replied, "not just my feet but my hands and my head as well!"

[10]Jesus answered, "A person who has had a bath needs only to wash his feet; his whole body is clean. And you are clean, though not every one of you." [11]For he knew who was going to betray him, and that was why he said not every one was clean.

[12]When he had finished washing their feet, he put on his clothes and returned to his place. "Do you understand what I have done for you?" he asked them. [13]"You call me 'Teacher' and 'Lord,' and rightly so, for that is what I am. [14]Now that I, your Lord and Teacher, have washed your feet, you also should wash one another's feet. [15]I have set you an example that you should do as I have done for you. [16]I tell you the truth, no servant is greater than his master, nor is a messenger greater than the one who sent him. [17]Now that you know these things, you will be blessed if you do them.

---

[a] 1 Or *he loved them to the last*

Jesus Predicts His Betrayal

[18]"I am not referring to all of you; I know those I have chosen. But this is to fulfill the scripture: 'He who shares my bread has lifted up his heel against me.'[a]

[19]"I am telling you now before it happens, so that when it does happen you will believe that I am He. [20]I tell you the truth, whoever accepts anyone I send accepts me; and whoever accepts me accepts the one who sent me."

[21]After he had said this, Jesus was troubled in spirit and testified, "I tell you the truth, one of you is going to betray me."

[22]His disciples stared at one another, at a loss to know which of them he meant. [23]One of them, the disciple whom Jesus loved, was reclining next to him. [24]Simon Peter motioned to this disciple and said, "Ask him which one he means."

---

[a] 18 Psalm 41:9

13:19 *I am:* See the note at 8:24.

13:21 *one of you is going to betray me:* See the notes at 13:2 and 13:11.

13:23 *the disciple whom Jesus loved:* In JOHN, one disciple is singled out in this way (19:26; 20:2). Although the identity of this disciple is never expressly stated, it has traditionally been assumed that this is John, the author of this Gospel. Obviously, this expression doesn't mean that Jesus didn't love the other disciples, but rather that there was a special bond between Jesus and this individual. See also the note at 21:24.

13:24 *Simon:* This is Simon Peter (see the note at 1:42).

13:18 Ps 41:9. **13:20** Matt 10:40; Mark 9:37; Luke 9:48; 10:16.

Washing the Feet by Jyoti Sahi, twentieth century. At Jesus' last supper with his disciples, he removed his outer garment, wrapped a towel around his waist, and began washing his disciples' feet. When he was finished he explained to them, "Now that I, your Lord and Teacher, have washed your feet, you also should wash one another's feet. I have set you an example that you should do as I have done for you." (See 13:1-17.)

13:26, 27 *Judas . . . Satan:* See the note at 13:2.

13:29 *the Feast:* The Feast of Passover (see the note at 2:13).

13:31 *Son of Man glorified:* See the note at 1:51 and the mini-article called "Son of Man," p. 130; see also the note at 7:39 (glorified).

13:34 *new command . . . Love one another:* Jesus' love for his followers is to be the standard for how they will love one another (15:12, 17; 1 John 3:23; 2 John 5).

13:36 *Simon Peter:* See the note at 1:42.

13:38 *before the rooster crows:* Since roosters crowed at dawn, Jesus is saying that Peter will deny that he knows Jesus three times before the next sunrise.

14:2 *In my Father's house are many rooms:* Jesus is talking about heaven. See the mini-article called "Heaven," p. 115.

14:5 *Thomas:* See the note at 11:16.

14:6 *I am the way and the truth and the life:* Jesus here claims that he is the "way" people can learn the "truth" about God and find "life" with God. See the mini-article called "Truth" on p. 1992.

13:29 John 12.6. **13:33** John 7.34.

[25] Leaning back against Jesus, he asked him, "Lord, who is it?"

[26] Jesus answered, "It is the one to whom I will give this piece of bread when I have dipped it in the dish." Then, dipping the piece of bread, he gave it to Judas Iscariot, son of Simon. [27] As soon as Judas took the bread, Satan entered into him.

"What you are about to do, do quickly," Jesus told him, [28] but no one at the meal understood why Jesus said this to him. [29] Since Judas had charge of the money, some thought Jesus was telling him to buy what was needed for the Feast, or to give something to the poor. [30] As soon as Judas had taken the bread, he went out. And it was night.

Jesus Predicts Peter's Denial

[31] When he was gone, Jesus said, "Now is the Son of Man glorified and God is glorified in him. [32] If God is glorified in him,[a] God will glorify the Son in himself, and will glorify him at once.

[33] "My children, I will be with you only a little longer. You will look for me, and just as I told the Jews, so I tell you now: Where I am going, you cannot come.

[34] "A new command I give you: Love one another. As I have loved you, so you must love one another. [35] By this all men will know that you are my disciples, if you love one another."

[36] Simon Peter asked him, "Lord, where are you going?"

Jesus replied, "Where I am going, you cannot follow now, but you will follow later."

[37] Peter asked, "Lord, why can't I follow you now? I will lay down my life for you."

[38] Then Jesus answered, "Will you really lay down your life for me? I tell you the truth, before the rooster crows, you will disown me three times!

Jesus Comforts His Disciples

14 "Do not let your hearts be troubled. Trust in God[b]; trust also in me. [2] In my Father's house are many rooms; if it were not so, I would have told you. I am going there to prepare a place for you. [3] And if I go and prepare a place for you, I will come back and take you to be with me that you also may be where I am. [4] You know the way to the place where I am going."

Jesus the Way to the Father

[5] Thomas said to him, "Lord, we don't know where you are going, so how can we know the way?"

[6] Jesus answered, "I am the way and the truth and the life. No one comes to the Father except through me. [7] If you really knew

---

[a] **32** Many early manuscripts do not have *If God is glorified in him.* [b] **1** Or *You trust in God*

me, you would know[a] my Father as well. From now on, you do know him and have seen him."

[8]Philip said, "Lord, show us the Father and that will be enough for us."

[9]Jesus answered: "Don't you know me, Philip, even after I have been among you such a long time? Anyone who has seen me has seen the Father. How can you say, 'Show us the Father'? [10]Don't you believe that I am in the Father, and that the Father is in me? The words I say to you are not just my own. Rather, it is the Father, living in me, who is doing his work. [11]Believe me when I say that I am in the Father and the Father is in me; or at least believe on the evidence of the miracles themselves. [12]I tell you the truth, anyone who has faith in me will do what I have been doing. He will do even greater things than these, because I am going to the Father. [13]And I will do whatever you ask in my name, so that the Son may bring glory to the Father. [14]You may ask me for anything in my name, and I will do it.

Jesus Promises the Holy Spirit

[15]"If you love me, you will obey what I command. [16]And I will ask the Father, and he will give you another Counselor to be with you forever— [17]the Spirit of truth. The world cannot accept him, because it neither sees him nor knows him. But you know

---

[a] 7 Some early manuscripts *If you really have known me, you will know*

14:8 *Philip:* See the note at 1:45 (Philip).

14:9 *Father:* See the note at 5:17. Jesus is saying that Philip and the other disciples will be able to do what Jesus has been doing—preaching the good news and working miracles (14:12). They will be able to do this because of the gift of the Holy Spirit (14:16).

14:16 *another Counselor:* Referring to the Holy Spirit (14:26). See the mini-article called "Holy Spirit" on p. 48.

14:17 *The world cannot accept him:* See the note at 12:31.

I AM

When God commanded Moses to lead Israel out of slavery in Egypt into the promised land (Canaan), God had declared, "I am the God of your father, the God of Abraham, the God of Isaac and the God of Jacob" (Exod 3:1-6). When Moses asked what God's name was, God replied, "I AM WHO I AM" (Exod 3:13-15).

The Hebrew name *Yahweh* is most likely related to the Hebrew verb "to be" and so may mean "I am the one who is" or "I will be what I will be" or "I am the one who causes to be." These possible meanings of the sacred name show that Yahweh is the God who *is, will be, and causes to be.* Yahweh, God, is the source of all that is and will fulfill his purpose for the people of God and for the whole creation.

In JOHN, Jesus uses the term "I am" to proclaim his divinity. He connects himself to these aspects of God's nature and with God's eternal existence, and he also describes the work God has given him to do. Jesus identifies himself as the one who supplies all needs ("I am the bread of life," John 6:35) and who brings the knowledge about God to people ("I am the light of the world," John 8:12). Jesus also uses this "I am" language to identify himself as the way for people to find God and become God's people ("I am the gate for the sheep," John 10:7-16; and "I am the way and the truth and the life," John 14:6). Using imagery from ISAIAH, Jesus says "I am the true vine" and that his people are "the branches," sharing in the common life of the new people of God (John 15:1, 5; see also Isa 5:1-7). By making these comparisons to the Jewish Scriptures, Jesus shows that he has always existed as the Son of God and has been in God's plan from the beginning: "Before Abraham was born, I am!" (John 8:58).

The Christian church believes that the Bible asserts that one God eternally exists in three persons. Christians are more familiar with the Father and the Son, but the Bible also contains a wealth of teaching about the Holy Spirit. The Holy Spirit represents the presence of God at work in the world. The Jewish Scriptures (Old Testament) declare that the Spirit of God was at work in the creation of the world (Gen 1:2), giving life to plants, animals, and humans (Ps 104:27-30). The leaders of Israel were given power and direction by the Spirit, including Moses and the seventy-two leaders chosen to help him (Num 11:24-30), Gideon (Judg 6:34), and Kings Saul and David (1 Sam 10:6-13; 11:6; 16:13; 2 Sam 23:1-4). The prophets were guided by the Spirit of God and given messages for the people (Isa 61:1; Ezek 2:2; 3:12-27; Mic 3:8; Zech 7:12).

The LORD promised to give his Spirit and message to his people so that they would become eager to obey his law and teachings (Isa 59:21; Ezek 36:24-29). The prophet Isaiah reminded the people that it was by the Spirit that God guided the history of Israel from the beginning (Isa 63:10-14). If God's people disobey the Spirit, they will be punished (Isa 63:10), but when they follow the Spirit, their lives and hearts will be transformed and purified (Ezek 36:26, 27). And ultimately, their hope for the future is that God's Spirit will renew them and their relationship with God (Isa 44:3-5; Ezek 11:19, 20), and send them a new ruler filled with wisdom and justice (Isa 11:2-5).

For the writers of the New Testament, Jesus is seen as the one who fulfills the vision that inspired the prophets. LUKE reports that an angel told Mary that the Holy Spirit would come upon her, and God's power would overshadow her and that her holy child, Jesus, would be called the Son of God (Luke 1:35). Jesus' relationship with God is again emphasized at his baptism when "the Holy Spirit descended on him in bodily form like a dove" (Luke 3:22). Jesus' baptism clearly involves the Father, the Son, and the Holy Spirit. At the beginning of his ministry Jesus read a passage from ISAIAH and declared that the Spirit of the Lord had come on him and had anointed him to preach the good news to the poor (Luke 4:16-19). Although Jesus' enemies accused him of having an evil spirit (Mark 3:28-30), Jesus claimed that it was by God's Spirit, not by Satan, that he was able to drive out demons (Matt 12:28). MATTHEW also claimed that Jesus was the chosen servant Isaiah said would be given the Spirit of God and bring justice to the nations (Matt 12:15-21; see also Isa 42:1-4).

In JOHN, Jesus tells his disciples he will send the Holy Spirit to help them; to teach them everything and remind them of what Jesus had already taught them; to show them what is true; and to guide them into all truth (John 14:15-17; 25, 26; 15:26; 16:4-15).

After Jesus died and was raised to life, he spent forty days with his apostles. He told them that they would be baptized with the Holy Spirit (Acts 1:3-5) and that the Spirit would give them the power to be Jesus' witnesses "to the ends of the earth" (Acts 1:8). Then, on the day of Pentecost, the Spirit came to the apostles who were gathered in Jerusalem (Acts 2:1-12). ACTS goes on to tell of the many ways the Holy Spirit guided and strengthened the apostles as they took the good news about Jesus to other lands and people (for example, see Acts 4:8, 31; 6:3-5; 8:29; 13:2-12; 20:22-28).

For Paul, it is the Spirit who sets free God's new people and who changes their lives so that they can have peace and be obedient to God (Rom 8:1-17). The Spirit gives them the ability to understand God's will, to live together in love, to see what the future will bring, and to carry out the different kinds of work that need to be done in the churches (1 Cor 12–14). The Spirit produces within them the love and the lifestyle that God wants for his people (Rom 8:9-13; Gal 5:22, 23).

him, for he lives with you and will be[a] in you. [18]I will not leave you as orphans; I will come to you. [19]Before long, the world will not see me anymore, but you will see me. Because I live, you also will live. [20]On that day you will realize that I am in my Father, and you are in me, and I am in you. [21]Whoever has my commands and obeys them, he is the one who loves me. He who loves me will be loved by my Father, and I too will love him and show myself to him."

[22]Then Judas (not Judas Iscariot) said, "But, Lord, why do you intend to show yourself to us and not to the world?"

[23]Jesus replied, "If anyone loves me, he will obey my teaching. My Father will love him, and we will come to him and make our home with him. [24]He who does not love me will not obey my teaching. These words you hear are not my own; they belong to the Father who sent me.

[25]"All this I have spoken while still with you. [26]But the Counselor, the Holy Spirit, whom the Father will send in my name, will teach you all things and will remind you of everything I have said to you. [27]Peace I leave with you; my peace I give you. I do not give to you as the world gives. Do not let your hearts be troubled and do not be afraid.

[28]"You heard me say, 'I am going away and I am coming back to you.' If you loved me, you would be glad that I am going to the Father, for the Father is greater than I. [29]I have told you now before it happens, so that when it does happen you will believe. [30]I will not speak with you much longer, for the prince of this world is coming. He has no hold on me, [31]but the world must learn that I love the Father and that I do exactly what my Father has commanded me.

"Come now; let us leave.

The Vine and the Branches

15 "I am the true vine, and my Father is the gardener. [2]He cuts off every branch in me that bears no fruit, while every branch that does bear fruit he prunes[b] so that it will be even more fruitful. [3]You are already clean because of the word I have spoken to you. [4]Remain in me, and I will remain in you. No branch can bear fruit by itself; it must remain in the vine. Neither can you bear fruit unless you remain in me.

[5]"I am the vine; you are the branches. If a man remains in me and I in him, he will bear much fruit; apart from me you can do nothing. [6]If anyone does not remain in me, he is like a branch that is thrown away and withers; such branches are picked up, thrown into the fire and burned. [7]If you remain in me and my

---

[a] 17 Some early manuscripts and is   [b] 2 The Greek for prunes also means cleans.

14:22 Judas (not Judas Iscariot): This Judas is Judas, the son of James mentioned in Luke 6:16 and Acts 1:13. See the notes at 6:70, 71 and 12:4 (Judas Iscariot).

14:26 the Holy Spirit: See the mini-article called "Holy Spirit," p. 48.

14:27 peace: The peace that Jesus gives here is more than simple contentment or the absence of conflict. It is complete well-being and wholeness of mind, body, and spirit.

14:28 I am going to the Father: Jesus is talking about going back to heaven to rule beside God the Father (Luke 24:50, 51).

14:30 prince of this world: See the note at 12:31.

15:1, 2 true vine ... more fruit: Jesus says that he is the main vine of the plant, which produces many smaller branches. A farmer who takes care of fruit-bearing vines needs to trim away (prune) old branches and branches that are not giving fruit. If the vine is not pruned, the plant won't produce as much fruit.

Only those branches that stay connected to the vine (Jesus) can produce fruit (15:5). The kind of "fruit" Jesus wants his followers to produce is based on loving God and other people. God's people, Israel, are sometimes pictured in the Jewish Scriptures as a vineyard that did not produce the kind of grapes the owner expected (Isa 5:1-7).

15:6 a branch that is thrown away and withers: Vine branches that no longer produce fruit are cut off the vine (15:1, 2) and burned after they dry out.

15:8 *bear much fruit:* See the note at 15:1, 2.

15:15 *servants . . . friends:* The word in the New Testament usually translated as "servant" actually means a slave who was owned or controlled by someone else, not a servant hired to do a certain job. Slaves or servants were not considered to be equal to their masters, and masters would not have talked with them as equals, the way two friends would talk together. See also the mini-article called "Slaves and Servants in the Time of Jesus," p. 128.

15:16 *bear fruit—fruit that will last:* See the note at 15:1, 2.
15:18 *world:* See the note at 12:31.

15:21 *They will treat you this way because of my name:* Jesus is saying that some people of the "world" who are not followers of Jesus will treat Jesus' followers badly. Some of Jesus' followers will be put to death, just as Jesus was.

15:22 *sin:* See the note at 5:14. Jesus came to offer all people a chance to turn to God and believe the truth. Many chose not to believe in Jesus' new message.
15:26 *Counselor:* See the mini-article called "Holy Spirit," p. 48.

16:2 *put you out of the synagogue:* See the notes at 9:22, 23 (put out) and 12:42.

15:12 John 13:34; 15:17; 1 John 3:23; 2 John 5. **15:20** Matt 10:24; Luke 6:40; John 13:16. **15:25** Ps 35:19; 69:4.

words remain in you, ask whatever you wish, and it will be given you. [8]This is to my Father's glory, that you bear much fruit, showing yourselves to be my disciples.

[9]"As the Father has loved me, so have I loved you. Now remain in my love. [10]If you obey my commands, you will remain in my love, just as I have obeyed my Father's commands and remain in his love. [11]I have told you this so that my joy may be in you and that your joy may be complete. [12]My command is this: Love each other as I have loved you. [13]Greater love has no one than this, that he lay down his life for his friends. [14]You are my friends if you do what I command. [15]I no longer call you servants, because a servant does not know his master's business. Instead, I have called you friends, for everything that I learned from my Father I have made known to you. [16]You did not choose me, but I chose you and appointed you to go and bear fruit—fruit that will last. Then the Father will give you whatever you ask in my name. [17]This is my command: Love each other.

The World Hates the Disciples

[18]"If the world hates you, keep in mind that it hated me first. [19]If you belonged to the world, it would love you as its own. As it is, you do not belong to the world, but I have chosen you out of the world. That is why the world hates you. [20]Remember the words I spoke to you: 'No servant is greater than his master.'[a] If they persecuted me, they will persecute you also. If they obeyed my teaching, they will obey yours also. [21]They will treat you this way because of my name, for they do not know the One who sent me. [22]If I had not come and spoken to them, they would not be guilty of sin. Now, however, they have no excuse for their sin. [23]He who hates me hates my Father as well. [24]If I had not done among them what no one else did, they would not be guilty of sin. But now they have seen these miracles, and yet they have hated both me and my Father. [25]But this is to fulfill what is written in their Law: 'They hated me without reason.'[b]

[26]"When the Counselor comes, whom I will send to you from the Father, the Spirit of truth who goes out from the Father, he will testify about me. [27]And you also must testify, for you have been with me from the beginning.

16 "All this I have told you so that you will not go astray. [2]They will put you out of the synagogue; in fact, a time is coming when anyone who kills you will think he is offering a service to God. [3]They will do such things because they have not known the Father or me. [4]I have told you this, so that when the time comes you will remember that I warned you. I did not tell you this at first because I was with you.

---

[a] **20** John 13:16   [b] **25** Psalms 35:19; 69:4

The Work of the Holy Spirit

[5]"Now I am going to him who sent me, yet none of you asks me, 'Where are you going?' [6]Because I have said these things, you are filled with grief. [7]But I tell you the truth: It is for your good that I am going away. Unless I go away, the Counselor will not come to you; but if I go, I will send him to you. [8]When he comes, he will convict the world of guilt[a] in regard to sin and righteousness and judgment: [9]in regard to sin, because men do not believe in me; [10]in regard to righteousness, because I am going to the Father, where you can see me no longer; [11]and in regard to judgment, because the prince of this world now stands condemned.

[12]"I have much more to say to you, more than you can now bear. [13]But when he, the Spirit of truth, comes, he will guide you into all truth. He will not speak on his own; he will speak only what he hears, and he will tell you what is yet to come. [14]He will bring glory to me by taking from what is mine and making it known to you. [15]All that belongs to the Father is mine. That is why I said the Spirit will take from what is mine and make it known to you.

[16]"In a little while you will see me no more, and then after a little while you will see me."

The Disciples' Grief Will Turn to Joy

[17]Some of his disciples said to one another, "What does he mean by saying, 'In a little while you will see me no more, and then after a little while you will see me,' and 'Because I am going to the Father'?" [18]They kept asking, "What does he mean by 'a little while'? We don't understand what he is saying."

[19]Jesus saw that they wanted to ask him about this, so he said to them, "Are you asking one another what I meant when I said, 'In a little while you will see me no more, and then after a little while you will see me'? [20]I tell you the truth, you will weep and mourn while the world rejoices. You will grieve, but your grief will turn to joy. [21]A woman giving birth to a child has pain because her time has come; but when her baby is born she forgets the anguish because of her joy that a child is born into the world. [22]So with you: Now is your time of grief, but I will see you again and you will rejoice, and no one will take away your joy. [23]In that day you will no longer ask me anything. I tell you the truth, my Father will give you whatever you ask in my name. [24]Until now you have not asked for anything in my name. Ask and you will receive, and your joy will be complete.

[25]"Though I have been speaking figuratively, a time is coming when I will no longer use this kind of language but will tell you plainly about my Father. [26]In that day you will ask in my name. I am not saying that I will ask the Father on your behalf. [27]No, the Father

---

[a] **8**Or *will expose the guilt of the world*

16:5 *I am going to him who sent me:* See the note at 14:28.

16:7 *Counselor . . . I will send him to you:* See the mini-article called "Holy Spirit," p. 48. The Spirit will show how wrong the world is about sin and reveal the right way to live. The Spirit teaches the truth about God and God's purposes.

16:8 *convict the world of guilt in regard to sin and righteousness and judgment:* Many believed that the laws and rules based on the Law of Moses were the whole truth about the righteousness God expected of God's people. Jesus made it clear that some had missed the true message of the Law and misunderstood what God expected. God's justice was meant for all people, not just a chosen few from Israel. Those who did not believe Jesus would have to face God's judgment.

16:11 *prince of this world:* See the note at 12:31.

16:20 *you will weep and mourn while the world rejoices:* Jesus was talking about the sadness and fear his followers would feel when he was put to death on a cross (19:17-30). This sadness would be severe, like the pain a woman feels before she gives birth to a baby. However, those who do not have faith in Jesus ("the world"), will be happy to get rid of him.

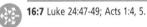

16:7 Luke 24:47-49; Acts 1:4, 5.

16:32 *you will be scattered . . . leave me all alone:* Even though the disciples said they knew who Jesus really was, his trial and death would test their courage and faith. Jesus tells them that they will not, at first, stand by him in his suffering (18:15-27; Mark 14:50, 51).

16:33 *I have overcome the world:* See the notes at 8:44 and 12:31.

17:1 *the time has come. Glorify your Son:* See the notes at 2:4 and 7:39 (glorified).

17:2 *eternal life:* See the mini-article called "Eternal Life," p. 38.

17:5 *before the world began:* See the note at 1:1-3.

17:9 *I am not praying for the world:* See the note at 12:31.

16:28 John 1:1-3; 13:3; 14:28.

himself loves you because you have loved me and have believed that I came from God. [28]I came from the Father and entered the world; now I am leaving the world and going back to the Father."

[29]Then Jesus' disciples said, "Now you are speaking clearly and without figures of speech. [30]Now we can see that you know all things and that you do not even need to have anyone ask you questions. This makes us believe that you came from God."

[31]"You believe at last!"[a] Jesus answered. [32]"But a time is coming, and has come, when you will be scattered, each to his own home. You will leave me all alone. Yet I am not alone, for my Father is with me.

[33]"I have told you these things, so that in me you may have peace. In this world you will have trouble. But take heart! I have overcome the world."

Jesus Prays for Himself

17 After Jesus said this, he looked toward heaven and prayed:

"Father, the time has come. Glorify your Son, that your Son may glorify you. [2]For you granted him authority over all people that he might give eternal life to all those you have given him. [3]Now this is eternal life: that they may know you, the only true God, and Jesus Christ, whom you have sent. [4]I have brought you glory on earth by completing the work you gave me to do. [5]And now, Father, glorify me in your presence with the glory I had with you before the world began.

Jesus Prays for His Disciples

[6]"I have revealed you[b] to those whom you gave me out of the world. They were yours; you gave them to me and they have obeyed your word. [7]Now they know that everything you have given me comes from you. [8]For I gave them the words you gave me and they accepted them. They knew with certainty that I came from you, and they believed that you sent me. [9]I pray for them. I am not praying for the world, but for those you have given me, for they are yours. [10]All I have is yours, and all you have is mine. And glory has come to me through them. [11]I will remain in the world no longer, but they are still in the world, and I am coming to you. Holy Father, protect them by the power of your name—the name you gave me—so that they may be one as we are one. [12]While I was with them, I protected them and kept them safe by that name you gave

---

[a] **31** Or *"Do you now believe?"*　[b] **6** Greek *your name*; also in verse 26

me. None has been lost except the one doomed to destruction so that Scripture would be fulfilled.

¹³"I am coming to you now, but I say these things while I am still in the world, so that they may have the full measure of my joy within them. ¹⁴I have given them your word and the world has hated them, for they are not of the world any more than I am of the world. ¹⁵My prayer is not that you take them out of the world but that you protect them from the evil one. ¹⁶They are not of the world, even as I am not of it. ¹⁷Sanctify[a] them by the truth; your word is truth. ¹⁸As you sent me into the world, I have sent them into the world. ¹⁹For them I sanctify myself, that they too may be truly sanctified.

---

[a] 17 Greek *hagiazo* (*set apart for sacred use* or *make holy*); also in verse 19

17:12 *the one doomed to destruction:* Jesus was talking about Judas Iscariot. See the notes at 6:70, 71 and 13:2.

17:15 *the evil one:* Satan (the devil). See the notes at 8:44 and 12:31; and the mini-article called "Satan," p. 126.

17:12 Ps 41:9; John 13:18.

TRUTH

In the Bible, truth refers to what is dependable, tested, and trustworthy. It is firm and never changes. This contrasts with some Greek philosophies, where truth is an idea or a principle that exists apart from the physical world that gets old and decays. Truth in the Bible is based on God's unchanging purpose for the world and all the people God created. The proper response to the truth of God, therefore, is trust in God's promises.

Trust is the basis for the special relationship between God and people throughout human history. Abraham trusted God's promises (Gen 15:6). Jacob gave thanks for the ongoing love and faithfulness that God showed him in spite of his disobedience (Gen 32:9-12). Moses praised God on Mount Sinai because God's love was continuing through each generation of his people (Exod 34:8, 9). God is always faithful, and God's promises and plans are true and trustworthy (Deut 32:3, 4). Just as plants always grow and the sun and stars always shine, so God's love and promises are forever dependable (Ps 85:10, 11).

In the New Testament, Jesus claimed that the prophet Isaiah's words were coming true because of the work the Spirit had anointed Jesus to do (Luke 4:16-21). In his teaching, Jesus frequently used the Hebrew word *amen* (translated in the NIV, "I tell you *the truth*") to emphasize that what he says about God's will for his people is completely true and reliable (Matthew 5:18; 6:2; 8:10; 18:18; 19:23; 24:2; 25:12). Jesus tells his disciples that his death on a cross and his resurrection fulfill promises recorded in the Jewish Scriptures, and so are surely true (Luke 24:27, 45-47).

In JOHN, Jesus is the true light (John 1:9) who brings God's true word. He is also the true bread (John 6:32), the true vine (John 15:1), and the true way to God (John 14:6), who brings the Spirit of truth (John 16:13). And Jesus is the truth of God (John 14:6). His people live by the actions and promises of God, and as a result, they are the people of truth (John 18:37) who hear and trust him as the living word of God.

In the later letters of the New Testament, truth comes to be understood in the more usual modern sense—as what is correct, in contrast to what is false. There are warnings against false teaching (1 Tim 1:3, 4; 2 Tim 2:16-18) and against those who are enemies of the truth (2 Tim 3:6-9) and who tell senseless stories (Titus 1:10-14). These letters say the church should fight for the true faith (1 Tim 6:11-21) and should see itself as "the pillar and foundation of the truth" (1 Tim 3:14, 15), which here means "right belief."

17:23 *let the world know that you sent me:* Jesus prays that his followers will be one with God and one with each other. The unity that Jesus' followers show will help convince the world (unbelievers) that Jesus really did come from God.

17:24 *loved me before the creation of the world:* See the note at 1:1-3.

18:1 *Kidron Valley:* This valley runs just east of the temple mount in Jerusalem. Across the Kidron Valley to the east is a high hill known as the Mount of Olives. Near the bottom of that slope was a grove of olive trees, which other Gospels call Gethsemane (Matt 26:36; Mark 14:32). See the map on p. 139.

This hill is where the prophet Zechariah said God would appear and defeat his enemies (Zech 14:1-4). It is in this place that Jesus' enemies arrest him.

18:2 *Judas . . . his disciples:* For more about Judas, see the notes at 6:70, 71 and 12:4. For more about "disciples," see the note at 6:67.

18:3-5 *a detachment of soldiers . . . chief priests and Pharisees . . . Jesus of Nazareth:* Roman soldiers were stationed in the Fortress Antonia near the temple. They were in charge of keeping order in the city. The chief priests and Pharisees may have persuaded the Roman soldiers to make the arrest by saying that Jesus was a dangerous rebel. See the notes at 7:32 (chief priests and temple guards) and 1:24 (Pharisees).

Jesus was often identified by adding his hometown (Nazareth) to his name, since there were probably many Jewish men named Jesus at the time he lived.

18:3-5 *I am he:* See the mini-article called "I Am," p. 47.

Jesus Prays for All Believers

[20]"My prayer is not for them alone. I pray also for those who will believe in me through their message, [21]that all of them may be one, Father, just as you are in me and I am in you. May they also be in us so that the world may believe that you have sent me. [22]I have given them the glory that you gave me, that they may be one as we are one: [23]I in them and you in me. May they be brought to complete unity to let the world know that you sent me and have loved them even as you have loved me.

[24]"Father, I want those you have given me to be with me where I am, and to see my glory, the glory you have given me because you loved me before the creation of the world.

[25]"Righteous Father, though the world does not know you, I know you, and they know that you have sent me. [26]I have made you known to them, and will continue to make you known in order that the love you have for me may be in them and that I myself may be in them."

JESUS' ARREST, TRIAL, AND DEATH ON A CROSS

The action in the next three chapters takes place in less than 24 hours. Shortly after Jesus is finished praying for his followers he is arrested and brought to trial. The Roman governor, Pontius Pilate, sentences Jesus to death on a cross to keep the crowd from starting a riot. Jesus' death comes quickly as he completes the work God has sent him to do.

Jesus Arrested

18 When he had finished praying, Jesus left with his disciples and crossed the Kidron Valley. On the other side there was an olive grove, and he and his disciples went into it.

[2]Now Judas, who betrayed him, knew the place, because Jesus had often met there with his disciples. [3]So Judas came to the grove, guiding a detachment of soldiers and some officials from the chief priests and Pharisees. They were carrying torches, lanterns and weapons.

[4]Jesus, knowing all that was going to happen to him, went out and asked them, "Who is it you want?"

[5]"Jesus of Nazareth," they replied.

"I am he," Jesus said. (And Judas the traitor was standing there with them.) [6]When Jesus said, "I am he," they drew back and fell to the ground.

[7]Again he asked them, "Who is it you want?"

And they said, "Jesus of Nazareth."

[8]"I told you that I am he," Jesus answered. "If you are looking for me, then let these men go." [9]This happened so that the words he had spoken would be fulfilled: "I have not lost one of those you gave me."[a]

[10]Then Simon Peter, who had a sword, drew it and struck the high priest's servant, cutting off his right ear. (The servant's name was Malchus.)

[11]Jesus commanded Peter, "Put your sword away! Shall I not drink the cup the Father has given me?"

Jesus Taken to Annas

[12]Then the detachment of soldiers with its commander and the Jewish officials arrested Jesus. They bound him [13]and brought him first to Annas, who was the father-in-law of Caiaphas, the

---

[a] 9 John 6:39

St. Peter Cuts Off Malchus's Ear, a painted ceiling panel from St. Martin's Church, Zillis, Switzerland, twelfth century. After praying for his disciples, Jesus went with them to a garden. Judas knew where they would be and brought Roman soldiers and temple police to arrest Jesus. Although Jesus let himself be arrested, Simon Peter reacted by cutting off the right ear of the servant of the high priest. But Jesus told Peter, "Put your sword away! Shall I not drink the cup the Father has given me?" (See 18:1-11.)

18:10 *Simon Peter ... Malchus:* See the note at 1:42. The sword that Peter used to strike the high priest's servant was actually a dagger, which is like a short, straight sword.

The name Malchus means "king." He may have come from Nabatea. He served Caiaphas, the high priest, but his exact position is not known.

18:11 *Shall I not drink the cup:* In the Scriptures a cup is sometimes used as a symbol of suffering (Isa 51:17; Jer 25:15; Rev 14:10; 16:19). To "drink the cup" is to suffer. See also the note at 4:34.

18:12 *detachment of soldiers with its commander and the Jewish officials:* The commander is a Roman tribune, who commanded 1000 soldiers. The Jewish officials may refer to the temple guard (see the note at 7:32).

18:13 *Annas ... father-in-law of Caiaphas:* Annas was the high priest of the Jewish people when Jesus was a child, but his sons and son-in-law, Caiaphas, were appointed by the Romans after Annas was forced to leave that position. Annas kept the title of high priest even though others took over the job from him. He was asked to give his advice on certain major problems, such as what to do with Jesus. See the note at 11:49 (Caiaphas).

18:11 Matt 26:39; Mark 14:35, 36; Luke 22:42.

18:15 *Simon Peter and another disciple:* See the note at 1:42 (Simon). The other disciple who risks his life to go with Jesus before the high priest is probably the same as "the disciple whom Jesus loved" (see the note at 13:23), who stood at the foot of the cross (19:25-27) and who went with Peter to the tomb (20:1-10).

18:15 *the high priest's courtyard:* According to tradition, Annas and Caiaphas, the high priest, lived in the upper part of the city, probably near the temple.

18:18 *the servants and officials:* The "officials" are probably part of the temple guard. See the note at 7:32.

18:19 *high priest:* See the notes at 11:49 and 18:13. In the other Gospels, Jesus goes on trial in front of the high priest and a whole council of Jewish leaders (see Matt 26:57-68; Mark 14:55-65; Luke 22:66-71).

18:20 *synagogues:* See the note at 6:59 and the mini-article called "Synagogues," p. 130.

18:24 *Annas sent him . . . to Caiaphas the high priest:* See the note at 18:13. This verse makes it sound as if Annas was the one questioning Jesus in 18:19, though he was not really the high priest.

18:27 *Again Peter denied it:* This is the third time Peter denies knowing Jesus (13:38).

18:28 *the palace of the Roman governor:* Pilate's official home was Caesarea on the Mediterranean coast. When he was in Jerusalem, he lived at the Antonia, a fortress that overlooked the temple area from the northwest. See the map on p. 139. See also the mini-article on "Pontius Pilate" on p. 57.

18:14 John 11:49, 50. **18:17** John 13:38. **18:26** John 18:10.

high priest that year. [14]Caiaphas was the one who had advised the Jews that it would be good if one man died for the people.

Peter's First Denial

[15]Simon Peter and another disciple were following Jesus. Because this disciple was known to the high priest, he went with Jesus into the high priest's courtyard, [16]but Peter had to wait outside at the door. The other disciple, who was known to the high priest, came back, spoke to the girl on duty there and brought Peter in.

[17]"You are not one of his disciples, are you?" the girl at the door asked Peter.

He replied, "I am not."

[18]It was cold, and the servants and officials stood around a fire they had made to keep warm. Peter also was standing with them, warming himself.

The High Priest Questions Jesus

[19]Meanwhile, the high priest questioned Jesus about his disciples and his teaching.

[20]"I have spoken openly to the world," Jesus replied. "I always taught in synagogues or at the temple, where all the Jews come together. I said nothing in secret. [21]Why question me? Ask those who heard me. Surely they know what I said."

[22]When Jesus said this, one of the officials nearby struck him in the face. "Is this the way you answer the high priest?" he demanded.

[23]"If I said something wrong," Jesus replied, "testify as to what is wrong. But if I spoke the truth, why did you strike me?" [24]Then Annas sent him, still bound, to Caiaphas the high priest.[a]

Peter's Second and Third Denials

[25]As Simon Peter stood warming himself, he was asked, "You are not one of his disciples, are you?"

He denied it, saying, "I am not."

[26]One of the high priest's servants, a relative of the man whose ear Peter had cut off, challenged him, "Didn't I see you with him in the olive grove?" [27]Again Peter denied it, and at that moment a rooster began to crow.

Jesus Before Pilate

[28]Then the Jews led Jesus from Caiaphas to the palace of the Roman governor. By now it was early morning, and to avoid ceremonial uncleanness the Jews did not enter the palace; they wanted

---

[a] **24** Or *(Now Annas had sent him, still bound, to Caiaphas the high priest.)*

to be able to eat the Passover. ²⁹So Pilate came out to them and asked, "What charges are you bringing against this man?"

³⁰"If he were not a criminal," they replied, "we would not have handed him over to you."

³¹Pilate said, "Take him yourselves and judge him by your own law."

"But we have no right to execute anyone," the Jews objected. ³²This happened so that the words Jesus had spoken indicating the kind of death he was going to die would be fulfilled.

³³Pilate then went back inside the palace, summoned Jesus and asked him, "Are you the king of the Jews?"

³⁴"Is that your own idea," Jesus asked, "or did others talk to you about me?"

18:31 *we have no right to execute anyone:* It is most likely that the Roman authorities did not allow Jewish officials to put anyone to death without a clear case of guilt. That right was reserved for the Roman government.

18:33 *king of the Jews:* If Jesus admitted to being a real king, he could be put on trial as a political rebel. This crime against Roman authority was punishable by death on a cross.

PONTIUS PILATE

Pontius Pilate was governor (prefect) of Judea from A.D. 26 to 36, during the time that Tiberius was the Roman emperor (A.D. 14-37), and Herod Antipas was governor (tetrarch) of Galilee (4 B.C. to A.D. 39). Pilate is mentioned by Roman, Jewish, and Christian writers. The Roman historian, Tacitus, tells in his Annals that Jesus was put to death by Pilate during the reign of Tiberius. Philos, a Jewish scholar from Alexandria, wrote that Pilate angered the Jews in Jerusalem by displaying metal shields at the governor's palace that bore the image and name of the emperor as though he were a god. The Jewish historian Josephus tells about the public outcry Pilate caused when he brought standards (images carried on poles) into Jerusalem picturing the emperor as a god, and when he took funds from the temple treasury to pay for an aqueduct to bring water into Jerusalem.

In the New Testament, Pilate is mentioned several times (Acts 3:13; 4:27; 13:28; 1 Tim 6:13), but he is most important in the Gospel accounts of Jesus' trial and execution. Mark 15:1-15, probably the oldest of these stories, says that when Pilate asked Jesus if he was the king of the Jews, Jesus answered, "Yes, it is as you say." Pilate saw no reason to put Jesus to death and was warned by his wife, because of a dream she had experienced, not to do so (Matt 27:19).

But when the crowd demanded that Jesus be crucified, Pilate gave in to their demands and ordered Jesus' death. Pilate washed his hands in public to show he did not intend to take the blame for Jesus' death. Luke is the only Gospel that mentions Pilate sending Jesus to Herod Antipas (Luke 23:7). In each of the Gospel accounts, Pilate gave in to the demands of the crowd that Jesus be crucified, and ordered Jesus' death. Pilate was in a political bind. When the chief priests shouted, "We have no king but Caesar" (John 19:15), they pointed out the dilemma. With his claim to be a king, Jesus was a threat to the empire. If Pilate let Jesus go, it would end his political career, and perhaps his life.

The Gospel accounts put the blame for Jesus' death on the Jews and their leaders. If Jesus had been put to death for breaking the Jewish law, his execution under Jewish authority would have been done by crushing him to death with stones. This was the form of punishment commanded in the Law of Moses and that was later used to kill the church's "first martyr," Stephen, (Acts 7:54-60; Deut 13:9, 10; 21:18-21). But Pilate had him put to death by crucifixion, the Roman method of execution. And the sign he had put on Jesus' cross said that Jesus claimed to be the king of the Jews (Matt 27:37; Mark 15:26; John 19:19).

18:40 *Barabbas had taken part in a rebellion:* Rebels like Barabbas stirred up trouble against the Romans in the hope of gaining freedom for the Jewish people.

19:1, 2 *flogged . . . crown of thorns:* In the Roman Empire, often before a condemned person was nailed to a cross (crucified) he would be mocked and beaten with a whip ("flogged"). The "crown of thorns" that the soldiers placed on Jesus' head may have been made from the branches of the spiny burnet plant that grows in Palestine.

19:4 *I find no basis for a charge against him:* See also Matt 27:24, which reports that Pilate washed his hands in front of the crowd as a sign that he was not responsible for Jesus' death.

19:6 *chief priests and their officials:* The "officials" were most likely temple guards. See the note at 7:32 (chief priests and temple guards).

19:6 *Crucify!:* See the mini-article called "Crucifixion," p. 111.

19:7 *according to that law he must die . . . claimed to be the Son of God:* See the mini-article called "Son of God" on p. 10. See also the note at 10:33 (claiming to be God).

19:11 *the one who handed me over to you:* The "one" mentioned here may be Judas, Caiaphas, or even Satan.

---

[35]"Am I a Jew?" Pilate replied. "It was your people and your chief priests who handed you over to me. What is it you have done?"

[36]Jesus said, "My kingdom is not of this world. If it were, my servants would fight to prevent my arrest by the Jews. But now my kingdom is from another place."

[37]"You are a king, then!" said Pilate.

Jesus answered, "You are right in saying I am a king. In fact, for this reason I was born, and for this I came into the world, to testify to the truth. Everyone on the side of truth listens to me."

[38]"What is truth?" Pilate asked. With this he went out again to the Jews and said, "I find no basis for a charge against him. [39]But it is your custom for me to release to you one prisoner at the time of the Passover. Do you want me to release 'the king of the Jews'?"

[40]They shouted back, "No, not him! Give us Barabbas!" Now Barabbas had taken part in a rebellion.

Jesus Sentenced to Be Crucified

19 Then Pilate took Jesus and had him flogged. [2]The soldiers twisted together a crown of thorns and put it on his head. They clothed him in a purple robe [3]and went up to him again and again, saying, "Hail, king of the Jews!" And they struck him in the face.

[4]Once more Pilate came out and said to the Jews, "Look, I am bringing him out to you to let you know that I find no basis for a charge against him." [5]When Jesus came out wearing the crown of thorns and the purple robe, Pilate said to them, "Here is the man!"

[6]As soon as the chief priests and their officials saw him, they shouted, "Crucify! Crucify!"

But Pilate answered, "You take him and crucify him. As for me, I find no basis for a charge against him."

[7]The Jews insisted, "We have a law, and according to that law he must die, because he claimed to be the Son of God."

[8]When Pilate heard this, he was even more afraid, [9]and he went back inside the palace. "Where do you come from?" he asked Jesus, but Jesus gave him no answer. [10]"Do you refuse to speak to me?" Pilate said. "Don't you realize I have power either to free you or to crucify you?"

[11]Jesus answered, "You would have no power over me if it were not given to you from above. Therefore the one who handed me over to you is guilty of a greater sin."

[12]From then on, Pilate tried to set Jesus free, but the Jews kept shouting, "If you let this man go, you are no friend of Caesar. Anyone who claims to be a king opposes Caesar."

[13]When Pilate heard this, he brought Jesus out and sat down on the judge's seat at a place known as the Stone Pavement (which in Aramaic is Gabbatha). [14]It was the day of Preparation of Passover Week, about the sixth hour.

"Here is your king," Pilate said to the Jews.

[15]But they shouted, "Take him away! Take him away! Crucify him!"

"Shall I crucify your king?" Pilate asked.

"We have no king but Caesar," the chief priests answered. [16]Finally Pilate handed him over to them to be crucified.

The Crucifixion

So the soldiers took charge of Jesus. [17]Carrying his own cross, he went out to the place of the Skull (which in Aramaic is called Golgotha). [18]Here they crucified him, and with him two others-one on each side and Jesus in the middle.

[19]Pilate had a notice prepared and fastened to the cross. It read: JESUS OF NAZARETH, THE KING OF THE JEWS. [20]Many of the Jews read this sign, for the place where Jesus was crucified was near the city, and the sign was written in Aramaic, Latin and Greek. [21]The

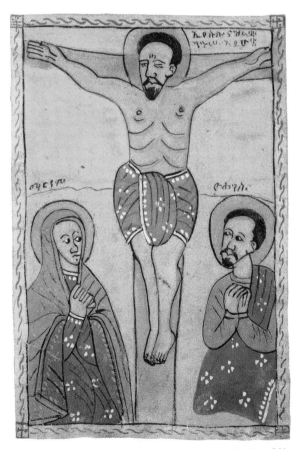

The Crucifixion, a painting on parchment, Coptic, fifth century. When Jesus was nailed to a cross he looked down and saw his disciple, John, standing near his mother Mary. He said to the disciple, "Here is your mother." From that time on, the disciple took Jesus' mother into his home. (See 19:26, 27.)

19:12 *Pilate . . . Caesar:* See the note at 19:4. At this time the Roman Emperor was Tiberius Caesar, who ruled the Roman Empire from A.D. 14–37.

19:13 *judge's seat . . . the Stone Pavement (which in Aramaic is Gabbatha):* The judge's seat was a platform from which the Roman governor could announce decisions. Its actual location is not clear, nor is the meaning of the Aramaic word, *Gabbatha*. Normally, Pilate would have sat down there to make his announcements.

19:14 *the day of Preparation of Passover Week, about the sixth hour:* This would refer to noon on the day before Passover. The time Jesus was being put on trial and sentenced to die on the cross, the Passover lambs were being slaughtered and prepared for the next day's Passover meal. See also the note on p. 7. (Lamb of God)

19:15 *We have no king but Caesar:* Though the chief priests are supposed to serve God, they showed their loyalty to the Roman emperor in order to get Pilate to sentence Jesus to death.

19:17 *the Skull (which in Aramaic is called Golgotha):* The place was probably given this name because it was near a large rock in the shape of a human skull. See the map on p. 139.

19:18 *crucified him:* See the mini-article called "Crucifixion," p. 111.

19:20 *Aramaic, Latin and Greek:* The sign over Jesus was written in all these languages, so that nearly everyone could read it. The Jewish people spoke Aramaic (a Semitic language similar to Hebrew). The official Roman language was Latin, though many Romans probably spoke Greek. Greek was the language of commerce commonly spoken throughout the Mediterranean world by many different peoples.

19:26 *the disciple whom he loved:* See the note at 13:23.

19:29 *jar of wine vinegar . . . a stalk of the hyssop plant:* Sometimes inexpensive wine or vinegar was mixed with a drug called gall (Matt 27:34). This mixture took away some of the pain that the person on the cross was suffering. Hyssop is a plant with a shrub-like base and stems that are stiff and strong.

19:30 *It is finished:* Jesus' words show not only that his earthly life was done, but that the work God had sent him to do, to sacrifice himself for the sins of the world (1:29), had been completed.

19:31 *a special Sabbath:* Since the Passover was set by the phase of the moon (see the note at 2.13), it could be on any day of the week. In Israel a day began at sundown. Here, the next day was also the Sabbath, so it was important that the dead body of Jesus not be left to decay on that doubly holy day. And anyone who touched a dead body would have to go through purification rites before being able to celebrate the Passover.

19:31 *have the legs broken:* This is the way that the Romans sometimes speeded up the death of a person who had been nailed to a cross. See the mini-article called "Crucifixion," p. 111.

chief priests of the Jews protested to Pilate, "Do not write 'The King of the Jews,' but that this man claimed to be king of the Jews." [22]Pilate answered, "What I have written, I have written."

[23]When the soldiers crucified Jesus, they took his clothes, dividing them into four shares, one for each of them, with the undergarment remaining. This garment was seamless, woven in one piece from top to bottom. [24]"Let's not tear it," they said to one another. "Let's decide by lot who will get it."

This happened that the scripture might be fulfilled which said,

> "They divided my garments among them
> and cast lots for my clothing."[a]

So this is what the soldiers did. [25]Near the cross of Jesus stood his mother, his mother's sister, Mary the wife of Clopas, and Mary Magdalene. [26]When Jesus saw his mother there, and the disciple whom he loved standing nearby, he said to his mother, "Dear woman, here is your son," [27]and to the disciple, "Here is your mother." From that time on, this disciple took her into his home.

The Death of Jesus

[28]Later, knowing that all was now completed, and so that the Scripture would be fulfilled, Jesus said, "I am thirsty." [29]A jar of wine vinegar was there, so they soaked a sponge in it, put the sponge on a stalk of the hyssop plant, and lifted it to Jesus' lips. [30]When he had received the drink, Jesus said, "It is finished." With that, he bowed his head and gave up his spirit.

[31]Now it was the day of Preparation, and the next day was to be a special Sabbath. Because the Jews did not want the bodies left

---

[a] **24** Psalm 22:18

QUESTIONS ABOUT JOHN 12:1—19:42

1. Shortly before he was put to death, Jesus visited Mary and Martha in Bethany (12:1-7). What did Mary do and what did it have to do with Jesus' death? What was Judas' complaint? How did Jesus respond to his complaint? What did Jesus mean (12:7)?
2. Read 12:23-26. What is the meaning of Jesus' words? Is anything worth risking death? If so, what?
3. Why did Jesus wash the feet of his disciples (13:1-17)? Why is this surprising? How can Christians serve one another?
4. What is the "new command" Jesus gave his followers (13:34, 35)? How can this command be followed?
5. Read 14:6 and 15:1-3. Explain what Jesus means by these statements.
6. How did Jesus promise to help his followers after he left to be with the Father (16:5-15)?
7. How did Jesus reply to Pilate's question (18:33-37)? What is Jesus' kingdom?

on the crosses during the Sabbath, they asked Pilate to have the legs broken and the bodies taken down. ³²The soldiers therefore came and broke the legs of the first man who had been crucified with Jesus, and then those of the other. ³³But when they came to Jesus and found that he was already dead, they did not break his legs. ³⁴Instead, one of the soldiers pierced Jesus' side with a spear, bringing a sudden flow of blood and water. ³⁵The man who saw it has given testimony, and his testimony is true. He knows that he tells the truth, and he testifies so that you also may believe. ³⁶These things happened so that the scripture would be fulfilled: "Not one of his bones will be broken,"ᵃ ³⁷and, as another scripture says, "They will look on the one they have pierced."ᵇ

The Burial of Jesus

³⁸Later, Joseph of Arimathea asked Pilate for the body of Jesus. Now Joseph was a disciple of Jesus, but secretly because he feared the Jews. With Pilate's permission, he came and took the body away. ³⁹He was accompanied by Nicodemus, the man who earlier had visited Jesus at night. Nicodemus brought a mixture of myrrh and aloes, about seventy-five pounds.ᶜ ⁴⁰Taking Jesus' body, the two of them wrapped it, with the spices, in strips of linen. This was in accordance with Jewish burial customs. ⁴¹At the place where Jesus was crucified, there was a garden, and in the garden a new tomb, in which no one had ever been laid. ⁴²Because it was the Jewish day of Preparation and since the tomb was nearby, they laid Jesus there.

Jesus Appears to His Followers

The last two chapters of JOHN focus on Jesus' appearances to a number of his followers after God has raised him from death. This final miracle shows God's power over death.

The Empty Tomb

20 Early on the first day of the week, while it was still dark, Mary Magdalene went to the tomb and saw that the stone had been removed from the entrance. ²So she came running to Simon Peter and the other disciple, the one Jesus loved, and said, "They have taken the Lord out of the tomb, and we don't know where they have put him!"

³So Peter and the other disciple started for the tomb. ⁴Both were running, but the other disciple outran Peter and reached the

19:38 *Joseph of Arimathea:* Arimathea was a small village twenty miles northwest of Jerusalem. Because Joseph was rich (Matt 27:57), he had money enough to prepare Jesus' body for a proper burial.

19:39 *Nicodemus:* See the note at 3:1.

19:39 *myrrh and aloes:* See the chart called "Spices and Perfumes," p. 129.

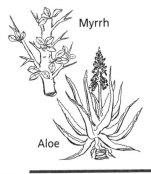

Myrrh

Aloe

19:40 *wrapped it, with the spices, in strips of linen:* See the note at 11:44.

19:41 *in the garden a new tomb:* The tomb and garden must have been near Golgotha (see the note at 19:17). This would have made it easier to finish the task of preparing and burying the body before the Sabbath.

19:42 *Jewish day of Preparation:* See the note at 19:31.

20:1 *Early on the first day of the week:* Early on the morning after the Sabbath ended, which would be Sunday.

20:1 *Mary Magdalene:* Mary was probably from Magdala, a town on the Sea of Galilee. Other Gospels tell how Jesus healed her (Mark 16:9; Luke 8:2). See also 19:25.

20:2 *Simon Peter and the other disciple, the one Jesus loved:* See the notes at 1:42 (Simon Peter) and 13:23 (the disciple whom Jesus loved).

19:24 Ps 22:18. **19:28** Ps 22:15. **19:36** Exod 12:46; Num 9:11, 12; Ps 34:20. **19:37** Zech 12:10; Rev 1:7. **19:39** John 3:1, 2.

ᵃ **36** Exodus 12:46; Num. 9:12; Psalm 34:20　ᵇ **37** Zech. 12:10　ᶜ **39** Greek *a hundred litrai* (about 34 kilograms)

20:5 *strips of linen:* See the note at 11:44.

20:12 *two angels:* See the mini-article called "Angels," p. 86.

20:16 *Rabboni:* See 1:38.

20:19 *disciples . . . the doors locked for fear of the Jews:* Jesus' followers were afraid that they would be identified and harassed for their beliefs, so they hid out in a locked room.

20:20 *he showed them his hands and side:* Jesus had nails driven through his hands (or possibly wrists) when he was put to death on the cross (see 19:18 and the mini-article called "Crucifixion," p. 111). Soldiers later pierced his side with a spear (19:34).

20:22 *Receive the Holy Spirit:* See the note at 1:32 (Spirit). Jesus gave the Holy Spirit to the disciples as he had earlier promised (14:16, 26; 16:7).

20:23 *forgive anyone his sins, they are forgiven:* In giving the Holy Spirit, Jesus gave the disciples the power to preach the good news about Jesus so that their sins might be forgiven. The Christian church has the power to proclaim that people's sins can be forgiven because of what Jesus has done (20:21).

tomb first. [5]He bent over and looked in at the strips of linen lying there but did not go in. [6]Then Simon Peter, who was behind him, arrived and went into the tomb. He saw the strips of linen lying there, [7]as well as the burial cloth that had been around Jesus' head. The cloth was folded up by itself, separate from the linen. [8]Finally the other disciple, who had reached the tomb first, also went inside. He saw and believed. [9](They still did not understand from Scripture that Jesus had to rise from the dead.)

Jesus Appears to Mary Magdalene

[10]Then the disciples went back to their homes, [11]but Mary stood outside the tomb crying. As she wept, she bent over to look into the tomb [12]and saw two angels in white, seated where Jesus' body had been, one at the head and the other at the foot.

[13]They asked her, "Woman, why are you crying?"

"They have taken my Lord away," she said, "and I don't know where they have put him." [14]At this, she turned around and saw Jesus standing there, but she did not realize that it was Jesus.

[15]"Woman," he said, "why are you crying? Who is it you are looking for?"

Thinking he was the gardener, she said, "Sir, if you have carried him away, tell me where you have put him, and I will get him."

[16]Jesus said to her, "Mary."

She turned toward him and cried out in Aramaic, "Rabboni!" (which means Teacher).

[17]Jesus said, "Do not hold on to me, for I have not yet returned to the Father. Go instead to my brothers and tell them, 'I am returning to my Father and your Father, to my God and your God.'"

[18]Mary Magdalene went to the disciples with the news: "I have seen the Lord!" And she told them that he had said these things to her.

Jesus Appears to His Disciples

[19]On the evening of that first day of the week, when the disciples were together, with the doors locked for fear of the Jews, Jesus came and stood among them and said, "Peace be with you!" [20]After he said this, he showed them his hands and side. The disciples were overjoyed when they saw the Lord.

[21]Again Jesus said, "Peace be with you! As the Father has sent me, I am sending you." [22]And with that he breathed on them and said, "Receive the Holy Spirit. [23]If you forgive anyone his sins, they are forgiven; if you do not forgive them, they are not forgiven."

Jesus Appears to Thomas

[24]Now Thomas (called Didymus), one of the Twelve, was not with the disciples when Jesus came. [25]So the other disciples told him, "We have seen the Lord!"

But he said to them, "Unless I see the nail marks in his hands and put my finger where the nails were, and put my hand into his side, I will not believe it."

[26]A week later his disciples were in the house again, and Thomas was with them. Though the doors were locked, Jesus came and stood among them and said, "Peace be with you!" [27]Then he said to Thomas, "Put your finger here; see my hands. Reach out your hand and put it into my side. Stop doubting and believe."

[28]Thomas said to him, "My Lord and my God!"

[29]Then Jesus told him, "Because you have seen me, you have believed; blessed are those who have not seen and yet have believed."

[30]Jesus did many other miraculous signs in the presence of his disciples, which are not recorded in this book. [31]But these are written that you may[a] believe that Jesus is the Christ, the Son of God, and that by believing you may have life in his name.

Jesus and the Miraculous Catch of Fish

21 Afterward Jesus appeared again to his disciples, by the Sea of Tiberias.[b] It happened this way: [2]Simon Peter, Thomas (called

---
[a] 31 Some manuscripts *may continue to*   [b] 1 That is, Sea of Galilee

20:24 *Thomas (called Didymus):* Didymus is Aramaic for "twin." See the note at 11:16.

20:28 *My Lord and my God:* See the note at 13:13 (Lord). Thomas is convinced that Jesus has been raised from the dead, because he can see the wounds Jesus received when he was put to death on the cross.

20:31 *these are written:* Verses 30, 31 have often been called the "theme verses" of JOHN. John tells about Jesus' miracles (signs), so that people who were not able to see and hear Jesus in person (20:29) would have faith in Jesus.

21:1 *Sea of Tiberias:* See the note at 6:1.

21:2 *Simon Peter, Thomas (called Didymus), Nathanael . . . the sons of Zebedee, and two other disciples:* See the notes at 1:42 (Simon Peter), 11:16 (Thomas), and 1:45 (Nathanael). James and John were the "sons of Zebedee" (Mark 3:17). The "two other disciples" are simply not named.

Doubting Thomas by Michael Smither, twentieth century. Thomas the Twin was not with the other disciples when Jesus appeared to them after God had raised him to life. Thomas told them he would not believe what they were telling him unless he could see and touch Jesus' wounds for himself. Later, Jesus appeared to the disciples again and invited Thomas to touch his wounds. Thomas immediately recognized Jesus, but Jesus said to him, "Because you have seen me, you have believed; blessed are those who have not seen and yet have believed." (See 20:24-29.)

21:7 *the disciple whom Jesus loved:* See the note at 13:23.

21:9 *fish . . . bread:* In JOHN these are not simply food. The bread represents the bread of the Lord's Supper (see the note at 6:53) and is a reminder that Jesus is the bread that gives life (6:35). In the early church a favorite symbol for Jesus was the fish.

21:3, 6 Luke 5:4-6.

Didymus), Nathanael from Cana in Galilee, the sons of Zebedee, and two other disciples were together. ³"I'm going out to fish," Simon Peter told them, and they said, "We'll go with you." So they went out and got into the boat, but that night they caught nothing.

⁴Early in the morning, Jesus stood on the shore, but the disciples did not realize that it was Jesus.

⁵He called out to them, "Friends, haven't you any fish?"

"No," they answered.

⁶He said, "Throw your net on the right side of the boat and you will find some." When they did, they were unable to haul the net in because of the large number of fish.

⁷Then the disciple whom Jesus loved said to Peter, "It is the Lord!" As soon as Simon Peter heard him say, "It is the Lord," he wrapped his outer garment around him (for he had taken it off) and jumped into the water. ⁸The other disciples followed in the boat, towing the net full of fish, for they were not far from shore, about a hundred yards.ᵃ ⁹When they landed, they saw a fire of burning coals there with fish on it, and some bread.

¹⁰Jesus said to them, "Bring some of the fish you have just caught."

¹¹Simon Peter climbed aboard and dragged the net ashore. It was full of large fish, 153, but even with so many the net was not torn. ¹²Jesus said to them, "Come and have breakfast." None of the disciples dared ask him, "Who are you?" They knew it was the Lord. ¹³Jesus came, took the bread and gave it to them, and did the same with the fish. ¹⁴This was now the third time Jesus appeared to his disciples after he was raised from the dead.

Jesus Reinstates Peter

¹⁵When they had finished eating, Jesus said to Simon Peter, "Simon son of John, do you truly love me more than these?"

"Yes, Lord," he said, "you know that I love you."

ᵃ **8** Greek *about two hundred cubits* (about 90 meters)

QUESTIONS ABOUT JOHN 20:1—21:25

1. Who were the first persons to go to Jesus' tomb on Sunday morning (20:1-9)? What did they find, and what were their reactions?
2. What task did Jesus give to his disciples when he met them after he was raised from death (20:21-23)? What does this mean for the church today?
3. According to 20:30, 31, why did the author write this Gospel? Compare this to Jesus' words in 20:29. How do people living two thousand years after Jesus come to have faith in Jesus as God's Son and the Messiah?
4. What command did Jesus give to Peter (21:15-19)? What did that mean for Peter? What does it mean for Jesus' followers (the church) today?

Jesus said, "Feed my lambs."

¹⁶Again Jesus said, "Simon son of John, do you truly love me?"

He answered, "Yes, Lord, you know that I love you."

Jesus said, "Take care of my sheep."

¹⁷The third time he said to him, "Simon son of John, do you love me?"

Peter was hurt because Jesus asked him the third time, "Do you love me?" He said, "Lord, you know all things; you know that I love you."

Jesus said, "Feed my sheep. ¹⁸I tell you the truth, when you were younger you dressed yourself and went where you wanted; but when you are old you will stretch out your hands, and someone else will dress you and lead you where you do not want to go." ¹⁹Jesus said this to indicate the kind of death by which Peter would glorify God. Then he said to him, "Follow me!"

²⁰Peter turned and saw that the disciple whom Jesus loved was following them. (This was the one who had leaned back against Jesus at the supper and had said, "Lord, who is going to betray you?") ²¹When Peter saw him, he asked, "Lord, what about him?"

²²Jesus answered, "If I want him to remain alive until I return, what is that to you? You must follow me." ²³Because of this, the rumor spread among the brothers that this disciple would not die. But Jesus did not say that he would not die; he only said, "If I want him to remain alive until I return, what is that to you?"

²⁴This is the disciple who testifies to these things and who wrote them down. We know that his testimony is true.

²⁵Jesus did many other things as well. If every one of them were written down, I suppose that even the whole world would not have room for the books that would be written.

21:15 *Simon son of John:* Simon Peter (see the note at 1:42).

21:15, 16 *Feed my lambs . . . Take care of my sheep:* Jesus called himself the good shepherd (10:14). His followers are his flock of lambs (sheep). Jesus tells Peter to take care of his sheep ("followers") by feeding them the message of Jesus, which includes offering the message of forgiveness of sins through Jesus (20:23).

21:18, 19 *you will stretch out your hands . . . lead you where you do not want to go . . . glorify God:* The phrase "stretch out your hands" probably means that Peter would die on a cross just as Jesus had. Peter's freedom would be taken away and he would be led where he does not want to go. Even so, his death would glorify God, just as Jesus' death glorified God (see the note at 12:27).

21:20 *the disciple whom Jesus loved:* See the note at 13:23.

21:24 *This is the disciple who testifies to these things and who wrote them down:* According to this verse, "the disciple whom Jesus loved" (21:20) is the one who wrote this true account of Jesus' words and works, though he had to choose them from the many stories and memories of what Jesus said and did (21:25)

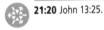

21:20 John 13:25.

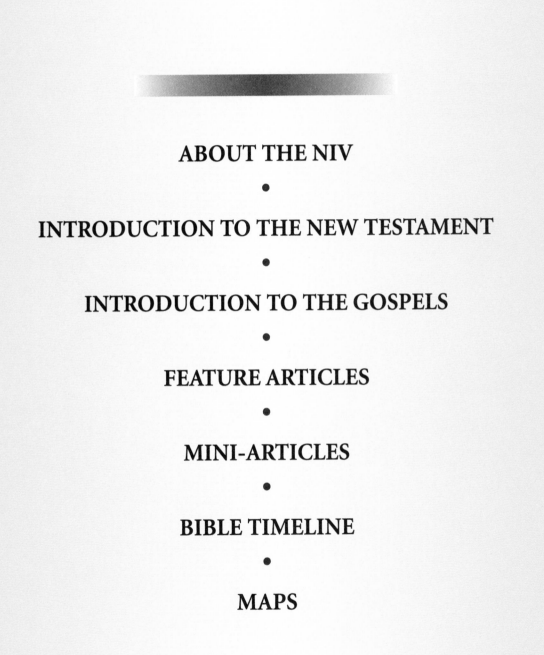

ABOUT THE NIV

•

INTRODUCTION TO THE NEW TESTAMENT

•

INTRODUCTION TO THE GOSPELS

•

FEATURE ARTICLES

•

MINI-ARTICLES

•

BIBLE TIMELINE

•

MAPS

ABOUT THE NIV

THIS NEW TESTAMENT of the *New International Version* of the Holy Bible is a completely new translation made by over a hundred scholars working directly from the best available Greek texts. It had its beginning in 1965 when, after several years of exploratory study by committees from the Christian Reformed Church and the National Association of Evangelicals, a group of scholars met at Palos Heights, Illinois, and concurred in the need for a new translation of the Bible in contemporary English. This group, though not made up of official church representatives, was transdenominational. Its conclusion was endorsed by a large number of leaders from many denominations who met in Chicago in 1966.

Responsibility for the new version was delegated by the Palos Heights group to a self-governing body of fifteen, the Committee on Bible Translation, composed for the most part of biblical scholars from colleges, universities and seminaries. In 1967 the New York Bible Society (now the International Bible Society) generously undertook the financial sponsorship of the project—a sponsorship that made it possible to enlist the help of many distinguished scholars. The fact that participants from the United States, Great Britain, Canada, Australia and New Zealand worked together gave the project its international scope. That they were from many denominations—including Anglican, Assemblies of God, Baptist, Brethren, Christian Reformed, Church of Christ, Evangelical Free, Lutheran, Mennonite, Methodist, Nazarene, Presbyterian, Wesleyan and other churches—helped to safeguard the translation from sectarian bias.

How it was made helps to give the *New International Version* its distinctiveness. The translation of each book was assigned to a team of scholars. Next, one of the Intermediate Editorial Committees revised the initial translation, with constant reference to the Hebrew, Aramaic or Greek. Their work then went to one of the General Editorial Committees, which checked it in detail and made another thorough revision. This revision in turn was carefully reviewed by the Committee on Bible Translation, which made further changes and then released the final version for publication. In this way the entire Bible underwent three revisions, during each of which the translation was examined for its faithfulness to the original languages and for its English style.

All this involved many thousands of hours of research and discussion regarding the meaning of the texts and the precise way of putting them into English. It may well be that no other translation has been made by a more thorough process of review and revision from committee to committee than this one.

From the beginning of the project, the Committee on Bible Translation held to certain goals for the *New International Version*: that it would be an accurate translation and one that would have clarity and literary quality and so prove suitable for public and private reading, teaching, preaching, memorizing and liturgical use. The Committee also sought to preserve some measure of continuity with the long tradition of translating the Scriptures into English.

In working toward these goals, the translators were united in their commitment to the authority and infallibility of the Bible as God's Word in written form. They believe that it contains the divine answer to the deepest needs of humanity, that it sheds unique light on our path in a dark world, and that it sets forth the way to our eternal well-being.

The first concern of the translators has been the accuracy of the translation and its fidelity to the thought of the biblical writers. They have striven for more than a word-for-word translation. Because thought patterns and syntax differ from language to language, faithful communication of the meaning of the writers of the Bible demands frequent modifications in sentence structure and constant regard for the contextual meanings of words.

The Committee on Bible Translation submitted the developing version to a number of stylistic consultants. Samples of the translation were tested for clarity and ease of reading by various kinds of people—young and old, highly educated and less well educated, ministers and laymen. Concern for clear and natural English motivated the translators and consultants. In view of the international use of English, the translators sought to avoid obvious Americanisms on the one hand and obvious Anglicisms on the other. A British edition reflects the comparatively few differences of significant idiom and of spelling.

As for the traditional pronouns "thou," "thee" and "thine" in reference to the Deity, the translators judged that to use these archaisms (along with the old verb forms such as "doest," "wouldest" and "hadst") would violate accuracy in translation. Greek does not use special pronouns for the persons of the Godhead. A present-day translation is not enhanced by forms that in the time of the *King James Version* were used in everyday speech, whether referring to God or man.

The Greek text used in translating the New Testament was an eclectic one. No other piece of ancient literature has such an abundance of manuscript witnesses as does the New Testament. Where existing manuscripts differ, the translators made their choice of readings according to accepted principles of New Testament textual criticism. Footnotes call attention to places where there was uncertainty about what the original text was. The best current printed texts of the Greek New Testament were used.

There is a sense in which the work of translation is never wholly finished. This applies to all great literature and uniquely so to the Bible. In 1973 the New Testament in the *New International Version* was published. Since then, suggestions for corrections and revisions have been received from various sources. The Committee on Bible Translation carefully considered the suggestions and adopted a number of them. These were incorporated in the first printing of the entire Bible in 1978. Additional revisions were made by the Committee on Bible Translation in 1983 and appear in printings after that date.

To achieve clarity the translators sometimes supplied words not in the original texts but required by the context. If there was uncertainty about such material, it is enclosed in brackets. Also for the sake of clarity or style, nouns, including some proper nouns, are sometimes substituted for pronouns, and vice versa. As an aid to the reader, italicized sectional headings are inserted in most of the books. They are not to be regarded as part of the NIV text, are not for oral reading, and are not intended to dictate the interpretation of the sections they head.

The footnotes in this version are of several kinds, most of which need no explanation. Those giving alternative translations begin with "Or" and generally introduce the alternative with the last word preceding it in the text, except when it is a single-word alternative; in poetry quoted in a footnote a slant mark indicates a line division. Footnotes introduced by "Or" do not have uniform significance. In some cases two possible translations were considered to have about equal validity. In other cases, though the translators were convinced that the translation in the text was correct, they judged that another interpretation was possible and of sufficient importance to be represented in a footnote. In the New Testament, footnotes that refer to uncertainty regarding the original text are introduced by "Some manuscripts" or similar expressions.

It should be noted that minerals, flora and fauna, architectural details, articles of clothing and jewelry, musical instruments and other articles cannot always be identified with precision. Also measures of capacity in the biblical period are particularly uncertain.

Like all translations of the Bible, made as they are by imperfect man, this one undoubtedly falls short of its goals. Yet we are grateful to God for the extent to which he has enabled us to realize these goals and for the strength he has given us and our colleagues to complete our task. We offer this version of the Bible to him in whose name and for whose glory it has been made. We pray that it will lead many into a better understanding of the Holy Scriptures and a fuller knowledge of Jesus Christ the incarnate Word, of whom the Scriptures so faithfully testify.

The Committee on Bible Translation
June 1978
(Revised August 1983)
Names of the translators and editors
may be secured from the
International Bible Society,
translation sponsors of the *New International Version,*
1820 Jet Stream Drive,
Colorado Springs, CO
80921-3696 U.S.A.

THE NEW TESTAMENT

THE "NEW TESTAMENT" is the second part of the Christian Bible. Its twenty-seven books continue the story of God's people begun in the Old Testament (the Jewish Scriptures). The word "testament" comes from a Latin word that means "will," which was used to translate the Greek word *diatheke*, which means "will," "agreement," or "covenant." The Old Testament tells of the covenant God made with the people of Israel. This covenant was based, in large part, on the Law of Moses. Those who obeyed God and lived according to this Law were God's people. But about six hundred years before the time of Jesus, the prophet Jeremiah announced a "new covenant" based on an inward relationship with God (Jer 31:31-34). Jesus used the language of a "new covenant" to describe what God was doing through him (Luke 22:20; 1 Cor 11:25), and other New Testament writers did the same (2 Cor 3:6; Heb 8:8; 9:15; 12:24). The apostle Paul says that this new covenant is not based on written law but comes from God's Spirit and brings new life (Gal 3:10-14).

The books of the New Testament were written during a period of about one hundred years following the time of Jesus. Many of the books focus on Jesus of Nazareth, who was born to Jewish parents and declared by Christians to be the Christ ("Messiah"), or Savior (Mark 8:29; 14:61, 62; Luke 2:11; John 20:30, 31; Acts 3:18-21). The four Gospels (MATTHEW, MARK, LUKE, and JOHN) tell about the life and teachings of Jesus, each from a different perspective. ACTS tells how the earliest apostles preached about Jesus and spread his message in the decades following Jesus. The Letters of the New Testament provide an understanding of the ways the message of Jesus was being preached and interpreted during the first years of the early Church as the good news about Jesus was being taken to new lands. They also give some clues about what the earliest Christians were experiencing. REVELATION, the last book in the New Testament, ends with the hope of a future in which God will bring a new heaven and a new earth.

It is impossible to give an exact date for the writings of the New Testament books, but most scholars now agree that some of the Letters of Paul are the oldest of the New Testament writings. The Gospels and ACTS actually were written later. MARK, probably the first Gospel to be put in writing, was most likely written sometime after A.D. 60.

Though Jesus and his disciples spoke Aramaic, the books of the New Testament were first written in the "everyday" Greek of that time. The New Testament writers also were familiar with the Greek translation of the Jewish Scriptures (called the Septuagint). A number of quotations found in the New Testament come directly from this Greek translation, while others were translated into Greek from the Hebrew of the Jewish Scriptures. The original manuscripts of the New Testament deteriorated or were destroyed long ago. But hand-made copies of the text of these books were made repeatedly down through the centuries. The earliest copy of the entire Greek New Testament dates from the fourth century, and the earliest fragment of a New Testament book dates from around A.D. 125. Also of value to biblical scholars are early translations of New Testament writings into Coptic, Syriac, and Latin. It took over three hundred years before the twenty-seven books that make up the New Testament became the accepted list followed in our Bibles today, but ever since then the Church has regarded these writings as equal in authority to the Old Testament Scriptures.

THE GOSPELS

THE FOUR GOSPELS (MATTHEW, MARK, LUKE, and JOHN) present various accounts of the life and teachings of Jesus Christ. ACTS gives a detailed report of what happened to some of Jesus' early followers as they carried the message about Jesus from Jerusalem to the other areas of the Roman empire.

The word "Gospel" comes from an Old English word that means "good news." The Greek word that is translated as "gospel" or "good news" is *euangelion* (see Mark 1:1). The English words "evangelist" and "evangelism" also come from this word. An evangelist is one who tells good news.

The Gospels were probably written down in their present form between thirty and sixty years after Jesus' crucifixion. Since Jesus himself left no writings, the Gospels record stories and eyewitness descriptions that had been passed on by word of mouth for a number of years. At first, Jesus' followers were so eager to tell the message about him that they didn't think it was necessary to write down what he had said and done. But as Jesus' first followers and eyewitnesses grew older and died, it became more important to have a written record of what Jesus did and taught, and to describe his death and resurrection.

Although other "gospels" about Jesus were written and circulated, the only ones accepted by the whole church as reliable and divinely inspired were MATTHEW, MARK, LUKE, and JOHN. It is not certain who actually wrote these Gospels, since the names of the authors are never given in the books themselves. Traditionally, Matthew and John, two of the 12 apostles, have been held as the authors of MATTHEW and JOHN; and the authors of MARK and LUKE are considered to be early followers of Christ who heard about Jesus from one or more of Jesus' first disciples. Some biblical scholars believe that all four of the Gospels were written by followers of Christ who heard about Jesus from his first disciples.

Many sources were used to write the Gospels. These sources probably included various collections of Jesus' sayings and stories that were available to the Gospel writers. For example, a number of Jesus' sayings are similar in MATTHEW and LUKE, so they may have been working with the same source. Both of them also appear to have used MARK for their basic outlines. But MATTHEW and LUKE also used different sources to describe the events surrounding Jesus' birth, since MARK has nothing to say about Jesus' childhood. MATTHEW, MARK, and LUKE have so much material in common and follow the same basic outline, that they are sometimes referred to as the "Synoptic" Gospels (from the Greek word *synopsis*, which means "seeing together").

The three Synoptic Gospels are more like each other than any of them is like JOHN. While MATTHEW, MARK, and LUKE focus on Jesus' public teaching and miracle working in Galilee, JOHN contains information about Jesus' early work in Judea. JOHN also contains some of Jesus' sayings that are not found in the other Gospels. These include the so-called "I am" sayings, such as "I am the bread of life" (John 6:35) and "I am the light of the world" (John 8:12). The order of events in JOHN does not follow the order shared by the Synoptic Gospels. And JOHN does not include any of Jesus' parables that are found in the other three Gospels.

The Bible is like a small library that contains many books written by many authors. The word "Bible" comes from the Greek word *biblia,* meaning "books." It took well over 1,000 years for all of these books to be written down, and it was many more years before the list of books now known as the Bible came together in one large book.

Passing Stories Along

Before anything in the Bible was written down, people told stories about God and God's relationship with the people we now read about in the Bible. This stage of passing on stories by word of mouth is known as the "oral tradition." This stage of relating stories by word of mouth lasted for many years as families passed along the stories of their ancestors to each new generation. In the case of the Jewish Scriptures (Old Testament), some stories were told for centuries before they were written down in a final form.

Long before the Bible was ever written, its stories, teachings, lists of ancestors, and poems were passed along from one generation to the next by word of mouth in storytelling gatherings. This is known as "the oral tradition."

Writing Down the Bible Stories

Eventually, as human societies in the Near East began to develop forms of writing that were easy to learn and use (around 1800 B.C.), people began to write down the stories, songs (psalms), and prophecies that would one day become a part of the Bible. These were written on papyrus, a paper-like material made from reeds, or on vellum, which was made from dried animal skins. But all the books found in the Old Testament were not written down at one time. This process took centuries. While some books were being written and collected, others were still being passed on in storytelling fashion.

The very first manuscripts of the books that make up the Old and New Testaments have never been found, and most likely wore out from continued use or were destroyed centuries ago. However, copies of these manuscripts were made by hand and became valued possessions of synagogues, churches, and monasteries. Before these copies wore out, new copies were made, and then eventually copies were made from these copies—and so on, from one generation to the next. Some very old copies of both the Old and New Testament writings have been preserved, and they are now stored in museums and libraries around the world in places like Jerusalem, London, Paris, Dublin, New York, Chicago, Philadelphia, and Ann Arbor, Michigan.

Collecting the Jewish Scriptures

It is not possible to know exactly when all the books of the Jewish Scriptures were finally collected. Some of the writings in the Jewish Scriptures may go back as far as 1300 B.C., but the process of bringing the books together may not have begun until around 400 B.C. The process of deciding which books would be part of the official Jewish Scriptures went on until almost A.D. 100. This work was often done by Jewish rabbis (teachers).

Once the stories of the Bible began to be written down, it became necessary to make new copies before the old ones wore out from repeated use and became unreadable. Sometimes several scribes made copies while another scribe read the text aloud.

Preparing the Bible for a Changing World

It was during this time that the Jewish Scriptures were translated into Greek. This translation is called the Septuagint, which means "seventy," and is often identified by the Roman numeral for seventy (LXX). The legend of how the Septuagint came to be and how it got its name is told in a document called the *Letter of Aristeas*. The legend says that seventy-two scholars began translating the Jewish Scriptures from Hebrew, all at the same time. The *Letter* goes on to say that they all finished at the same time, in seventy-two days, and that all seventy-two scholars discovered that their translations were exactly the same! All the seventy-some numbers in this story gave the translation its name. This Greek version of

the Bible was used by Jewish people scattered throughout the Roman world, because most of them spoke Greek instead of Hebrew. The oldest copies of the Septuagint date from the second century B.C., more than one hundred years before Jesus was born. The Septuagint was also the main version of the Jewish Scriptures used by early Christians.

It is not exactly clear how it was decided which books should be considered holy enough to be included in the Jewish Scriptures. We do know that around A.D. 100, a group of Jewish scholars met at Jamnia, a center of Jewish learning west of Jerusalem. During this time, the scholars debated which books should be in the Jewish Scriptures. Probably these scholars' discussions were a large part of the Jewish community's decision that thirty-nine books should be on the holy list (canon). Seven books, sometimes called the Deutero-canonical books (meaning "second list"), were not included on the list. Today, most Protestant churches follow the original list of thirty-nine books and call it the Old Testament. The Roman Catholic, Anglican (Episcopal), and Eastern Orthodox churches include the Deuterocanonical books in their Old Testament.

The Stories of Christ and His First Followers

Jesus and most of his followers were Jewish, and so they used and quoted the Jewish Scriptures. After Jesus died and was raised to life around A.D. 30, the stories about Jesus, as well as his sayings, were passed on by word of mouth. It probably wasn't until about A.D. 65 that these stories and sayings began to be gathered and written down in books known as the Gospels, which make up about half of what Christians call the New Testament. The earliest writings of the New Testament, however, are probably some of the letters that the apostle Paul wrote to groups of Jesus' followers who were scattered throughout the Roman empire. The first of these letters, probably 1 THESSALONIANS, may have been written as early as A.D. 50. Some scholars feel that all the New Testament writings were written by the end of the first century A.D.; others feel that a portion of the New Testament was written early in the second century.

The New Testament books were written in Greek, an international language during this period of the Roman empire. They were often passed on and read as single books or letters. For nearly three hundred years (A.D. 100-400), the early church leaders and councils debated which New Testament writings should be considered inspired by God and treated with the same respect given to the Jewish Scriptures. In A.D. 367, Athanasius, the bishop of Alexandria, wrote a letter that listed the twenty-seven books he said Christians should consider authoritative. His list included the books already in widest use in the Christian churches, and the writings he named are the same twenty-seven books that today we call the New Testament.

Translating the Bible

When the New Testament books were written, the Greek language was understood all over the Mediterranean world. But by the late second century A.D., local languages were becoming popular again, especially in local churches. Translations of the Bible were then made into Latin, the language of Rome; Coptic, a language of Egypt; and Syriac, a language of Syria. In A.D. 383, Pope Damasus I assigned a scholar priest named Jerome to create an official translation of the Bible into Latin. It took Jerome about twenty-seven years to translate the whole Bible. His translation came to be known as the Vulgate and served as the standard version of the Bible in Western Europe for the next thousand years. By the Middle Ages, only scholars could read and understand Latin. But by the time Johannes Guttenberg invented the modern printing press (around 1456), the use of vernacular (local or national) languages was becoming acceptable and widespread in official, educational, and religious settings. And as more people began to learn to read, there was a new demand for the Bible in vernacular languages. And so translators like Martin Luther, William Tyndale, Cassiodoro de Reina, and Giovanni Diodati began to translate the Bible into the languages that people spoke in their everyday lives.

The process of Bible translating continues today, and it has been helped by some recent discoveries. For example, many ancient Greek manuscripts of the New Testament have been found in the last 150 years. In 1947, some very old manuscripts of the Jewish Scriptures were found in caves at Qumran, Murabba'at, and other locations just west of the Dead Sea in Israel, and have become known as the Dead Sea Scrolls. These manuscripts, which date from between the third century B.C. and the first century A.D., have helped modern scholars to better understand the wording of certain texts and to make decisions about how to best translate specific verses or words.

The Bible is a very old book that has come to us because many men and women have worked hard copying and studying manuscripts, examining important artifacts and ancient ruins, and translating ancient texts into modern languages. Their dedication has helped keep the story of God's people and the record of God's revelation alive.

The faith of Israel, now more commonly known as the Jewish faith, did not begin as a set of religious practices or system of beliefs. Rather, it began when God commanded Abraham to leave his home and take his wife Sarah and family to a new land called Canaan. Along with this command, God promised Abraham three things: (1) he would have many descendants who would become a great nation; (2) his descendants would be famous and have a land they could call their own; and (3) God would bless Abraham's descendants, and everyone on earth would be blessed because of them (Gen 12:1-3; 15:1-6; 17:1-8).

In return for these promises, Abraham and his descendants were to trust in God alone and obey what God told them to do. A special agreement (also known as a "covenant") had been formed. Abraham confirmed this agreement with God by having his son and all his male descendants circumcised (Gen 17:9-27). Having male children circumcised became an important sign of belonging to God's special people.

The following things made the faith of Israel unique among the religions of the ancient world:

1. They believed that God (*Yahweh*) had selected them to be God's special (chosen) people.

2. They believed God acted in history and was involved in the life of the whole community. God's relationship was with all the people, not just with a few individuals or the community's leaders.

3. They believed only in *Yahweh* and did not worship any other gods.

The LORD Gives His Chosen People the Law

The Bible describes how God was at work in the history of the Hebrew people, the Israelites. When they went to Egypt to escape a famine (Gen 42), God took care of them. Later, God helped them escape, led by Moses, from slavery in Egypt (Exod 12–14). The festival called Passover commemorates this important event, and is observed by Jewish people today. Remembering God's blessings and guidance has been an important part of their worship life as God's people.

God made an important agreement with the Israelite people at Mount Sinai, a place in the desert where Moses and the Israelites arrived after escaping from Egypt (Exod 19:1, 2). This happened before they entered Canaan, the land God promised to give them. At Sinai, God gave the Law to Moses and the people. This Law includes the Ten Commandments (Exod 20:2-17; Deut 5:6-21) and other instructions about how the Israelite people should live together and worship God. Other sections of this Law of Moses are given in Exodus 19–34, LEVITICUS, and DEUTERONOMY. The Law includes rules about making sacrifices to God, about how to treat others, and about who would be in charge of Israel's worship. It also included instructions about observing special festivals and holy days and explained what should happen if someone broke a law. At this point in their history, the people of Israel did not need a system of government or a constitution because they were supposed to live according to the Law of Moses. God promised that if the people followed the Law they would be rewarded. But if they were unfaithful to God and did not live according to the Law, they could expect to be punished (Exod 20:5, 6; Lev 25:14-46).

The People Enter the Land God Promised Them

In addition to the Law, God also gave Moses instructions for making the tabernacle (also known as the Tent of Meeting). The people would gather to worship God and offer sacrifices (Exod 25–30). This tent had three sections:

1. **The outer area.** This is where animals were sacrificed and burned on an altar. There was also a bronze basin in this area for the priests to wash their hands (Exod 27:9-19; 30:17-21).

2. **The Holy Place.** This area had a table, a golden candlestick, and an altar where incense was burned. The altar and table were made of acacia wood and covered with gold. A special kind of bread called the bread of the Presence was kept on the table. Twelve loaves of bread, one for each of Israel's tribes, were to be set out on the table every Sabbath (the day of rest), and only the priests were permitted to eat it (Lev 24:5-9). The lampstand was made of gold and had seven branches that curved upward. An oil-burning lamp was placed on each of the seven branches (Exod 25:31-40). The lampstand had seven branches probably because seven was a holy number that symbolized the Sabbath, the seventh day of the week (the day God rested after creating the world; see Gen 2:1, 2).

3. **The Most Holy Place.** This is where God was said to be present and where the ark of the covenant containing the stone tablets of the Law was kept. The ark of the covenant was covered with gold and measured about 4-feet long and was just over 2-feet wide and high. Gold rings were put on each side, so the people could carry the chest with them when they moved from place to place (Exod 25:10-22). The lid of the box was called the atonement cover (traditionally "mercy seat" because this is where God "sat" to be among the people, to receive their sacrifices, and to meet a representative of the people, Exod 26:34). Only Moses, and later the high priest, were allowed to enter the Most Holy Place. It was separated from the rest of the tent by a curtain, and inside the Most Holy Place was a lamp that was to be kept burning (Exod 27:20, 21).

Each of the areas of the tabernacle was separated from the others by curtains. A frame made of forty-eight acacia wood planks supported the whole tent, and it measured about 150 feet by 75 feet. The people carried the tabernacle and ark of the covenant with them as they journeyed. When they finally entered the land of Canaan, the tabernacle was set up at Shiloh (Josh 18:1). Later it was moved to Nob (1 Sam 21:1-6), then Gibeon (1 Chr 16:39), and finally to Jerusalem (2 Chr 5:4-6).

The agreement God had made with Abraham and Sarah was beginning to take shape. *Yahweh* had led the people of Israel out of slavery in Egypt and had helped them get their own land. With each new generation, the people of Israel grew in number and began to enjoy the blessings of living in the promised land. But the people had a difficult time being completely loyal to God, so problems arose.

JUDGES describes how God raised up special leaders, called judges, to help the people in times of crisis. The Israelites lived in this way for many years, until the people begged the judge and prophet named Samuel to give them a king like the ones who ruled neighboring countries. Samuel thought the people's request showed a lack of faith, but God eventually told Samuel to choose Saul as Israel's first king (1 Sam 8–10). Later, a shepherd named David was anointed king (1 Sam 16; 2 Sam 2:4). David captured Jerusalem and made it the capital of Israel and the single place of worship for all the tribes (2 Sam 5, 6). He even set up the tabernacle in Jerusalem on a hill that was known as Zion.

David's son Solomon built the first temple to take the place of the tabernacle. Solomon asked King Hiram of Tyre to supply some materials and skilled builders to help the Israelites construct the temple. In

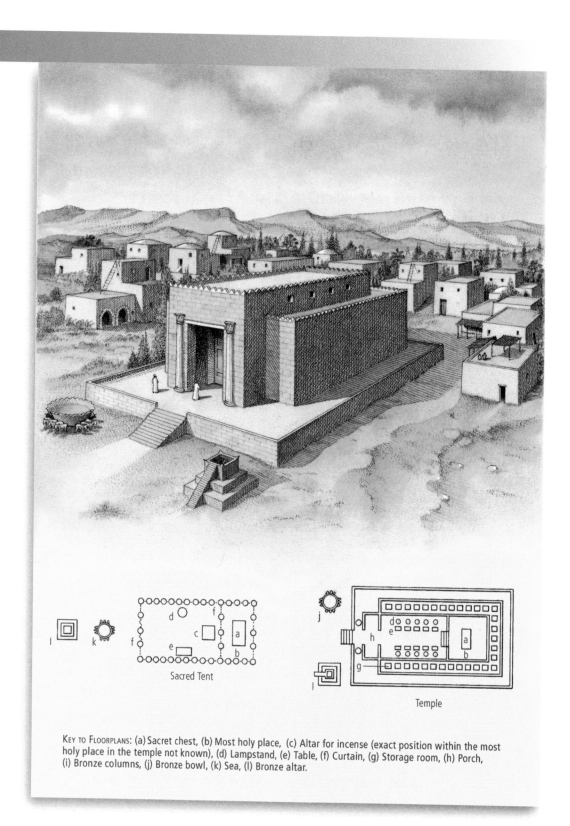

KEY TO FLOORPLANS: (a) Sacret chest, (b) Most holy place, (c) Altar for incense (exact position within the most holy place in the temple not known), (d) Lampstand, (e) Table, (f) Curtain, (g) Storage room, (h) Porch, (i) Bronze columns, (j) Bronze bowl, (k) Sea, (l) Bronze altar.

Sacred Tent

Temple

exchange for grain and olive oil from Israel, King Hiram gave Solomon lumber for the temple. People from both kingdoms worked together and the two nations were at peace with one another (1 Kgs 5). The temple was built using cedar, olive wood, and brick, with beautiful decorations made of gold and ivory. Like the tabernacle, the temple had three areas, but in the temple a large olive wood door, instead of a curtain, separated the Holy Place from the Most Holy Place (1 Kgs 6:16; 7:13—8:13). It took seven years to build Solomon's temple, which was dedicated sometime between 960 and 950 B.C. during the Feast of Tabernacles (1 Kgs 8:62-66).

After King Solomon died, the ten northern tribes of Israel broke away and made Shechem and then Tirzah their capital. They created several places of worship (1 Kgs 12:25-33), and some of the northern leaders, such as Ahab and Jezebel, encouraged the people to worship the Canaanite god Baal (1 Kgs 18). They also built idols (such as "Asherah poles") to worship the local gods (1 Kgs 14:15). This was one of the things God and God's prophets had warned the people not to do. Because the people did not remain loyal to *Yahweh* alone, they were punished. In 722 B.C. the Assyrians invaded the northern kingdom (Israel) and took most of the people from their homeland to live in Assyria (2 Kgs 17). The people of the southern kingdom (Judah) saw this as God's punishment for the northern tribes' disobedience to their agreement with God.

Later the people of Judah also disobeyed God and were invaded by the Babylonians, who destroyed Jerusalem and the temple in 586 B.C. Solomon's temple had stood for nearly 400 years, but the Babylonian invasion put a temporary end to worship at the temple. Israel's priests and prophets were forced to discover how Israel's faith could survive in exile, far away from Jerusalem in captivity in Babylon.

Israel Returns and Rebuilds the Temple

The people of Israel lived in exile in Babylon for about 50 years, but the priests and teachers of Israel did not let their faith die. Although the temple was destroyed, and they were far from home, they still had God's Word in the Scriptures and in their hearts. Some scholars believe that the time of exile marked a renewed commitment to God and to studying Scripture. The Jewish people probably continued to meet for worship, but they had to do so in private homes.

In 540 B.C. the Persians defeated the Babylonians. The Persian ruler, Cyrus, followed the Persian custom of allowing captured people to return to their homelands and to worship freely, as long as they promised not to start a revolt against the Persians. Many, but not all Israelites, did return to Judah beginning in 539 B.C. They completed work on a new, smaller temple ("the second temple") in 515 B.C. (Ezra 3–6). They physical splendor of this temple could not compare with Solomon's temple, but it was used for nearly 500 years, somewhat longer than Solomon's temple was used.

Two men, Ezra and Nehemiah, were especially important leaders during the first hundred years after the people returned to Judah from exile. Ezra, a Jewish priest and scribe, studied the Law of Moses and taught it to the people (Neh 8). Copies of the Law of Moses and the historical records were recovered and again became the basic guidelines for the relationship between the God and the people of Israel. Nehemiah, who was appointed by the Persian king to be governor of Judah, supervised the reconstruction of the walls of Jerusalem (Neh 2-6).

During the centuries after the second temple was built and before Jesus was born, the people of Israel were often under the rule of foreign powers. This caused them to start thinking of themselves more as a religious group than as a nation with

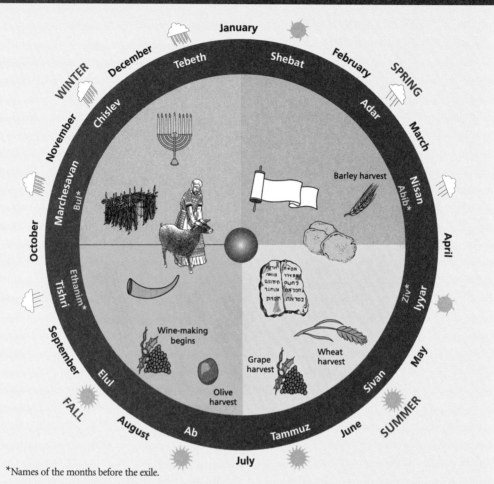

January · WINTER · December · Tebeth · Shebat · February · SPRING · Adar · March · Barley harvest · Nisan / Abib* · Chislev · April · November · Marchesavan · Bul* · Ziv* / Iyyar · October · Ethanim* / Tishri · Wheat harvest · May · Wine-making begins · Grape harvest · Sivan · September · Elul · Olive harvest · SUMMER · FALL · August · Ab · Tammuz · June · July

*Names of the months before the exile.

THE CALENDAR IN THE ANCIENT WORLD

As in other parts of the ancient Near East, the people of Israel developed a calendar that was based on the yearly movement of the sun and on the phases of the moon. The year was divided into twelve months, based on the observation that the moon's phases changed about twelve times in the period of days that made up a year. The number of days in the lunar (moon-based) year was about eleven days shorter than the solar (sun-based) year, so the Israelites periodically added an extra month to the calendar to make sure that the festivals they celebrated would continue to fall at their expected times in relation to the weather patterns (seasons) and agricultural cycles (planting and harvesting).

Early in Israelite history the year was considered to begin in the seventh month (around the fall fruit harvest). Later, it began in the spring on the first new moon after the vernal equinox (one of two times in the year when day and night are equal in length).

Time was measured, however, more often by season than by names of months. The year was divided into the dry season (April to September) and the rainy season (October to March). These, in turn, were divided into times for planting grain (November to December) and times for harvesting (April to June). Time was also measured by the agricultural activities that were undertaken in specific months. For example, wheat was harvested in March and April, grapes matured in June and July, and summer fruit was picked in August and September.

The months themselves had religious significance for the people of Israel. The beginning of each month (when the moon is "new") was considered a holy time and a time when the New Moon Festivals were celebrated (Num 28:11-15). Most of the yearly religious festivals had traditional associations with agricultural events, as well as to the events in Jewish history they commemorated.

FALL FESTIVALS

FEAST OF TRUMPETS
(ROSH HASHANAH, FIRST DAY OF TISHRI, THE SEVENTH MONTH)

A day to celebrate the New Year and to remember the agreement God made with the people at Mount Sinai. This holiday marks the beginning of the festival year.
Lev 23:23-25; Num 29:2-6.

DAY OF ATONEMENT
(YOM KIPPUR, TENTH DAY OF TISHRI)

The day of the year when the people expressed their sorrow

for their sins by going without eating (fasting) and the priest purified the Most Holy Place by sacrificing a bull for his own sins and a goat for the sins of the people. A second goat (called a scapegoat) was released into the desert to show that the people's sins were being taken away.
Lev 16:1-34; Num 29:7-11.

FEAST OF TABERNACLES
(SUCCOTH, FIFTEENTH DAY OF TISHRI)

A week-long celebration to remember how the people

wandered for forty years in the desert before entering into the land God promised to them.
Lev 23:33-43.

FEAST OF DEDICATION
(HANUKKAH, TWENTY-FIFTH DAY OF CHISLEV)

A week-long celebration to remember the rededication of the temple by Judas Maccabeus in 164 B.C. The story of Judas and his brothers is told in a book called *1*

Maccabees, which describes events in Jewish history from 175 to 134 B.C.
1 Maccabees 4:36-59; John 10:22.

SPRING FESTIVALS

PASSOVER AND THE FEAST OF UNLEAVENED BREAD
(FIFTEENTH DAY OF NISAN)

A week-long festival to recall how God delivered the people

from slavery in Egypt and to give thanks for the yearly production of food crops and flocks.
Exod 12:23-25.

FEAST OF WEEKS (PENTECOST)
(SHAVUOTH, SIXTH DAY OF SIVAN)

A day to celebrate the grain harvest and the beginning of the season when the first fruits were offered. It was also a day to recall how God delivered the nation from Egypt and provided a land that could supply the needs of the people.
Lev 23:15-21; Deut 16:9-12.

PURIM
(THIRTEENTH DAY OF ADAR)

A day to celebrate how Queen Esther helped stop Haman's plot against the Jews in the time of King Xerxes of Persia.
Esth 9:20-32.

PILGRIMAGE FESTIVALS

Three times a year, Jewish men were required to go to Jerusalem to celebrate these special festivals:

FEAST OF TABERNACLES

FEAST OF UNLEAVENED BREAD

FEAST OF WEEKS (PENTECOST)

SABBATH: A WEEKLY FESTIVAL

The word Sabbath comes from the Hebrew verb *shab-bat*, to "stop" or to "rest," and refers to the seventh day of the week, from sunset on Friday to sunset on Saturday. The ancient Israelites, like modern Jews, worshiped on the Sabbath and rested from their work.

The Bible's description of the Sabbath's origin is found in Genesis 2:1-3. These verses at the end of the creation story tell how God rested from the work of creation on the seventh day and made it a special, holy day. In EXODUS a connection is made between God's resting from creation and commanding Israel to rest from work on the Sabbath and worship the LORD (Exod 20:8-11; 31:17). This resting was not only for Israelites, but for their animals, servants (including slaves), and any foreigners living in Israel as well (Exod 23:12; Deut 5:14, 15).

Related to the weekly Sabbath observance is the biblical command that every seven years the land must be allowed to rest for a full year. During this Seventh Year (or "sabbatical year") the land was not

to be plowed or planted. This was done to honor the LORD, the one to whom the land truly belonged (Exod 23:10,11; Lev 25:1-7). Any crops that grew on their own were to be left in the fields for the poor and for work animals. The Seventh Year was also a time when debts were cancelled (Deut 15:1-3).

In addition, the Bible speaks of a Year of Jubilee. Each seventh Sabbatical Year (that is, every forty-nine years), land that had been sold was to be returned to its original owner, and all slaves were to be freed to their families (Lev 25:8-34). This year began on the Day of Atonement with the blowing of the ram's horn.

The Sabbath observance was one of the most important elements in Israelite religion. It reminded people of their special status as God's chosen people and that God was the Creator of the world. The three Sabbath observances of rest and freedom point to God's desire to free all of creation. Celebrating them reminds people of their own need for continual re-creation.

physical boundaries and a political leadership of its own. At this time, the most important feature of Israel's religion, which had come to be known as Judaism, was its stress on keeping the Law of Moses. To be a Jew meant following the Law of Moses. This included observing all the religious festivals as well as the special rules for priests and worship in the temple.

The second temple was at the center of an important event in Israel's history in the second century B.C. The Syrian king Antiochus IV Epiphanes set up an altar to the Greek god Zeus in the temple in 167 B.C. This was a horrible offense against God and the Jewish people, so the Jewish people revolted against Antiochus and restored the temple in 164 B.C. The Maccabean priests who led the revolt to free the Jews from Syrian rule set up a Jewish state with themselves as kings. It lasted until the Romans invaded in 63 B.C.

Herod Rebuilds and Enlarges the Temple

In 37 B.C., the Romans named a local leader ruler of Judah. In 20 B.C., Herod received permission to rebuild and expand the temple. Most of the building was completed in a year and a half, but work continued on the temple for another forty to fifty years, into the time when Jesus began his teaching (John 2:20). This expanded second temple, sometimes called "Herod's temple," was built on a huge four-sided platform that was almost a mile around its base. Its largest stones were as big as 40 feet long and 6 feet high. Some of these stones are still in place today on the temple site in Jerusalem. What is left of this "temple mount" can be seen clearly at the site called the "Western Wall" (or "Wailing Wall"), where many Jews still go to pray. The temple itself was surrounded by a large wall that had many different entrances. The outer area of the temple grounds included a court of the Gentiles, where anyone was allowed to visit. In this outer area, birds and animals suitable for

sacrifice were sold to pilgrims, and foreign money was exchanged so pilgrims could pay their temple tax. In addition to the traditional sections discussed earlier—an altar area where burnt offerings were sacrificed by the priests, a holy area, where only priests were allowed, and the Most Holy Place where only the high priest was allowed to go—the second temple also included a women's court.

The religious life of the temple went on in clear view of the Romans, who occupied the Antonia Fortress (also called the Praetorium) built right outside the northwest corner of the wall surrounding the temple area. This fortress was the living quarters for a large number of Roman soldiers, whose job was to keep peace in Jerusalem (Acts 21:34-37). The Roman governor's official residence was in Caesarea, but he usually stayed at this fortress while in Jerusalem.

During the time of Herod's temple, the Romans were in charge of Jerusalem and Judea. They did, however, allow a council of local Jewish leaders, including the high priest and other important religious and business leaders, to have some control over settling local matters, especially those having to do with the temple and religious issues. For example, no Gentile (non-Jew) was allowed in the inner parts of the temple. If someone broke this law, the Jewish leaders could call upon the Roman authorities to put the offender to death.

In Jesus' day, the temple continued to be the center of the Jewish faith. Jewish men and many of their family members traveled to Jerusalem to celebrate yearly festivals such as Passover and Pentecost. The temple priests and the rituals surrounding the temple were important to the Jewish people. Some Jews, such as the Pharisees, also emphasized the importance of studying and interpreting the Jewish Scriptures. This means that there were a number of different and important ways that Jewish people expressed their faith. If this had not been true, the Jewish faith might have died out when the temple was destroyed in A.D. 70.

Jesus' prediction that the temple would be destroyed (Mark 13:1, 2) came to pass when the Romans destroyed Herod's temple while putting down a Jewish revolt that lasted between A.D. 64-70. The Roman emperor Hadrian (A.D. 117-138) crushed a second Jewish revolt about A.D. 131. In 132, Hadrian built a temple to honor the Roman god Jupiter on the same site, and in the seventh century A.D., Muslims built a mosque called the Dome of the Rock on the temple site. The shrine and mosque are still standing today, as are a few parts of Herod's original temple area.

The Role of Israel's Priests

According to the agreement God made with Moses, all the people of Israel were to serve God as priests (Exod 19:5, 6). They would be God's holy nation. The Law of Moses also set aside special priests to represent the whole people in their relationship with God. The priests of Israel were to be from the tribe of Levi. Those who were not born into this tribe could not serve as priests.

The priesthood of Israel appears to fall into three levels. In the lowest level were those Levites who were not direct descendants of Moses' brother Aaron (see Num 3:5-13). They were to help the priests and take care of the furnishings in the tabernacle (and later, in the temple). At the next level were the priests who were responsible for offering sacrifices and leading the worship. These priests were also from the Levite tribe, but had to be direct descendants of Aaron. The Levites and the priests were divided into twenty-four groups or shifts. Each group served in the temple for one week on a rotating basis. With twenty-four groups, a particular priest might serve for a total of two or, very occasionally, three weeks each year. At the head of the priesthood was the high priest. He was in charge of the other priests, and was the only priest who could enter the Most Holy Place to offer sacrifices on the Day of Atonement (Lev 16:1-25).

The priests wore special clothes made of linen and other fine materials. For a

The Arch of Titus. *Rome, built in A.D. 81, celebrates how this Roman general put down the Jewish Rebellion in Palestine eleven years earlier. This relief from the Arch shows how Titus brought the temple treasures, including the gold lampstand (menorah), to the emperor and paraded them through the streets of Rome.*

description of these, see Exod 28:1—29:30. The high priest wore a special vest (ephod) and a breastpiece. The breastpiece was made partly of metal (gold) and partly of cloth (fine linen) and was to have four rows of precious stones with three in each row, representing the twelve tribes of Israel. In the early days of the priesthood, the breastpiece had a pouch in it that contained the "Urim and Thummim," objects the high priest could use to get a "yes" or "no" answer from God (Exod 28:30). Most likely, by the time the Jewish people returned from their exile in Babylonia, the use of the Urim and Thummim had been discontinued. Another distinctive part of the high priest's attire was a turban. It had a gold rosette with the words "HOLY TO THE LORD" engraved on it (Exod 28:36; 39:30).

When the Jewish people returned to Jerusalem after exile in Babylon, the Persian king would not allow them to have their own king. Because they could not have a king, the high priest became an even more significant person in the life of the people. In the centuries before Jesus and during Jesus' lifetime, the high priest was the head of the temple and of the Jewish people.

Worship and Festivals

The worship practices of Israel included the offering of sacrifices, prayers, and Scripture reading. Selected texts were read for certain occasions, and sometimes songs were sung. PSALMS includes prayers and songs that were sung or said in worship by the whole people or used by individuals in private prayer. The text of Deuteronomy 6:4 ("Hear, O Israel," called the *Shema*) was to be said in prayer every morning and evening.

One of the most important aspects of the religious life of the Jewish people, both before and after the exile, was the keeping of the Sabbath (Exod 20:8-11; Exod 31:12-17). On the Sabbath, the seventh day of the week, Jews are commanded not to do any work and to rest, just as God rested after creating the world in six days (Gen 1:1—2:4). The Sabbath is also devoted to prayer and to remembering how God brought the Israelite people out of slavery in Egypt. On this day, they and their children, their servants, their visitors, and even their livestock should rest and not work (Deut 5:12-15).

The festival celebrations that were commanded in the Law of Moses and established by Jewish tradition greatly influenced Israel's life of faith. These celebrations can be grouped according to the time they were to take place as well as by purpose. See the chart on the previous pages for an explanation of the major festivals in the Jewish calendar.

Both the faith of Israel and the faith of the early Christians developed in cultural contexts steeped in other religious traditions. The people of Israel encountered religions with many similar beliefs and rituals in Palestine and Egypt. Christianity came into being as one among many religions and philosophies spread around the Mediterranean world by merchants and soldiers.

The People of Israel and Canaanite Religions

The people of Israel believed in one God. This belief is known as "monotheism." Many of the other religions in the ancient Mediterranean world recognized a number of different gods. When the Israelite people entered Canaan well over one thousand years before Jesus was born, they came into contact with the various gods of their neighbors. The Law of Moses commanded God's people to remain loyal to the one true God, *Yahweh*, who had led them out of slavery in Egypt and into the promised land of Canaan (Exod 20:1-5). Once they settled there, they were often tempted to follow the other gods, and often did.

The Gods of Israel's Neighbors. Among the Canaanites, one of the most common names for god was El. The Canaanites did not believe that El was the only god, but they did believe that El was the one who ruled over all the other gods. They believed El was the creator of the universe and the kind, compassionate father of the whole human race. El was worshiped in Palestine before the Israelites took over the land. In the Jewish Scriptures, "El" also frequently refers to the God of Israel. Some examples of the use of this name are found in the Old Testament.

Some of the enemies of El were known as Yamm (the sea), Mot (death) and Leviathan (the sea monster). See Psalm 104:26 and Isaiah 27:1.

Another name for a god in the ancient Near East was Baal, which means "master," "husband," and "lord." Baal was worshiped by the Canaanites as a god of fertility who ensured good and abundant crops. Baal was also connected to storms that came into Syria and Palestine from the sea in the winter and early spring. Since rain was essential for the growth of crops, people believed that the storms that came from the sea were powerful gods. Some ancient people believed that parts of nature itself were filled with god-like spirits, so they worshiped things like trees, rivers, fountains, and caves.

Some people in the ancient world believed goddesses provided fertility for crops and flocks and helped human beings to have children. The Canaanite goddess Asherah was pictured as the mother of the gods. She was identified as the wife of El. King Manasseh of Judah had a carved image of Asherah placed in the temple of the LORD in Jerusalem (2 Kgs 21:7). Asherah poles were put up on hilltops as symbols of fertility (1 Kgs 14:23; 16:33).

NAMES OF GOD

NAME	SCRIPTURE PASSAGES
El Elyon (God Most High)	Gen 14:18-20
El Olam (Eternal God)	Gen 21:33
El Berith (God of the Covenant)	Judg 9:46
El Shaddai (God All-Mighty or God of the Mountains)	Gen 17:1; 35:9-11; Exod 6:3

The goddess Anath was also a fertility goddess. She was famous for performing acts of violence against those who opposed her. An important city in Israel, Anathoth, was named for her (Josh 21:18; Jer 1:1; 11:21). This means that she was probably worshiped in this town at an earlier time. Even during the time when Nehemiah (about 445 B.C.) was helping restore Israel to the land and reminding the people to practice God's law after the exile in Babylon, the city's name remained Anathoth (Neh 7:27; 11:32).

The Philistine people who lived in the narrow strip of land between Judah and the Mediterranean Sea often battled with Israel. Their chief god was Dagon (1 Sam 5:1-5). The people of Moab, another of Israel's enemies when the Israelites were settling in Canaan, worshiped the god named Chemosh.

When the people of Israel worshiped other gods, God punished them. Ahab, the king of Israel, married Jezebel, the daughter of king Ethbaal of Sidon. Part of Jezebel's name, *Zebul*, was a form of Baal's name. Ahab went against the Law of Moses when he built a temple with an altar to worship Baal in his capital city, Samaria (1 Kgs 16:31, 32), and when he allowed Jezebel to encourage him to support hundreds of prophets of Asherah (1 Kgs 18:19). Many of the people of Israel were led to worship *Yahweh*, Israel's God, as well as Baal and Asherah. This worship broke the commandment God had given to Moses: "You shall have no other gods before me" (Exod 20:3). Because of their sins, God allowed Israel's neighbors to defeat them and carry many of the people into exile (2 Kgs 17).

Other Religions Outside of Palestine. In the ancient world, many cities or city-states had their own gods. Often people would build altars and places of worship (shrines) where they could bring sacrifices for their gods. These sacrifices were intended to please the gods in the hope that they would then protect the people of the city and give them good crops. In ancient Babylonia, for example, each city built temples to its protector gods.

Astrology, the belief that the sun and the stars control human life, came out of Babylonia and had a great influence throughout the Greek and Roman empires. The people of Israel rejected this belief in the influence of the stars as contrary to monotheism. They believed that God created the sun, moon, and stars (Gen 1:14-19; Ps 8:3; 147:4). Since these heavenly bodies are created, they cannot be gods.

In Egypt, the cults of Isis, Osiris, and Serapis were popular. In Syria, Israel's northern neighbor, people worshiped the great sky-god named Hadad, and helped spread the belief in astrology, common in Babylonia, to the Greeks. From Persia, a nation that conquered the Babylonians and ruled Palestine before the Greeks invaded the land, came the cult of Mazdaism. This was connected to the religion taught by Zoroaster, a teacher whose ideas would later influence Gnostic beliefs (see below). The most important of the cults popular in Asia Minor was the cult of Cybele, also known as the Great Mother. The Greeks identified Cybele with Rhea, the mother of the Greek gods, and with Artemis, who is mentioned in the Bible as the goddess of the Ephesians (Acts 19:21-41).

The Christian Church in the Greek World

Greek Religions. In the centuries before Jesus was born, the number of religions, cults, and forms of philosophy in the Mediterranean world had grown rapidly. The letters of the New Testament provide glimpses of how various religions, philosophies, and cult teachings opposed Christian followers. (For examples, see 1 Cor 8; 10; Gal 1:6-9; 1 John 2:26, 27; Rev 2:2-6,14-16, 20-25.)

The greatest religious influences and new philosophies came from the ancient Greeks. When Alexander the Great and his heirs took over Syria and Palestine after 330 B.C., they gave new names to the local gods and goddesses and introduced new deities.

There was the Greek god of time, Chronos, and Zeus, the chief of the Greek gods. The Greeks also worshiped goddesses, such as Artemis, goddess of the hunt, and the Egyptian goddess Isis. Isis is not mentioned in the New Testament, but it is known that many people in the Mediterranean world at this time believed in her as the one who made crops and flocks fertile every year. Belief in Isis was spread by merchants and soldiers and became a very important religion. The worship of Isis competed with the spread of Christianity in the first three centuries A.D. Asklepios, the god of healing, was also popular at this time. The desire of Christians to show the superiority of Jesus over this god may have influenced the way some of the miracle stories about Jesus' power to heal were shaped by the writers of the New Testament.

Various "mystery cults" were popular throughout the Greek world as well. Mystery cults had secret beliefs, so becoming a member usually required going through initiation ceremonies or practicing specific kinds of rites or sacraments. Participants in these cults believed that the ceremonies brought a person into the very life of the gods. The most popular Greek mystery cults were the cults of Demeter and Dionysus. Demeter was the goddess of grain and of the tamed or cultured aspects of nature. Dionysus was the god of wine and of the wild, untamed aspects of nature. The spirit of Dionysus was said to be in the animal (and possibly human) flesh that was eaten as part of the cult rituals. Members who participated in the rite believed they were consuming part of Dionysus when they ate. To many people at

The Egyptian fertility goddess Isis holding her son Horus. Although this goddess is never mentioned in the Bible, she was worshiped throughout the Greek and Roman world in the time of Jesus and his apostles.

this time, Christians also seemed to be a mystery cult, because when they celebrated the Lord's Supper, Christians ate the bread and drank the wine that Jesus described as his body and blood (Mark 14:22-24). Dionysus was also believed to make new birth possible for his followers. These beliefs would have seemed similar to the Christians' claim that Jesus had the power to renew the life of his people (John 3:1-21).

Other religions in the first century were based on fate, fortune, astrology, and magic. Some people believed that the supreme god was Tyche ("Fortune"), who ruled the lives of human beings. If someone became rich, it was because of Fortune; if that person suddenly lost his or her wealth, that was because of Fortune, too. Similarly, some people believed in a ruler known as "Fate." Fate was thought to determine everything that would happen in the universe, including the actions of all people. Good things and bad things alike were caused by Fate, and human beings were simply thought to be the means Fate used to carry out present and future events already determined.

This type of thinking opened the way for the religions based on astrology. In astrology, it was believed that the movement of the sun, moon, and planets determined a person's life. In Greece, astrology was combined with science in order to develop "horoscopes" (maps of the positions of planets) for predicting the future of individuals. Those who did not like the idea that their lives were controlled by the planets or by fate turned to magic. They wore charms or amulets and recited spells in order to hold off the power of evil.

Greek Philosophies. In Greece during the third and fourth centuries before Christ, the Greek philosophers Socrates, Plato, and Aristotle were concerned with how people could live a virtuous life that was in harmony with their city, their culture, and the natural world. Disciples of these great teachers would later form a number of schools of philosophy. By the time of the early Christian church, the teachings of these schools had spread throughout the Mediterranean world. Plato and Aristotle especially had a profound effect on later Christian writers and thinkers.

Originally worshiped as a goddess of fertility and successful childbearing, Fortuna was believed to control both good and bad luck. She is often represented holding a cornucopia and a steering oar.

Socrates of Athens lived from about 469 to 399 B.C. The Greek philosophers who lived before Socrates were concerned with trying to discover what the world was made of, but Socrates believed that philosophy could also tell people how to live a good life. To do this, Socrates developed two forms of gathering and presenting information, called induction (to suggest general conclusions from specific examples) and definition (to try to clearly describe what is meant by the general quality of a thing), and a method of using logic in discussions called "dialectic," which involved asking and answering questions. Because of his interest in virtue, Socrates is usually considered the founder of ethics.

Plato, a student of Socrates, lived from about 428 to 348 B.C. and started a school called the "Academy," which continued for more than nine hundred years. Plato's teachings, written in his *Dialogues,* have been among the most influential in the history of Western Civilization. Plato believed that Reason (in Greek, called *logos*) was the nature of the universe, controlling things from within. When he thought about how the world was constantly changing, Plato looked for things that do not change, which are represented in the things that do change. He called these "Forms" or "Ideas." Plato thought that when we call things by a general name, such as Beauty or Courage, we do so because there is a permanent Idea or Form of Beauty or Courage underlying each individual example of it. He believed that these Ideas or Forms, which are the meanings behind physical laws and material things, are what is truly real. Plato also believed that the human soul was immortal, and that the soul is superior to the body. According to Plato, it is the soul that makes us what we are, and that the highest responsibility of people is to "tend the soul," so that it is acceptable to the gods.

Aristotle lived from about 384 to 322 B.C. and was a student of Plato at the "Academy." When Plato died, Aristotle left Athens and became a teacher of Alexander the Great. When Aristotle returned to Athens, he began a school called the "Lyceum," where he taught that the knowledge of a thing requires an understanding of what caused it. Unlike Plato, he believed that form caused matter to move, and that the only pure form was God, who was the cause and goal of all motion. Aristotle's teachings, recorded by his students, cover many fields, including ethics and logic, the natural sciences, politics, physics, and poetry.

Cynics were followers of the Greek philosophical school founded by Antisthenes, a student of Socrates who lived from about 444 to 370 B.C. The most famous Cynic philosopher was Diogenes of Sinope (a town on the shore of the Black Sea). Diogenes believed that happiness came from following virtue for its own sake, and by living a life free from grasping after material possessions and pleasures. It is not clear why the Cynic school (from the Greek word *kyon* meaning "dog") was given its name. It may be a reference to their harshly critical style, in response to what they thought was a corrupt society. Or it may refer to the "Cynosarges," a school where the followers met to discuss philosophy. Cynic philosophers were not tied to one place and their wandering style was copied by some early Christian apostles. This is evidenced when Paul preached at the Areopagus in Athens, and his audience thought he was a wandering philosopher (Acts 17:16-34).

Stoicism was founded by Zeno of Citium (a town in Cyprus), who lived from around 336 to 261 B.C. The name "stoicism" comes from the Greek word *stoa.* Zeno and his students used to meet regularly at a pillared porch, the *Stoa Poikile,* on the north side of the marketplace in Athens (see the illustration). The Stoics thought that the whole universe was a divine being, and that the gods were simply various names of the one cosmic God. They believed that virtue was living in harmony with the rational force of nature. To find peace of mind, the Stoics said, people should learn what is in their power and what isn't, and should concern themselves only with the things in their power. The Stoics concluded that people had the power to live in

Porch-like structures called "Stoas" were gathering places for people in the Greek and Roman worlds. A group of philosophers came to be known as the Stoics because they met in the Stoa in Athens.

harmony with the cosmic God, which they called virtue. They believed that people should live according to virtue (the rational force of all nature) and be indifferent (the Greek word *apatheia*) to all things—like wealth, pleasure, good or bad fortune—that might prevent them from living a virtuous life. (In English today, the word "stoic" has come to mean patient, disciplined, or self-restrained.) Like all Stoics who would come after him, Zeno preached the equality of the sexes and was strongly opposed to slavery. Stoics had many beliefs in common with early Christians. Most significantly, however, they did not believe in the divinity of Christ, his resurrection, or the judgment of the world. Stoic influences can be found in the writings of the Jewish teacher Philo of Alexandria (who lived from around 25 B.C. to A.D. 50). The apostle Paul also uses Stoic terms to communicate with his Greek-speaking audience. (See Acts 17:28; 1 Cor 7: 32-35; and Phil 4:11-13)

Epicureanism was founded in Athens by Epicurus, who lived from about 342 to 270 B.C. The main goal of life for Epicureans was to find true happiness. They believed true happiness was gained by encouraging serenity (the Greek word *ataraxia*) and by avoiding pain. They did not believe that fate or destiny ruled their lives; instead, they believed in free will. Since they did not believe that the gods influenced a person's life, they were considered by some to be atheists. For them, true pleasure came from living nobly and justly and with a healthy lifestyle. They believed intellectual pleasure was superior to bodily pleasure. The Epicureans valued friendship as a way for people to support each other in the search for happiness. They believed death was the end of existence, but that it was not to be feared because it brought peace and an end to pain. Epicureanism was probably most popular among the upper classes of the Roman Empire.

Gnostics is a term historians have given to a number of religious groups in the second and third centuries A.D. Some of the letters of the New Testament, such as COLOSSIANS and 1 JOHN, seem to be battling early forms of Gnosticism. *Gnosis* is the Greek word for knowledge, and Gnostics believed they possessed a special or secret knowledge. Many sects who have been identified as Gnostics believed that the world was ruled by evil forces (called "archons"). Among these evil forces, they included the God of the Old Testament. Archons held humanity captive in a state of ignorance and suffering. Gnostics believed that Jesus was a godlike being (rather than a living person) who had been sent to restore people's knowledge of their origin in the true God. People, they said, were made of body, soul, and spirit. People who lived only the life of the body could not be saved. Christians might achieve a lower form of salvation through their faith, but real salvation came through a superior knowledge *(gnosis)* of the life of the spirit and soul, which is the divine element in human beings. In the early centuries after Christ, Gnosticism was a serious challenge, leading to the rise of elitist sects within Christianity. Gnostics were a very diverse group of sects, but some of their general characteristics have been described by historians.

Emperor Worship. The Jews and early Christians faced the problem of emperor worship in the centuries just before and after Jesus was born. Beginning in the fourth century B.C., Alexander the Great (356-323 B.C.), the Macedonian king who conquered much of the Near East, claimed that he was divine. Rulers who took over after he died made similar claims. They demanded that all their subjects honor them as gods. One of these rulers, Antiochus IV Epiphanes put up a statue of Zeus in the Jerusalem temple. This set off the Maccabean revolt of 168-165 B.C., in which the Jewish people reclaimed the temple and gained their freedom for a brief period of time.

Roman emperors, whose armies conquered Palestine in 63 B.C., also claimed that they were gods. The Roman emperor Gaius Caligula (ruled A.D. 37-41) wanted to put up a statue of himself in the temple, but he died before he could make this happen. Around the end of the first century, the emperor Domitian ordered people to address him as "Lord and God." REVELATION pictures a prostitute and a horrible beast which likely symbolized the Roman empire's attempt to destroy God's people and their worship of "the Lamb" (Christ), and to force Christians to honor the emperor as divine instead (Rev 17).

The Bible and the Beliefs of the Ancient World

Jews and Christians encountered the various religions and philosophies described in this article, and many others as well, particularly as they moved away from Palestine and settled in other parts of the Roman empire. Many of these systems of belief were not compatible with the monotheism of Judaism and Christianity. Sometimes, however, they adapted some of the teachings from these other systems of thought in response to the situations they faced. In light of these situations, both the Jewish Scriptures (Old Testament) and the New Testament contain direct and indirect references to these other forms of belief. It is, therefore, important to become aware of these other beliefs in order to understand the Bible more fully.

The Bible is a book of faith, telling the story of how God acted in history to protect and save humankind. Miracles are an important part of that story. God's actions in miracles on behalf of the faithful are contrasted with the situation of those who looked to other gods and relied on magic, reading the stars, or calling on the spirits of the dead. Throughout the Bible, the miracles of God are extraordinary acts. These miracles are often unexplainable by the expectations, common at the time, of how nature works. Many of these miracles can be described in the categories shown on the chart below.

The people praised God for these miracles, including God's amazing actions in Israel's history (Deut 7:19; 11:1-4; 34:10-12). The writers of the PSALMS and the later teachers of the Law of Moses saw God working in these miracles to preserve and reward the Israelite people, and to keep them living in God's ways (Ps 105; 107; 136; see also Neh 9).

Throughout the Bible, miracles are presented as signs that point to a larger meaning. This is evident, for example, in the descriptions of the Israelites' experiences in the desert of Sinai, which show God's special purpose for the people. Not only do they survive their ordeal, but they are brought into the land God promised to them so that they can worship the LORD (Deut 4:23-34; 6:21-25; 26:5-11; Josh 24:17). Miracles also helped the Israelites believe God's promises because the Israelites could see them being fulfilled. Even a Babylonian king came to believe that Israel's God had miraculous power after he saw how God preserved the three faithful young Israelite men in the fiery furnace (Dan 3).

HOW GOD USES MIRACLES

TYPE OF MIRACLE	SCRIPTURE PASSAGES
God's power revealed to the people	Gen 15:17; Exod 3:1-6; Josh 3:14-17; 1 Kgs 18:16-39; Luke 8:22-25; John 2:1-12; John 6:16-21; Acts 2
God helps women unable to have children	Gen 17:15-22; Judg 13; 1 Sam 1; Luke 1:5-25
God's power used to judge evildoers and rebellious people	Gen 6–9; 19:1-29; Exod 7:14—12:30; 1 Kgs 18:1-40; Jer 18; Acts 5:1-11
God helps Israel in battle	Josh 5:13—6:27; 10:1-15; Judg 6:33—8:21; 1 Sam 17:41-54
God saves or delivers people from trouble	Exod 14; Dan 3, 6; Acts 12:6-17; 16:16-34
God provides food and other blessings	Exod 16:1—17:7; 2 Kgs 4:1-7; Luke 5:1-11; John 6:5-15; 21:1-14
God heals and restores health	Num 21:4-9; 2 Kgs 5:1-14; Mark 5:21-43; Luke 18:35-43; Acts 3:1-10
God's purposes and glory revealed in a vision	Isa 6; Ezek 1; Zech 1:7—5:11; Acts 9:1-19; 10:1-48
God overcomes death	2 Kgs 4:18-37; Matt 28:1-7; Luke 7:11-17; John 11:1-44; Acts 9:36-43
God chooses servants and gives them special gifts	Gen 41; Exod 4:1-17; Judg 6:11-24; 1 Sam 3:1-18; Dan 2; Luke 1:26-38; Acts 2:1-13; 1 Cor 12:1-11

Jesus' Miracles Show God's Love and Power

The New Testament reports Jesus' many miracles (see the chart below). Yet, when Jesus' opponents tried to test him by making him perform a miracle to prove that God was with him, Jesus refused (Matt 16:1-4; Mark 8:11, 12; John 6:30, 31). Also, Jesus sometimes warned people not to tell anyone about his miracles (Mark 1:44; 5:43), possibly because non-believers would have thought Jesus was just a magician. Often, it seemed that Jesus' miracles only worked for people who believed (Mark 2:5-12; 5:34). His miracles were not for showing off. Instead, they demonstrated God's love for the people (Luke 4:18-21) and announced the presence of the kingdom of God.

Miracles in the Early Church

At the time of the early church, public miracles helped people recognize that God was at work (Acts 2:19-22, 43; 4:30; 5:12; 8:13).

At the same time, some people wrongly thought that the ability to heal and do miracles was a result of magical powers. In Acts 8:9-24 a magician named Simon claimed to be converted to Christianity, but he still had to learn that God's power was a gift, and not some magic power that could be bought. The apostle Paul claimed that God helped him perform miracles to confirm the good news about Jesus and Paul's own role as an apostle (Rom 15:15-19; 2 Cor 12:12).

Magic, Sorcery, and Witchcraft

In the ancient world, the belief in magic, sorcery, and witchcraft were common. The people of Israel claimed that the miracles performed by their prophets and leaders were different from these things because they were based on God's power. The writers of the Scriptures often contrasted these "true" miracles with unusual acts done by the prophets and priests of other peoples and religions. For example,

SOME WELL-KNOWN MIRACLES OF JESUS

MIRACLE	SCRIPTURE PASSAGE
Turns water into wine in Cana	John 2:1-11
Orders the wind and waves to be quiet	Mark 4:35-41
Walks on the water of the Sea of Galilee	Matthew 14:22-33
With five loaves and two fishes, feeds a crowd of more than 5,000 people	Matthew 14:13-21
Raises his friend Lazarus to life	John 11:17-44
Raises a dead girl to life	Matthew 9:18-26
Gives sight to a man born blind	John 9:1-41
Cures the woman who had been bleeding for twelve years	Matthew 9:20-22
Cures a man of evil spirits and sends the spirits into a herd of pigs	Mark 5:1-20
Heals ten men with leprosy	Luke 17:11-19
Heals a crippled man in Capernaum	Mark 2:1-12
Heals a man who was deaf and could hardly talk	Mark 7:31-37
Heals the high priest's servant after the man's ear is cut off	Luke 22:49-51

Joseph used God's help to interpret the dreams of the king of Egypt after the king's own magicians and wise men could not (Gen 41:1-36). Later, when the Egyptian king's magicians turned their walking sticks into snakes, Moses and his brother Aaron used God's power to do the same thing, and their snake ate the snakes created by the Egyptians (Exod 7:8-13). This showed the superiority of the God of Israel. In another case, Elijah showed that the power of Israel's God was greater than that of the god Baal when God helped Elijah win a contest against the prophets of Baal (1 Kgs 18:16-40).

Witchcraft was forbidden by the Law of Moses (Lev 19:26), because relying on spirits or powers other than God showed a lack of faith and trust in the one true God. Disobeying the command against witchcraft could lead to harsh punishment (Exod 22:18; Deut 18:10-13). When King Saul, Israel's first king, was afraid of the approaching Philistine army, he did not pray to God for help. Instead, he broke the law forbidding witchcraft and asked a woman from Endor who talked to spirits to call on Samuel, who died some time before (1 Sam 28:4-20). In another example, when the people of the northern kingdom (Israel) disobeyed God by worshiping the stars and using magic, or by worshiping idols like Asherah and Baal, God became so furious with them that he allowed them to be defeated by the Assyrians and carried away as prisoners (2 Kgs 17:16-18). Later, King Manasseh of the southern kingdom (Judah) sinned against God by worshiping the stars and planets, by practicing magic and witchcraft, and by asking fortune tellers for advice. Apparently, the advice he received included offering his own child as a sacrifice (2 Kgs 21:4-7). For Manasseh's terrible sins, the whole nation suffered God's judgment and punishment (2 Kgs 21:8-16). In another example, King Balak of Moab hired Balaam to put a curse on the Israelites, but Balaam would not do it (Num 22–24).

Parts of the New Testament make clear that sorcery and fortune telling were caused by evil spirits. In one case, a slave girl lost her power to tell fortunes after Paul ordered an evil spirit to leave her. This angered her owners because she could no longer make money for them by telling fortunes (Acts 16:16-19). In GALATIANS, Paul includes witchcraft on the list of acts done by those who obey their own selfish desires instead of obeying God's Spirit (Gal 5:20). And in REVELATION, a beast fooled people into believing in the beast who opposed God by doing magical miracles, such as making an idol speak as if it were alive (Rev 13:11-15).

Medicine and Healing

What does the Bible reveal about doctors in the ancient world? In one part of the Old Testament, it says that King Asa's death may have come from his depending only on human physicians, and not asking for God's help (2 Chr 16:12, 13). God is seen as the main healer in the Old Testament (Exod 15:26; Ps 41:1-4; Jer 17:14; Hos 6:1). In fact, often the priests were seen as healers on God's behalf (Lev 13:1-3; 14:1-32). That is perhaps one reason why Hannah went to the temple to pray for God's help once she realized that she could not have children (1 Sam 1:1-18). (In ancient times, this was seen as sickness in a woman.)

Some parts of the Bible reflect the belief that disease and sickness are caused by failing to live according to God's Law (Deut 28:21-23, 27-29, 34, 35), while health and well-being were seen as the reward for trusting God (Exod 15:26; Deut 7:12-15;). Other parts of the Bible temper this perspective (Job 2; 42:7; Eccl 8:10-13, 9:2; John 9:1-7). People with certain diseases were set apart from the rest of God's people because they were considered unclean (Lev 13; Num 12:9-14). While this was done primarily for religious reasons, those who had these diseases were not allowed to worship or be among their friends and neighbors until they were cured and had gone through a ritual cleansing ceremony (Lev 14).

Jesus knew these laws about sickness and being cleansed, but he also showed himself to be a great healer. Many of Jesus' miracles included healing people considered unclean (see the chart on the previous page). He encouraged the ten men he healed of leprosy to show themselves to the priests, probably so they could go through the ritual cleansing and be welcomed back into the community of God's people (Luke 17:11-14). Another time, Jesus' power healed a woman who had spent all her money and had gone to many doctors without finding a cure (Mark 5:25-34). Jesus offered his healing also to those who were not part of the Jewish people (Luke 4:23-29), just as the prophets before him had done (1 Kgs 17:1-24; 2 Kings 5:1-14). This was surely amazing to many people, and was a way of showing that God's love is for everyone.

Around the time of Jesus, Greeks and Romans went to the shrines of a god of healing, hoping to be cured of their ailments. The early stages of modern medicine began in these shrines, but some of the cures developed there, like eating the liver of a fox or drinking juice from an iris plant, had no connection with the cause of the diseases.

The Bible tends to teach trust in God and prayer and fasting as the way to be healed from illness, rather than trusting solely in human doctors or medicine. The Bible is not against doctors and medicine though, and biblical authors were not aware of modern scientific techniques. After all, Luke, a companion of the apostle Paul, was said to be a doctor (Col 4:14). Also, modern medicine can be seen in light of the biblical command to love one's neighbor (Luke 10:25-37). Jesus instructed his followers to go heal the sick (Luke 10:9). The Bible also stresses the value and dignity of human life, teaching that all human beings are created by God and in God's likeness (Gen 1:26, 27). This belief has probably influenced the practice and ethics of modern medicine as well.

In conclusion, the Bible's accounts of miracles, magic, and medicine are all stories about God's power and love. They are not scientific explanations of supernatural events, but a faithful witness to the all-powerful nature of God, the Creator.

Healing was an important part of Jesus' ministry on earth. The apostle Paul listed healing as one of the gifts the Spirit gives the church so that God's people can take care of one another (1 Cor 12:9) and grow stronger in their faith.

A prophet is someone who speaks God's message. The message the prophet speaks is called a "prophecy." And to speak as a prophet is to "prophesy." In general culture, prophets are sometimes compared with fortunetellers or those who predict future events. The prophets of the Old Testament, however, were somewhat different. Their task was to deliver God's message for their time and place. But those prophecies weren't simply reactions to the events and situations of the day. God's message did not depend on the needs of the audience, and did not have to agree with the popular human wisdom of the times, even from the perspective of the prophet himself. As 2 Peter 1:20, 21 states, "No prophecy of Scripture came about by the prophet's own interpretation. For prophecy never had its origin in the will of man, but men spoke from God as they were carried along by the Holy Spirit." The messages of the prophets were given both to God's people and to those who did not trust in Israel's God. Sometimes the message was a reminder to the people or their leaders that they were not obeying God, and that they should change their ways. This kind of message sometimes included strong warnings about God's judgment. At other times, the proph-ets brought words of hope in tough times, or said that even though things were bad in the present, God would cause things to change for the better in the future.

Prophets in the Old Testament

The Old Testament includes sixteen books written by or called by the names of different prophets, but these sixteen are not the only prophets who had an impact on the people of Israel. At least one prophet mentioned in the Old Testament was not part of God's chosen people, the Israelites: Balaam of Pethor was hired by the king of Moab to put a curse on Israel (Num 22:1—24:25). Using the very broad definition of prophet as one who speaks God's message, certain people from Israel's earliest history were called prophets: Abraham (Gen 20:7), Aaron (Exod 7:1), Miriam (Exod 15:20), Moses (Deut 18:18; 34:10), and Deborah (Judg 4:4). Moses certainly passed God's message to the people of Israel, but he also spoke to God for them. This was also the task of prophets. Samuel, the last of Israel's judges, was known as a prophet (1 Sam 3:20). He followed God's command to anoint Saul as Israel's first king (1 Sam 10:1).

The Old Testament often mentions the existence of false prophets who exerted influence in Israel. In contrast to the LORD's true prophets, they typically gained the favor of Israel's wicked kings. At one point some of these prophets had a contest with Israel's prophet, Elijah (875-845 B.C.), to try to prove who was stronger, Israel's God *Yahweh,* or the Canaanite god, Baal. The prophets of Baal acted like they were caught up in a trance. As they cried out to Baal they had what looked like a seizure and began to dance around. They even used their swords to cut themselves until blood poured out (1 Kgs 18:24-29). Elijah also opposed King Ahab of the northern kingdom of Israel and his wife Jezebel, who encouraged the people to worship the Canaanite god Baal (1 Kgs 17–21).

A few other examples of Old Testament prophets include the prophet Nathan, who gave King David the good news that his descendants would always rule the people of Israel (2 Sam 7:4-17), but Nathan also delivered God's angry message after David had arranged the death of a man named Uriah so that he could have Uriah's wife Bathsheba. Because of this evil action, Nathan told David that David and Bathsheba's son would die (2 Sam 12:1-14). Another prophet named Micaiah warned King Ahab that he would die in battle against the Aramean (Syrian) army (1 Kgs 22:5-38). Elisha became Elijah's assistant and eventually took his place (1 Kgs 19:19-21; 2

King David and the Prophet Nathan from a Byzantine Psalter (around A.D. 950). The Bible tells of many prophets who brought difficult news to powerful rulers. Nathan told King David that David's son would die because of his sin.

warned the leaders and the people who had grown rich to care for the poor and stop worshiping idols. About the same time or a little later, the prophets Micah and Isaiah de-livered their prophecies in the southern kingdom (Judah). Isaiah warned that a king would come from the east to take over the land and force the people to leave. He called the people to obey God in order to avoid the punishment that he predicted, but he also gave them the promise that God would help them triumph in the end. The suffering they would undergo was to be seen as punishment from God. Though Isaiah's message be-gan in the 700s B.C., many scholars believe that followers of Isaiah continued writing prophecy in his name even after the Babylonian exile in 586 B.C. Jeremiah, Ze-phaniah, Nahum, and Habakkuk were prophets in Judah during the time just before it was defeated by Babylon and many of its people

Kgs 2:1-18). God used Elisha to bring healing to Naaman, the commander of the army of Aram (2 Kgs 5:1-14). Another proph-et, Huldah, gave advice to King Josiah (640-609 B.C.) when Josiah asked what he should do with *The Book of the Law* that had been found in the temple (2 Kgs 22:14-20).

The Writings of the Prophets

The kingdom of Israel split into two sections (northern and southern) around 931 B.C., after the death of King Solomon. Each of these kingdoms had its own temple and king, and prophets in both parts of Israel gave warnings and encouragement to the rulers and the people. The first books of the prophets probably date back to just after 800 B.C. The prophecies of Amos and Hosea were written for the rulers and the people of the northern kingdom (Israel). They

were taken off as captives in 586 B.C. About the time Jeremiah was finishing his work as a prophet, Ezekiel began to bring God's message to the people. His prophecies were given to the people of Judah before they were taken away from their homes and forced to live in exile, and continued into the period of the exile in Babylon, where Ezekiel was also taken as captive. The last part of his prophecy includes a great vision of the future when God would rebuild the temple in Jerusalem and bring a new day for God's people (Ezek 40–46).

After the people of Judah were allowed to leave Babylon and return home, the prophets Haggai and Zechariah delivered God's message. Speaking around 520 B.C., Haggai told the people that God wanted them to rebuild the temple. About the same time Zechariah told the people the LORD's chosen king would again rule in Jerusalem and that all people on earth would someday worship Israel's God. Still later came the prophecies of Malachi, who told the priests to be faithful to the agreement the LORD had made with Israel. The time of the prophet Obadiah is unclear, though he probably wrote some time after 587 B.C. when the country of Edom helped Babylon defeat Judah. It is not clear when the prophet Joel delivered his message of both judgment and hope, though it was most likely some time after the people returned from captivity in Babylon.

JONAH is different from the other prophetic books, because it gives only one sentence of what Jonah preached (3:4). The rest of the book tells about how Jonah tried to run away when God told him to preach to the people of Nineveh, the capital of Assyria, who were enemies of Israel. The first half of DANIEL tells about Daniel and what happened to him as he lived in exile in Babylon. The second half of DANIEL tells of Daniel's vision of the future when God would help bring victory to his people. Daniel's vision belongs to a kind of writing known as "apocalyptic."

Prophecy and the New Testament

The New Testament focuses on the life and work of Jesus Christ. The New Testament writers used the Jewish Scriptures, especially the writings of the prophets, to show that Jesus was God's promised Messiah. For example, MATTHEW often uses the phrase, "to fulfill what was said by the prophet" which is followed by a quote from one of the Old Testament prophets (Matt 1:22; 2:5, 17; 4:14-16). Each quote is meant to show that Jesus' life fulfills what was said by one of the prophets hundreds of years earlier. In his letters, the apostle Paul quoted the Old Testament prophets to show that Jesus was God's chosen one who had come to save all people, Jews and Gentiles alike (Rom 9:25, 26, 33; 15:11, 12).

The New Testament writers also used the words of the prophet Isaiah to show

that John the Baptist was the one who had been sent to prepare the way for Jesus (Matt 3:1-3; Luke 3:3-6). And John preached like a prophet, telling the people to turn to God and get ready for the one (Jesus) who was coming to baptize them with the Holy Spirit (Mark 1:7, 8; Luke 3:15-17).

Jesus quoted the Old Testament prophets to show that he was the Son of Man who would come from heaven with power and great glory (Matt 24:29, 30 quotes Isaiah 13:10; 34:4; Matt 26:64 quotes Dan 7:13, 14). Jesus also said that he was the shepherd who would be rejected and struck down (Matt 26:31 quotes Zech 13:7). He applied the writing of the prophet Isaiah to himself, explaining why he had come to earth (Luke 4:16-21 quotes Isa 61:1). Paul

St. John the Baptist *by Sally Barton Elliott. John, like many of the prophets of the Old Testament, gave the people of his time strong warnings and told them to turn to God and get ready for the one God was sending to save them.*

said it was because God's purpose for people and all creation was fulfilled in Jesus (1 Cor 15:20-28), who overcame the powers of evil.

Prophecy and the Church

Some of the followers of Jesus received the special gift of prophecy from God's Spirit (Rom 12:6; 1 Cor 12:27-31). These New Testament prophets were to use this gift to speak God's messages of truth (1 Cor 14:29-32). God's followers are also warned in the New Testament to watch out for false prophets who would try to lead them away from the truth about God (1 Tim 6:3-5; 2 Pet 2:1-3). REVELATION warns of a false prophet who would perform fake miracles and make false predictions in an effort to trick God's people (Rev 13:11-15), and the faithful are told to be careful to listen only to the message of God's true prophets (Rev 22:18, 19).

Jesus was born in the town of Bethlehem in the province of Judea during the reign of Augustus Caesar, the first Roman ruler called emperor. About sixty years earlier, the Romans had invaded Palestine as they continued expanding their great empire throughout the lands surrounding the Mediterranean Sea and beyond. At the time of Augustus, the Roman empire ruled over fifty million people from many different nationalities—from Palestine and Syria in the east to Spain in the west, including most of northern Africa and much of Europe. Because the Romans were well organized and had a strong army, their empire was actually very stable. Travel and trade between areas was easier than it had ever been. Historians have observed that the international peace brought by Roman rule and the superior system of Roman roads helped disciples to spread a new religion based on Jesus' teachings.

When Jesus began preaching the good news of the kingdom of God to the people of Galilee and Judea in the first century A.D. the Romans were in control of the entire Mediterranean world.

Palestine before Roman Rule

The centuries leading up to Jesus' birth were not politically stable in the area known as Palestine. The Jewish people who returned to Judah from exile in Babylon had been allowed to rebuild their cities and the temple in Jerusalem, but they were ruled by the Persians. Then the Greeks, led by Alexander the Great, defeated the Persians and drove them out of Palestine. Alexander's generals and their descendants ruled the land for many years, bringing with them Greek (Hellenistic) culture. One Greek ruler from the Seleucid family (Antiochus IV Epiphanes) tried to force the Hellenistic way of life on the Jewish people in Palestine. When he put up a statue of a pagan god in the holy Jewish temple in 168 B.C., Jewish people were enraged and rebelled. Led by Judas Maccabeus, the people defeated the Seleucids, reclaimed the temple, and created their own government.

For nearly one hundred years the Jewish people were again in charge of the land, led by members of Judas Maccabeus' family (the Hasmoneans), who took over as kings and priests of Israel. Yet many thought that the Hasmonean rulers were as selfish and cruel as the foreign kings who had ruled before them, so Jews did not fight back when the Romans invaded the country in 63 B.C.

During these two centuries before Jesus was born, a number of different Jewish religious groups were formed, each having different ideas about how to interpret the Scriptures and live the Jewish faith. These groups with their competing ideas appear in the New Testament and will be discussed individually later in this article.

Roman Rule in Palestine

Though many peoples and cultures contributed to the cultural life in Palestine in Jesus' day, the Romans were by far the most powerful. They controlled the land with strong, well-trained armies. The Roman emperor appointed a governor (procurator) who was in charge of collecting taxes and preventing the people from rebelling against Rome. The Romans placed heavy taxes on land, on goods and food that were bought and sold, and on inheritances. They also charged tolls for people traveling through the areas they controlled. The taxes went to support the Roman army and to maintain control of Palestine. Farmers and the poor suffered the most under this system of taxes.

The Romans made contracts with local people in order to collect taxes. These local tax collectors would often collect much more than the amount they were supposed to turn over to the Romans. They kept the rest. In Palestine, this led to bad feelings between the Jewish people and their neighbors who agreed to collect taxes for the Romans. Tax collectors were often seen as traitors by the Jewish religious leaders. Some called them sinners, and said they were not welcome to be part of the Jewish people or to worship with them. When Jesus ate with tax collectors and welcomed them (Luke 5:27-32; 19:1-10), he offended those who wanted to keep the tax collectors apart from Jewish social life.

Roman policy was to respect local customs and the laws of the peoples they ruled. They let local people form councils to control local affairs. In Judea the local ruling council (Sanhedrin) was made up of the high priest and chief priests and wealthy supporters of the Roman government. Their participation in the work of the council made them become even wealthier.

The Romans also set up rulers in the areas that were under their control. These local kings and governors reported to the Roman senate or to the emperor's representatives. For example, in 37 B.C. the Romans appointed Herod the Great as king of Palestine, partly because Herod's father had helped the Romans take control of the region. Herod ruled until 4 B.C. and was responsible for rebuilding the temple in Jerusalem, which attracted many worshipers and visitors from all over the Roman empire during the days of Jesus. The outer court of the temple, called the Court of the Gentiles, was a place where non-Jews (Gentiles) could come to see the beauty of this great building. The high priest was the person in charge of the temple. He was able to hold this position because of the support of the Roman authorities. The income from gifts and offerings to the temple was the major source of money for the whole people of Israel.

When Herod died, his three sons were appointed by the Romans to rule Galilee and Perea, the land east of the Jordan River. Under the Herods, the priests and their supporters on the council gained greater power and wealth. Although John the Baptist and Jesus were born during the time of Herod the Great, it was Herod's son, Herod Antipas, who was in power when they came to trial. Herod Antipas ordered the death of John the Baptist (Matt 14:1-12). During Jesus' trial, the Roman governor, Pontius Pilate, sent Jesus to see Herod Antipas because Jesus was from Galilee, the area under this Herod's rule. Usually, the Roman governors did not want to get mixed up in local problems and arguments. This is why Pilate sentenced Jesus to death only after the leaders of the people almost started a riot and argued that Jesus claimed to be a king of the Jews. This claim meant Jesus was considered guilty of rebellion against Rome and could therefore be put to death according to Roman law.

Class and Rank in the Roman Empire

The Roman empire had a class structure based on wealth, birth, and citizenship. At the very top of Roman society was the emperor, who was considered the empire's "first citizen." Some emperors even declared themselves to be equal with the gods. Below the emperor were six hundred senators, who were the empire's wealthiest citizens. Next came a group known as "knights," who had reached a certain level of wealth. They were well-educated and often were recruited to serve in the government of the empire. Beneath them were wealthy local citizens, known as "honorable men," who formed city councils. The upper classes in Roman society wore special clothes and got the best seats at special events.

Below these top groups came the large group of ordinary working people. They were divided into levels. First came those who were not wealthy but still had the privileges of Roman citizenship. Rome recognized only a small group of its subjects as full citizens. Citizens had the freedom and protection of their personal rights. For example, the apostle Paul was able to have his trial in Rome because he was a Roman citizen (Acts 16:37; 22:27). Jesus was not a Roman citizen, so he could be condemned to death without a formal trial by the personal decision of the Roman governor, Pontius Pilate.

Below citizens in the class structure was a large group of non-citizens who were free but did not have the special privileges allowed to Roman citizens. And beneath these non-citizens, at the very bottom of the class structure, were slaves, who could legally be bought or sold, beaten or tortured, as their owners saw fit. Slaves worked mostly as household servants for the rich. At the time of Jesus, almost one-third of the population of Italy were slaves. Slavery was very common and accepted throughout the Roman empire in Jesus' day.

Jewish Groups in Palestine

As mentioned above, the Romans allowed the various peoples in their empire to develop their own local councils. These councils usually included the wealthy and powerful people in a region, who were free to make laws and to force the people in that region to obey them. The chief priests and the rich people who worked with the Roman authorities formed the Jewish council based in Jerusalem. The Greek word for this council was the *synedrion*.

The Jewish people in Palestine had different opinions about the best way to deal with the Roman authorities who had control of their land. Even though they may have had different outlooks on these kinds of matters, they all turned to the Law of Moses and discussed it passionately in public and in their meeting places (synagogues).

The Jews began to use this name spelled in Hebrew (*Sanhedrin*) for the group that replaced the priests as the organizers and lawmakers of the Jewish people. It was the Sanhedrin who began to write down formulas for applying the Law of Moses. These interpretations developed into what today are known as the "Mishnah" and "Talmud."

The Jews in the time of Jesus had different opinions about what it meant to be the people of God. Here is a summary of some of the key groups that formed and how each one interpreted the Law of Moses:

Zealots. The Maccabees, as discussed earlier, insisted that the Jewish people have their own king. They were defeated when the Romans took over the land in 63 B.C. Later attempts to win freedom and create an independent Jewish state failed in A.D. 70 and again in

EMPEROR

600 Senators

Wealthy Knights

Honorable Men

Common Workers (citizens)

Common Workers (non-citizens)

Slaves

A.D. 135. The Jewish nationalists who tried to organize the revolt against the Romans were called Zealots. Scholars disagree about whether this term applies to a single, well-organized group or to any number of groups of dissatisfied Jews who wanted to be rid of their Roman rulers. At one time, this term also meant "someone who was strongly devoted to God and God's law." In the New Testament the term is even applied to one of the followers of Jesus (Luke 6:15; Acts 1:13).

Pharisees. By Jesus' day, it was common for Jewish people to meet in private homes for worship and to study the Scriptures. This practice had begun in the later second century B.C. and continued in the first century A.D. One group that did this would become very powerful within the Jewish community. They called themselves "Pharisees," which meant "The Separate Ones" in Hebrew. They wanted to renew and protect Judaism by having all Jewish people strictly follow the laws concerning the Sabbath, fasting, and the purity of food. Most Pharisees had regular jobs and were involved in the Roman culture of the day. But their special meetings and the strict way they followed the Sabbath law forbidding work on the seventh day of the week set them apart. As a result, they had a strong sense of group identity. There were also Pharisaic groups in cities outside Palestine. The apostle Paul, who was from Tarsus in southeastern Asia Minor, said he was once a Pharisee who strictly observed the law (Phil 3:5).

The Pharisees taught the Law of Moses as well as other traditional laws not found in the Scriptures. Their interpretation of traditional laws are included in the Mishnah and Talmud. The Pharisees were popular with the common people and established synagogues (Jewish meeting places) and schools. Unlike some other Jewish groups, they believed in life after death (resurrection) and future rewards and punishments (see Acts 23:6).

Sadducees. This group's name may come from Zadok, the high priest of Israel at the time of King David. The Sadducees also may have been descendants of the Zadokites, who had controlled the temple as high priests for many years until the middle of the second century B.C., when they were forced from power by Jonathan, the first Maccabean high priest. The Sadducees stayed close to the priestly families and tried to influence the business of the temple. They were willing to work with the Romans when they came to rule Palestine. Unlike the Pharisees, the Sadducees did not accept interpretations of the Law, but believed in following only the Law of Moses. They also did not believe in the resurrection (Mark 12:18; Acts 23:8). As long as the Sadducees followed the main teachings of the Law and stayed friendly with the Romans, they expected to continue in positions of power and wealth among their people. After the Jewish revolt led to the destruction of the temple in A.D. 70, the Sadducees no longer existed as a group.

Essenes. The Essenes may have been formed as a group at about the same time as the Sadducees. Instead of trying to influence the priesthood and religion of Israel from the inside, they withdrew from Jewish society, met secretly to study, and had their own special interpretation of the Jewish Scriptures. As a group, they disagreed completely with the priests and other official leaders of the Jews, and like the Pharisees, they believed in life after death.

The Essene communities were very structured. Each group had a leader who controlled who was allowed into the group, decided how property and belongings would be shared among group members, and made rulings concerning the law. Some scholars think that the Dead Sea community was an Essene group. Whether they were or not, the Essenes' beliefs show how deeply disappointed many Jews were with their religious leaders. The Dead Sea group withdrew from Jewish society and lived on a bluff overlooking the Dead Sea until the Roman army invaded the land in A.D. 66 to put down the Jewish revolt and completely destroyed the community there.

Scribes. The earliest scribes in the Jewish Scriptures (Old Testament) served kings as secretaries, such as Shebna under Josiah (2 Kgs 18:18, where the Hebrew word for "scribe" is translated "secretary"). Because they could read and write in a time when many people could not, scribes were very valuable to kings and governments. They had the authority to write legal papers and served as keepers of official records. Like Jeremiah's scribe, Baruch, they took dictation and then read it aloud for people to hear (Jer 36:4-18).

From the exilic period on, the scribes were scholars who studied, interpreted, and taught the Jewish Scriptures. In the New Testament, they are referred to as "teachers of the law" and addressed as rabbis (Matt 23:7). The scribes were not the same as the Pharisees, but most of these teachers belonged to the party of the Pharisees. They sometimes argued with Jesus about the meaning of traditional Jewish laws (Matt 9:3; 15:1, 2; Mark 2:16; 7:1, 2; Luke 5:30; 6:7).

Samaritans. Another group mentioned a few times in the New Testament are the Samaritans. The ancestors of the Samaritans came from the ten Israelite tribes that rebelled against King Solomon's son Rehoboam and formed a separate kingdom known as Israel, or the northern kingdom. They had their own temple on Mount Gerizim near Shechem, and their own priests. They followed the laws about the Sabbath in a very strict way, and they said that their holy Mount Gerizim was more important than Mount Zion, where the temple in Jerusalem was located. The Jewish people did not like the Samaritans and believed they were not really part of God's chosen people. The writers of the Gospels, however, record that Jesus reached out to them (Luke 17:11-19; John 4:3-9), and used one as a positive example when explaining to an expert in the Law of Moses what it means to have compassion and be a neighbor (Luke 10:25-37).

Jesus faced this complicated political and cultural situation as he tried to preach his message of good news. When he defended the poor and reached out to accept people such as tax collectors, Samaritans, and prostitutes, he offended the local religious leaders. The arguments described by the New Testament writers are mainly between different groups who have different ideas about who could or could not be part of God's people. The Romans controlled Palestine but were not very interested in getting involved in these local arguments, unless they led to rebellion against Roman authority.

The list of the descendants of Noah's sons comes to an end (Gen 11:26) with Abram ("exalted father"). He later became known as Abraham ("father of many"). God told Abram (Gen 12:1-3) to move from his home in Ur of the Chaldeans (in southern Mesopotamia) to the land of Canaan. God promised that his family would become "a great nation" with a special relationship to God. And all nations would be blessed because of Abraham and his wife Sarah and their descendants (Gen 12:1-3; 15:1-21). So Abraham went with Sarah and his nephew Lot. After passing through places that would be important in the later history of Israel (Shechem and Bethel; Gen 12:4-9) and after a long stay in Egypt, they settled in the land of Canaan. Lot settled east of the Jordan River, and Abraham settled to the west, where he lived by the great trees of Mamre near Hebron (Gen 13).

God promised Abraham that he would have many descendants, even though he had no son (Gen 15). Finally, when Abraham was a hundred years old, Sarah bore him a son. This son was named Isaac, meaning "he laughs"—a pun on the fact that both Abraham and Sarah laughed at the idea that they would have a child in their old age (Gen 17:17-19; 18:9-15). Abraham trusted God's promise and the child was born. Isaac was circumcised as a sign of Abraham's special relationship with God (Gen 21:1-7). Abraham's trust in God continued even when God told him to kill Isaac as a sacrifice. But God spared Isaac and once again promised Abraham that his numerous descendants would be a blessing to all the nations of the earth (Gen 22:1-19).

In the New Testament, in addition to being called the "father" of all who have genuine faith (Rom 4:16, 17), Abraham is frequently given as an example of human trust in the promises of God (Acts 7:2-8; Rom 4:1-25; Gal 3:1-29; Heb 6:13-15; 7:1-10; 11:8-19).

ANGELS

The word "angel" in English is based on the Greek word *angelos*, which means "messenger." Most often in the Bible, this is exactly what angels do—bring messages from God to people. Sometimes angels deliver messages or give orders in a personal meeting (Num 22:22-35; Luke 1:11-20, 26-38). At other times they bring messages to people in their dreams (Gen 31:10-13; Matt 1:20, 21). Angels often are present in visions. Angels may guide human beings to a vision and they may interpret the meaning of a vision (Zech 1:7-17; 5:5-11; Acts 10:3-23; Rev 10:1-11). In some instances, the angel is designated as "the angel of the LORD" (as in Gen 16:7-12) and was probably a special messenger or a preincarnate manifestation of Christ.

But angels are more than messengers. They carry out God's will by acting as God's agents. They protect God's people (Exod 14:19; 23:23; Ps 34:7; Dan 6:22) or punish them when they have sinned against God (2 Sam 24:11-17). God's angels also punish the enemies of God's people or punish other evil forces (Exod 12:23, 29, 30; Isa 37:36; Matt 13:49, 50; Rev 14:14-20; 20:1-3). Angels are said to be part of a council that surrounds God in heaven (Job 1:6; Zech 3:1). Angels came to help Jesus after his time of being tested by the devil in the wilderness (Matt 4:11), and one rolled back the stone of Jesus' tomb so others could enter and see that Jesus had risen (Matt 28:2).

Angels are often pictured in art as beings in long robes with wings. But in the Bible they appear in many forms. Moses saw the angel of the LORD in a burning bush (Exod 3:2). Jacob saw angels going up and down a ladder between heaven and earth (Gen 28:12). Two of the three "men" who ate with Abraham and told him that he would have a son apparently were angels, while the third was actually the LORD (Gen 18:1-10; 19:1). The being who appeared in the fiery furnace was said to "look like a son of the gods," and may have been an angel (Dan 3:21-25, 28). The winged guardians (seraphim or cherubim) of the Most Holy Place in the temple (Isa 6:1-7; Ezek 10:1-5) were angelic beings. The angel who helped Peter escape from prison appeared in a flash of light and somehow made Peter invisible to the prison guards (Acts 12:6-10).

Some angels in the Bible have names. DANIEL mentions Gabriel (Dan 9:21), who also later appears to Mary (Luke 1:26-28), and Michael, who is called a protector of God's people (Dan 10:13; 12:1). It is possible that Satan may have been part of God's council of angels (Job 1:6; Zech 3:1). In the New Testament period, angels became known more and more as spiritual beings who helped God battle against and defeat Satan and his helpers, the demons.

BAPTISM

The English word "baptism" comes from the Greek verb that means "to dip in water." In the Jewish Scriptures there were laws that required priests to wash themselves before they could offer sacrifices to God (Exod 40:12-15). The high priest had to bathe himself before and after he went into the Most Holy Place inside the tabernacle or the temple to make the sacrifice on the Day of Atonement (Lev 16:4, 23, 24).

The prophets of Israel instructed the people to "wash" themselves, symbolically speaking, by turning from their sins and doing what God wanted them to do (Isa 1:15-17; Jer 4:14). At the site of the religious community in Qumran, archaeologists discovered a pool with a set of steps that the members used to walk down to the water and back up. These steps made it possible for members to wash themselves as a way of showing that they wanted their lives to be pure. During the same period in Israel's history John the Baptist began preaching in the Jordan Valley. John told people to be baptized as a way of preparing themselves for the coming of someone who would be more powerful than he was, and who would bring the Holy Spirit to God's people (Luke 3:15-17).

Jesus did not baptize anyone himself during his earthly ministry, but his disciples did baptize people with Jesus' approval (John 3:22; 4:1, 2). And later, before Jesus was taken up to heaven, he told his disciples to teach and to baptize people of all nations (Matt 28:18-20). His disciples obeyed his command, and ACTS is full of accounts of how Jesus' disciples baptized new believers as they became part of the Christian church. These new members were baptized to show that they wanted to stop sinning, turn away from their old way of life, and show that they were ready to enter a new life of obedience to God (Rom 6:1-4).

ACTS begins with the story of how the Holy Spirit was sent to the church on the Day of Pentecost and how 3,000 new Christians were baptized (Acts 2:41). As the good news of Jesus spread throughout Judea and across Asia Minor, new members were baptized, including many who were not Jews: Samaritans (Acts 8:12), an Ethiopian official (Acts 8:38), a Roman army officer (Acts 10:47, 48), and a wealthy Greek woman (Acts 16:15). The apostle Paul wrote letters to local churches explaining that those who are baptized should make a break with their past life and become part of the people of faith (Rom 6:1-4; Col 2:11, 12). Just as God saved Noah from the flood, and just as God raised Jesus from the dead, so baptism signifies that God's new people are saved from the power of death, made acceptable to God, and welcomed into God's family (1 Pet 3:18-22).

BURIAL

The people of Israel and the other countries of the ancient Near East considered it very important to honor those who had died by giving them a proper burial. Because of the warm climate in Palestine it was important to bury people within twenty-four hours after

Left: Perfume bottles from burial caves in Jerusalem, 6th to 5th centuries B.C.
Right: First-century tomb near Jerusalem.

they died. In fact, Jewish law required that a dead person should be buried before sunset (Deut 21:23). To let a loved-one's body decay above ground where vultures and dogs could eat it was considered a serious dishonor.

There is no complete description in the Bible of how Jewish people prepared a body for burial. However, it is known that the body was washed (Acts 9:37), anointed with spices (Luke 24:1), and wrapped in cloth (Matt 27:59; John 11:44).

Most ancient Hebrews were buried in caves or in trenches dug in the ground. Sarah and Abraham were buried in the cave of Machpelah near Hebron (Gen 23:19; 25:9, 10). Later, tombs cut out of rock were used for burying the dead. Some tombs could only hold one body, others could hold several and were used by families. Because touching a corpse, even accidentally, made a person ceremonially unclean according to Jewish law, tombs were clearly marked. After the flesh had rotted away in the tomb, the bones would be collected in a box (called an ossuary). Then the level place where the dead body had been could be used to receive the body of another person who died.

Greeks, Romans, and Canaanites often burned (cremated) the bodies of people who died. Jewish people saw this as a dishonor and did this only if a body was already in an advanced state of decay. The bodies of Saul and his sons were burned probably to prevent further abuse by the Philistines (1 Sam 31:12). The dead bodies of people who had disobeyed God's law were sometimes burned (Josh 7:25).

Burial ceremonies centered on the family's mourning for the dead person and the carrying of the body to the place of burial. The bodies of the dead were put on wooden frames and carried to the place of burial (2 Sam 3:31; Luke 7:11-15). After the burial, those who handled the body were considered unclean and had to undergo a cleansing ceremony in order to be part of the community again (Num 19:11-20). There is no evidence that the Jewish people of Jesus' day performed funeral services to honor the dead.

CIRCUMCISION

"Circumcision" was the ceremony of cutting off the foreskin of a male's penis. This was a common rite among many people in the ancient Near East, though the reasons why are not clear.

Circumcision is first mentioned in the Bible in connection with God's promise to make Abraham's descendants a great nation and to give them a land they could call their own. In return, Abraham and his descendants were to obey God. To show that they were keeping their promise to God, every male descendant of Abraham was to be circumcised (Gen 17:1-14). Even non-Israelite men who wanted to be part of the Israelite people were to be circumcised (Gen 34:21-24). Circumcision became a requirement of the Law of Moses (Lev 12:3). The New Testament reports that both John the Baptist and Jesus were circumcised eight days after being born (Luke 1:59; 2:21).

The prophet Jeremiah warned that the outward practice of circumcision alone was not a true sign of being one of God's people, since other nations also practiced circumcision. The important thing was to worship God. His strong words to the people of Judah were, "The whole house of Israel is uncircumcised in heart" (Jer 9:25, 26). Later, he described a final and permanent renewal of the covenant with God that would be written on the people's hearts and minds (Jer 31:31-34). The writer of HEBREWS in the New Testament used Jeremiah's words to back up his message that the first covenant based on God's Law has been replaced by a new covenant brought by Christ (Heb 8).

The practice of circumcision caused arguments and division among early Christians. Some Jewish Christians who had lived according to the Law of Moses felt that they and any Gentile (non-Jewish) follower of Christ should obey all the Jewish laws and practice all the Jewish rituals, including circumcision (Acts 11:1, 2; 21:17-24). Others, especially the apostle Paul, challenged the belief that Gentiles had to be circumcised in order to be acceptable to God. Paul had been circumcised and was a strict follower of the Law of Moses (Phil 3:4-6). But he came to believe that Gentile men could be acceptable to God and become part of God's true people, even if they were not circumcised. Paul argued that being circumcised is worthwhile only if a person can obey the whole Law of Moses. If someone does not obey the whole Law, circumcision cannot make that person "a real Jew." Like Jeremiah, he believed true circumcision is something that happens in the heart (Rom 2:25-29). People are acceptable to God, not by doing everything the Law requires, but because they have faith (Rom 3:28; Phil 3:7-9).

Paul also criticized the Jews who insisted that Gentile believers must practice the Jewish rites, such as circumcision (Gal 6:12-14; Phil 3:2). Paul said it was wrong for them to argue that being circumcised was the way to complete what God's Spirit started (Gal 3:1-3). In the end, Paul said simply, "Neither circumcision nor uncircumcision means anything; what counts is a new creation" (Gal 6:15).

CRUCIFIXION

Crucifixion was a common way to punish criminals and to publicly humiliate them in the ancient world. In Jesus' day, the Romans used crucifixion to put criminals to death. A person was tied with cords or nailed to a wooden cross that was shaped like a T or like a plus sign (+). Usually the worst criminals, slaves who had done wrong, and those who had led revolts were crucified.

After a criminal was sentenced to die on the cross, he had to carry his cross to the crucifixion site. Sometimes he carried only the crosspiece. Before being put on the cross, he would be beaten and stripped. Then he would be fastened on the cross with his arms stretched out. This painful position made it difficult for the

A condemned man carries the crosspiece to the place of execution.

Some criminals were nailed to crosses and some were tied with ropes.

A condemned man's crime was written on a sign and nailed to the cross.

condemned man to breathe, and eventually he would die from suffocation. He might use his legs to push up for breath, so the legs would eventually be broken to speed up death (John 19:31).

In God's law, execution was usually by stoning (Lev 24:23; Num 15:36). Sometimes the Romans (who ruled Palestine at this time) allowed for executions (such as Stephen, Acts 7:59), but normally they retained the right to give the death penalty. That was why the Jewish leaders went to Pilate when they wanted Jesus to die (Matt 27:22). Crucifixion of Jesus would remove the blame from themselves, as well as provide a method of execution that, according to their law, would carry a curse (Deut 21:22, 23). So Jesus was accused of starting a revolt against the Romans by allowing himself to be called "King of the Jews." A sign with this title was placed on his cross (Matt 27:37).

God overcame the death of Jesus by bringing him back to life after he died on the cross. That's why the cross became the major symbol for God's power to forgive sins and give new life to people (1 Cor 1:18-24).

DATES IN B.C. AND A.D.

The initials B.C. have traditionally been an abbreviation for "Before Christ." If Luke's dating (in Luke 2:1, 2) is correct, then Jesus was born at least four years before the years known as A.D. began. (A.D. stands for the Latin phrase "in the year of our Lord.") Christian dating was actually not introduced until A.D. 526 by a monk named Dionysius Exiguus. He was given the job of creating a calendar for the feasts of the church. He fixed the birth of Jesus in the Roman year 754, which was selected as the first year of the Christian era beginning on January 1. Dionysius apparently misjudged Herod's reign by about five years.

The initials B.C.E. (Before the Common Era) and C.E. (in the Common Era) are sometimes used for the traditional B.C. and A.D.

DAY OF THE LORD

The "day of the LORD" refers to a future time when the LORD will act in history to punish his enemies and to save those who have been faithful. In the Old Testament, the day of the LORD (or simply, "the day") is described most often in the books of the prophets. It usually refers to some future historical event, rather than to a final judgment when God's enemies receive eternal punishment and God's faithful people receive eternal life. This idea of a final judgment day is more common in the New Testament (see below).

Perhaps the oldest passage in the Bible that mentions the LORD's day of judgment is found in AMOS (Amos 5:18-20). This and other passages from the prophets describe the day of the LORD as a dark day of disaster when the LORD will punish the wicked. The "wicked" may be other nations (Isa 13:1-6; Amos 1:3—2:3; Obad 15), the people from Israel and Judah (Ezek 7:2-13; Joel 1:15), or the people of the earth in general (Isa 2:12-22; Zeph 1:14-18). Punishment connected with the day of the LORD can take the form of an invasion by an enemy nation (Isa 10:5-12; Hos 10:10-15) or natural disasters such as swarms of locusts (Joel 1:4-7; Amos 7:1, 2), earthquakes and darkness (Joel 2:10; Amos 8:9), and famine (Ezek 5:13-17).

The day of the LORD also is described as a time when God will restore the people of Israel and Judah and save those who have been faithful. This time of restoration follows a time of punishment. For example, the prophets Isaiah, Jeremiah, and Ezekiel each warned the people that their exile in Babylon was punishment for being unfaithful to the LORD. But the LORD would forgive them and lead them back to Jerusalem, where they could once again be a "light" among the other nations (Isa 40:1-11; 49:8-13; Jer 23:7, 8; Ezek 37:15-23;

see also Amos 9:11-15). Often this time of restoration is described as a time of peace when the people would once again be ruled by an anointed ruler (Messiah) from the family of David (Isa 11).

A few Old Testament passages hint that God's saving love and judgment affect more than events in this life. For example, the prophet Daniel speaks of a time when the dead will rise from death. At this time, some people will receive eternal life and others will receive eternal shame (Dan 12:1-3; see also Job 19:25-27; Isa 26:19). These passages and later passages that come from writings dating to the period between the Testaments (first and second century B.C.) laid the foundation for the many New Testament passages that describe a coming day of judgment.

Jesus refers to a day of judgment (Matt 10:15; 11:22, 24; 12:36), and describes a time of coming judgment that sounds a great deal like the disastrous day of the LORD described above (Mark 13). But his words introduce the idea that the coming time of disaster is a warning that the end of time is near and soon the Son of Man will return and gather his chosen ones (Mark 13:27). One of Jesus' parables describes a coming time of judgment that is meant to encourage people to help their neighbors in this lifetime (Matt 25:31-46).

When the apostle Paul speaks of the coming day of the Lord he connects it to the return of Christ (1 Cor 1:8; 5:5; Phil 1:9, 10; 2:16; 1 Thes 5:2). REVELATION describes the future day when God will finally defeat the forces of evil as "the battle on the great day of God Almighty" (Rev 16:14). Death itself will be thrown into the lake of fire along with all those whose names are not written in the book of life (Rev 20:14, 15). Then God will create a new heaven and new earth (Rev 21:1-7). Some New Testament passages suggest that people face judgment or reward immediately after they die (Luke 16:19-24; 23:39-43).

ELIJAH

Elijah was a prophet who lived in Israel from around 899 to 850 B.C. This was after the Israelite kingdom of David and Solomon had divided into northern (Israel) and southern (Judah) kingdoms. In Elijah's day, many people in the northern kingdom were worshiping foreign gods such as Baal and Asherah. The worship of these gods was encouraged by Israel's King Ahab and his Phoenician queen, Jezebel (1 Kgs 16:30-33). At this time, Elijah seems to have been the only prophet who had the courage to challenge the influence of powerful people.

Elijah challenged the priests of Baal to see whose god was stronger (1 Kgs 18:15-40). He confronted Ahab and Jezebel because they killed a man named Naboth just so they could take his land and vineyard (1 Kgs 21). After this, he challenged Ahab's son, Ahaziah, when Ahaziah turned to the god Baal-Zebub for guidance instead of turning to the LORD (2 Kgs 1:1-4). And finally, Elijah challenged the false worship and cruel behavior of Jehoram, king of the southern kingdom, Judah (2 Chr 21:12-15).

Elijah was also known for his miracles. He predicted a drought (1 Kgs 17:1), provided food that would not run out (1 Kgs 17:14), raised a dead boy back to life (1 Kgs 17:17-24), and called for fire to come from heaven (1 Kgs 18:36-38; 2 Kgs 1:12).

Elijah did not die, but was taken to heaven in a whirlwind (2 Kgs 2:11). Many centuries later, some people believed that John the Baptist was Elijah himself come back from heaven (John 1:21), which John clearly denied. Others thought Jesus was Elijah (Matt 16:13, 14; Luke 9:8). The people's identification with them as the prophet Elijah was due to the prophet Malachi's prediction that "Elijah" would come to prepare God's people for the coming of the Messiah (Mal 4:5). Jesus identified John the Baptist not as the returned Elijah himself but as the one prophesied by Malachi who would be like Elijah (Matt 17:10-13, see also Luke 1:17).

Elijah and Moses appeared on the Mount of Transfiguration with Jesus (Matt 17:3, 4; Mark 9:4, 5; Luke 9:30-33).

FAITH

In the Bible, faith often means trust in God, but it can also refer to a set of beliefs or religious ideas. A Hebrew word sometimes translated as "faith" is *Amen*, which is used in English in prayers and hymns. It means to rely on what is firm and dependable, especially on God, whose words and works are completely reliable.

The importance of this trust relationship with God is shown powerfully in Genesis 15:1-6, where God tells Abraham that he will have a son and heir, even though he and his wife have not been able to have any children. God had earlier promised to bless all the families of the earth because of Abraham and his descendants (Gen 12:3; 17:3-7). These promises were not based on what Abraham could accomplish, but on what God would provide out of love and overwhelming kindness. Abraham's only response was to trust God's promises. This is what God's people are called to do: trust God's promises no matter what their problems and difficulties are (Ps 25:5; 32:10; Prov 16:20; Jer 39:17, 18).

In the Gospels, the charge that Jesus' disciples and others do not have faith (Mark 4:40; 6:6) is not a matter of their lack of correct beliefs, but their failure to trust God's power at work in Jesus. But those who do trust in Jesus experience that power, as did the father of the dying girl and the sick woman who reached out to touch Jesus (Mark 5:21-43).

After Jesus died and later was raised from death, his disciples and the apostle Paul urge men and women everywhere to put their trust ("have faith") in Jesus, who acts as a sacrifice to bring forgiveness of sins (Rom 1:3-6; 3:22-26) and is raised from death to bring God's promise of eternal life (Acts 2:36-39; 1 Cor 15:12-24; Eph 1:15-23). Those who trust in what Jesus has done are considered part of God's family (Gal 3:23-29).

In the Bible the term "salvation" refers to what God has done and is still doing to free humans from sin, sorrow, sickness, death, and the powers of evil. God wants human beings to live as God created them to live in the beginning (Gen 1, 2). When sin entered the world (Gen 3), people needed to "be saved" from the power that death now had over them.

The people of Israel knew that God acted to save them (Exod 12:17; Deut 6:20-24; Ps 44:1-8; 78:4). God saved the Israelites from slavery in Egypt, and then helped them defeat their enemies and settle in the land of Canaan. God also saved some of them many centuries later after they had been forced to go and live in Babylonia (Isa 43:14-16).

Israel's worship also centers on what God has done to save them from the suffering they had to face (Deut 26:6-10). They offered sacrifices in the temple to show that they were sorry for breaking God's laws and to ask for God's saving help, so they could continue to be God's holy people.

God also promised to give new life to them and to the whole earth, bringing peace and taking care of all their needs (Isa 65:17-25). The prophets of Israel said that a savior would bring good news to those who were brokenhearted or imprisoned or poor. This savior would also make a new covenant with God's people in the presence of all the nations of the world (Isa 61:1-11). And God would overcome the powers of evil and make his rule over the world last forever (Dan 7:27).

The New Testament describes Jesus as the one who "will save his people from their sins" (Matt 1:21). He is the one who has been sent "to seek and to save what was lost" (Luke 19:10). His healings and his telling about God's forgiveness are signs that he is bringing salvation (Mark 5:34; Luke 7:50; 19:9). Jesus' death saves human beings and sets them free from their sins (Mark 10:45). By rising from death, he saves and frees people from the power of death (Rom 4:25; 5:10).

The ancient Hebrews spoke of heaven as a great ocean in the sky. A dome was said to cover the earth and kept back the heavenly ocean (Gen 1:6, 7). Rain was said to fall on earth when God opened windows in the heavenly ceiling (Gen 7:11, 12; Isa 24:18; Mal 3:10). Because this heavenly dome was so heavy, it had to be held up by pillars (Job 26:11).

God lives and rules in heaven (1 Kgs 8:30; Isa 66:1). Heaven is also where God's court meets (Job 1:6; 2:1). Some of Israel's prophets had visions of God in heaven (1 Kgs 22:19), and the prophet Elijah was taken up to heaven in a whirlwind (2 Kgs 2:1-12). The apostle Paul also spoke of being taken up into a "third heaven," where he heard wonderful things (2 Cor 12:1-4). John had a vision of heaven that revealed secrets about the future (Rev 1:1; 4:1).

The Old Testament does not describe heaven as a place where God's faithful will live with God after they die. In fact, it was only in the fifth or sixth century B.C. that we see the Israelites express a clear belief in eternal life after death. The prophet Daniel had a vision of the people whose names were written in "*the book*." These people were to rise from death and be given eternal life (Dan 12:1-3). But even this vision does not say that those who are raised from death will live in heaven.

The New Testament also describes heaven as the place where God lives and rules (Matt 5:34). The angels who announced the birth of Jesus praise God in heaven (Luke 2:14). When Jesus was baptized, God's voice came from heaven and called Jesus "my Son" (Luke 3:22). Jesus described God as a Father in heaven (Matt 6:1, 9; 18:14; John 6:32). Jesus himself came from heaven (John 6:38-42) and returned there after death (Luke 24:50, 51). And he will come back from heaven in the future (Matt 24:30, 31; 1 Thes 4:16).

When Jesus spoke of the kingdom of heaven (Matt 4:17; 5:3; 13:44-47), he usually meant where God's will and purposes were done, rather than God's home. The promise of life after death is common in the New Testament. Jesus told his disciples that he will go to his Father's house to prepare a place for them (John 14:1-3). The apostle Paul said that those who are raised from death will have new bodies like those who are in heaven (1 Cor 15:45-54). Paul also said that those who have faith in Christ are citizens of heaven. Christ will make their poor earthly bodies like his own glorious body (Phil 3:20, 21). Other New Testament books say that heaven and earth will be destroyed or replaced and made new (2 Pet 3:10-13; Rev 21:1—22:5).

ISRAEL

The name "Israel" is used in several different, but interrelated, ways in the Bible. The following summary describes these different uses.

The Name. The Hebrew word for "Israel" means "one who wrestles with God" or "May God join in the struggle!" The second meaning implies "May God defeat the forces that oppose God and the people of God." The name "Israel" was given to Jacob, the son of Isaac and Rebekah and grandson of Abraham and Sarah, after Jacob wrestled with someone who seemed to be a human but later turned out to be God (Gen 32:22-32). Later, Israel's twelve tribes were named for the sons of Jacob (Israel) and for two of his grandsons (Gen 48, 49).

The Nation (Land). About 1000 B.C. the people from the separate tribes began to come together under their first king, Saul (1 Sam 9, 10). But it was King David who brought all the tribes together in one unified nation under one ruler (2 Sam 5:1-5). Jerusalem became the nation's capital and the central place for the people to worship God. David's son, King Solomon, built a temple in Jerusalem where all Israel could come together to worship the LORD (2 Sam 7; 1 Kgs 6). Under Solomon, the territory known as Israel stretched from the Gulf of Aqaba and the northern boundaries of Egypt in the south to Kadesh and the Euphrates River in northern Syria.

After Solomon died (924 B.C.), the ten northern tribes broke away from the two southern tribes known as Judah. These northern tribes built their own temple in the north at Samaria, and called themselves "Israel" (1 Kgs 12; 16:32). In 722 B.C. the Assyrians invaded from the north and deported the people of the northern kingdom (Israel), sending them into various regions in the Assyrian kingdom. The people in the southern kingdom (Judah) were not captured by the Assyrians, but in 586 B.C. Judah was defeated by the Babylonians and many of its people sent to live throughout Babylonia. This period in the history of Israel is known as "the exile." During the time before and after the exile, "Israel" was often used by the prophets as the name for all God's people (Ezek 36; Hos 4, 5).

God's Holy People. After the time of the Babylonian exile, the Israelites who returned to Judah were governed by the Persians and, later, by the Greeks. At this time the people of Israel, regardless of where they lived, came to be known as "Jews," a term derived from the Greco-Latin term "Judea," meaning Judah. Because they lived in so many different places, the Jewish people did not base their identity so much on the geographic area they controlled or on political power, but on their commitment to following God's Law. This desire to obey God is what set them apart from other nations. At the time of Jesus, the people of Israel were ruled by the Romans but continued to follow the traditions, ceremonies, and festivals that made them God's holy people.

ISRAEL'S PRIESTS

The people of Israel were holy, or "set apart for God," and they were to obey God's commandments. In Exodus 19:6 God tells Moses to tell the Israelites, "You will be for me a kingdom of priests and a holy nation." The prophet Isaiah repeated this promise and challenge. He said to the people who mourned in Jerusalem, "You will be called priests of the LORD, you will be named ministers of our God" (Isa 61:6).

Even though all the people were like priests, God commanded that special priests be selected from the tribe of Levi (Num 1:49-51; 3:5-13) to serve first in the tabernacle, and then later in the temple that would be built in Jerusalem. These priests are described according to their duties: (1) the Levites, who did basic work in preparing sacrifices and cleaning the Holy Place; (2) the priests, who offered the sacrifices and performed various ritual acts; and (3) the high priest, who was in charge of the Holy Place, and who was the only one who could go into the inner part of the temple (Most Holy Place), the LORD's throne room on earth (Ps 28:2; 47:8).

The priests wore special robes (Exod 28), a golden crown with the words, "HOLY TO THE LORD," and a breastplate marked with the names of the twelve tribes of Israel. Israel's priests had two main purposes: (1) to keep contact with God in the holy place of worship (the tabernacle, and later the temple); and (2) to help the people become pure.

The Jewish people returned to Jerusalem from exile in Babylon beginning in 538 B.C. Soon after, the prophets told the people to rebuild the temple that the Babylonians had destroyed in 586 B.C. and once again worship God there (Hag 2:15-18; Zech 4:9; 8:9). In the second century B.C., the Syrian king, Antiochus IV, put a statue of a foreign god in the temple and tried to force Jews to offer sacrifices to it. The Jewish people were greatly offended by this and revolted until once again proper worship of God in the temple was restored.

Some of the priests helped lead the revolt that set up an independent Jewish nation. This nation existed from 165 to 63 B.C., when the Romans invaded and took over Palestine. Israel's priests then began to cooperate with the Romans, who let King Herod build a great new temple in Jerusalem. Israel's priesthood came to an end in A.D. 70 when the temple was destroyed by the Roman army during another Jewish rebellion. The temple has never been rebuilt.

Until this final destruction of the temple, it was the job of the priests to offer sacrifices to thank God and to gain God's forgiveness for the sins of the people. The New Testament says that Jesus offered himself on the cross (Mark 10:45) and that God sent Jesus as a sacrifice in order to set people free from their sins (Rom 3:25, 26). In HEBREWS Jesus is seen as the great high priest, whose death on the cross was the full and final sacrifice for the sins of the world (Heb 4:14—5:10; 10:1-23).

JERUSALEM

Jerusalem, in the hill country eighteen miles west of the north end of the Dead Sea, began as a small settlement around 3500 B.C. It grew around the Gihon Spring, one of only two sources of water in the area around what would later be called the "temple mount." The city is mentioned in ancient Egyptian writings and at one time was known as Salem (Gen 14:18).

When David became king of Israel, he captured the walled city of Jerusalem around 1000 B.C. from the Jebusites (2 Sam 5, 6) and made it Israel's new capital. This decision helped to unify the country, since this neutral city was located between the feuding northern and southern tribes of Israel. The city grew under David's son, King Solomon, who extended the city to the north and built his palace and a temple to the LORD on the eastern hill. King Hezekiah (ruled 727-688 B.C.) further enlarged the city to include the western hill. In 586 B.C., when Judah's most important citizens were taken off to Babylonia as prisoners, much of Jerusalem was left in ruins.

Under the Jewish Maccabean kings (140-63 B.C.), it became prominent once again. By the time of Herod's rule (40-4 B.C.) Jerusalem covered more than 200 acres and had a population of forty thousand.

Solomon's temple, which the Babylonians destroyed in 586 B.C., was rebuilt on a smaller scale (516 B.C.) by returned exiles led by Zerubbabel after the Persians allowed the Jews to return to their land, then known as Judea (445 B.C.). When Alexander the Great (356-323 B.C.) conquered the Near East, the influence of Greek culture began to spread throughout the world. The Syrian (Seleucid) rulers who took over control of Palestine after Alexander's death had been influenced by the Greeks, and so began to turn Jerusalem into a typical Greek-style city. In 168 B.C., Antiochus IV of Syria made the temple a shrine to the Greek god Zeus. He also built a fortress just north of the temple so that his troops could keep an eye on the city and surrounding area. When the Jewish family known as the Maccabees came to power around 140 B.C., they made the western hill their seat of government.

The Romans took over Judea in 63 B.C., but it wasn't until 37 B.C. that Herod was able to capture Jerusalem. He expanded the city by enlarging the temple area on the eastern hill. He built a huge stone platform for the temple and its courtyards that covered more than one and a half million square feet. He lived in a palace on the western hill, surrounded by his wealthy supporters. Massive towers protected the palace, and a bridge crossed the valley between two hills. Another huge tower was built north of the temple area. A grand staircase led south from the temple mount to the older, poorer part of the city below. The northern city wall connected the tower overlooking the temple with Herod's palace. All of these structures would still have been in place in Jesus' day.

During the first Jewish revolt against the Romans (A.D. 66-70), the temple and much of the city were destroyed. After the second revolt (A.D. 130-135), the Romans built a new temple to their god Jupiter on the temple mount. They renamed the city Aelia Capitolina, and would not allow the Jews into the city in an effort to prevent any new uprisings. Since then, many different groups have controlled Jerusalem, including Byzantine Christians, Islamic rulers, Latin Christians, and Ottoman Turks. Today it is the capital of the Jewish state of Israel, as well as a holy city for Jews, Christians, and Muslims around the world.

JOHN THE BAPTIST

John is sometimes called the "last Old Testament prophet" because of the warnings he brought about God's judgment and because he announced the coming of God's "Anointed One" (Messiah). LUKE reports that John was born to an old couple named Elizabeth and Zechariah, who had learned from the angel Gabriel that God was going to give them a son. This son would have special work to do in preparing the way for God's Messiah (Luke 1:13-17, 57-66). In the Gospels, John is described as a prophet who preached in the desert and warned people that they should get ready for the new thing God was going to do (Matt 3:1-12; Mark 1:4-8; Luke 3:1-20). John wore clothes made of camel hair (2 Kgs 1:8), and he ate locusts and wild honey (Lev 11:20-23). He told the people of Israel that they could not count on being accepted by God simply because they were descendants of Abraham. They had to realize how they were disobeying God, and they needed to know how they could get ready to accept the new powerful messenger God was going to send to live among them (Luke 3:16).

John baptized people who were sorry for their sins. Many people thought he was the Messiah (Luke 3:15). But John told everyone that the Messiah would be more powerful than he was (Matt 3:11, 12; Luke 3:16, 17). Jesus compared John with Elijah, the prophet who many believed would come back before God judged the world (Matt 11:14), and he said that John's work was to prepare people for the coming of God's kingdom (Matt 11:10; Luke 7:27). Herod Antipas, a son of Herod the Great and brother of Archelaus (Matt 2:19-22), ordered that John the Baptist be killed (Matt 14:1-12; Mark 6:14-29).

LAW

The Hebrew word that the NIV usually translates "Law" is *torah.* It means "teaching" or "instruction." Because the instruction that God gave Moses at Mount Sinai (Exod 20:1—Num 10:10) is so important, it became known as "the Law." The Law was never meant to be just a set of rules to be obeyed in order to earn God's favor. God had already set the people free from slavery in Egypt when he gave them the Law. Its purpose was to help the people stay in God's favor and to remain free.

Actually, the five books GENESIS through DEUTERONOMY also became known as the *Torah* or the Law. They tell the story of God's love for and activity on behalf of Israel and the world. The instruction that God gave to Moses cannot fully be understood apart from the story of God's love for the world.

After the exile, Jewish scribes and rabbis were responsible for interpreting the Law, helping the understanding and application of the Law to meet new situations. Jesus continued to do this. (See, for example, Matt 5:21-39.) Jesus stated, "Do not think that I have come to abolish the Law or the Prophets; I have not come to abolish them but to fulfill them" (Matt 5:17). Jesus repudiated the Pharisees' emphasis on mere external obedience to the Law apart from a heart commitment to the underlying principles of the Law. Jesus summarizes

the full meaning of the Law as loving God and loving one's neighbor (Matt 22:37-40; compare Deut 6:4, 5; Lev 19:18).

The apostle Paul also continued to interpret the Law, helping the understanding of the Law to change and grow. Like Jesus, Paul summarizes the full meaning of the Law as love (Rom 13:8-10). Paul also said that all people are welcome in God's kingdom, regardless of what they eat, what day they worship on, or whether they are circumcised. This goes against many of the rules found in GENESIS to DEUTERONOMY. But Paul said that people are saved by God's love shown in Jesus, not by following any set of rules (Rom 10:4; Gal 5:1-6). According to Paul, the Law is useful because it points out our sin (Rom 3:20; Gal 3:19) and because it shows what is holy and good (Rom 7:12).

Certain psalms (Ps 1; 19; 119) celebrate the Law as the means for people to stay in God's favor and receive God's blessings. Happiness and true life come from listening to and obeying God's instruction, rather than trying to please oneself (Ps 1:1, 2; 19:7, 8; 119:1, 92, 174).

LORD (TITLE FOR JESUS)

The Greek word for "Lord" is *kyrios,* which ordinarily meant "master" or "sir." "Lord" should not be confused with "LORD," the word found throughout the Old Testament which is printed in all capital letters and used to represent God's special name "Yahweh." In the Roman empire, "Lord" was used for Caesar and indicated his absolute power as monarch, but did not mean that he was a god. "Lord" appears as a title for Jesus in the New Testament and declares his royal authority as the one who has been raised from the dead to sit at God's right hand. Practically speaking, "Lord" functions in the same way as "Christ," another royal title. When Peter addressed the crowd on the day of Pentecost, he said, "Let all Israel be assured of this: God has made this Jesus, whom you crucified, both Lord and Christ" (Acts 2:36). Another example of the royal meaning of this title is found in its Aramaic form, *maran*, which means "Our Lord," and was used to designate the king in the royal courts. In two places in the New Testament (1 Cor 16:22; Rev 22:20) the Christian community calls upon Jesus to return soon by using the expression *maranatha* ("Come, O Lord").

The apostle Paul repeatedly refers to Jesus as "Lord," and twice his letters contain the specific expression, "Jesus is Lord" (Rom 10:9; 1 Cor 12:3). It is one of the shortest and oldest statements of belief in the New Testament. Since "Lord" is used in the Septuagint (the Greek translation of the Hebrew Scriptures) to translate *Yahweh*, Paul was undoubtedly asserting Christ's deity and his authority over every other power. To affirm Christ as Lord gave great confidence to the early Christians who suffered for their belief that God raised Jesus from death and gave him the highest place and honored his name above all others. As one ancient hymn that Paul quoted said, "Therefore God exalted him to the highest place and gave him the name that is above every name, that at the name of Jesus every knee should bow, in heaven and on earth and under the earth, and every tongue confess that Jesus Christ is Lord, to the glory of God the Father" (Phil 2:9-11).

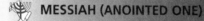

MESSIAH (ANOINTED ONE)

The Hebrew word "Messiah" means "anointed one." Anointing is the practice of pouring oil on the head of a person who is chosen to serve God and God's people. For example, priests were anointed (Lev 8:5-12; 1 Chr 29:22); prophets were sometimes anointed (1 Kgs 19:16); and Cyrus, a Persian king, was even called the LORD's "anointed" when God chose him to help the people return to Judea from their exile in Babylon (Isa 45:1).

In the Jewish Scriptures, it is the king who is most often called "the LORD's

anointed" (1 Sam 16:6; 24:5-7). Several psalms about the king make it clear that as God's "Anointed One" (Ps 2:2) or "Son" (Ps 2:7), the king is responsible for establishing God's justice and peace on earth. This means rescuing victims of oppression (see Ps 9:8, 9).

God's covenant with King David was that one of his descendants would always be king (Ps 89:4). But when Jerusalem was destroyed and the exile began in 586 B.C., the kingdom of David and his descendants was ended (Ps 89:38-45). After the exile, some people looked for the restoring of the kingship of David's line. Others suggested that all of God's people were now responsible for doing what the kings had done.

This matter was still being discussed hundreds of years later when the early Christians expressed their belief that Jesus was God's "anointed one." The early Christians saw in Jesus a "chosen one" who rescued the poor and established peace by inviting all people into God's kingdom. The Gospel of MARK uses the two titles for the king from Psalm 2 and applies them to Jesus: "Christ" (which is Greek for "anointed one") and "Son of God" (Mark 1:1; see Ps 2:2, 7). MATTHEW identifies Jesus as a descendant of David and so places him in David's royal line (Matt 1:1). Jesus became known as "Jesus Messiah" (or Jesus Christ; Mark 8:29; 14:61, 62), and confessing Jesus to be the Messiah set early Christians apart from their Jewish contemporaries (John 9:22, 23; 1 John 2:22).

MONEY CHANGING IN THE TEMPLE

People came to Jerusalem at the time of the yearly celebration of Passover and for other religious holidays. Part of the celebration and worship involved sacrificing animals and making offerings of grain to God. Different sacrifices required different types of animals (for example, see Lev 3:1-13; 14:10, 21; Num 28:16-25), so many merchants set up animal pens and cages in the outer court of the temple, which was called the court of the Gentiles. This court was the only part of the temple that Gentiles (non-Jewish people) were allowed to enter. It was also here that money changers often set up money tables where out-of-town Jewish visitors could change their money into the special kind of money used at the temple. The people used this money to pay the annual temple tax. Jesus became angry that these merchants had turned the court of the Gentiles into a place not of worship but of merchandising. Even worse, sometimes these merchants overcharged people, and the money changers did not give a fair amount of money back to people in return for the foreign money they had exchanged. So Jesus accused these sellers and money changers of being robbers (Mark 11:17). He was also making the point that Amos the prophet had made eight centuries earlier: Offering sacrifices was not as important as worshiping God and being fair to people (Amos 5:21-24). The chief priests and other temple officials, as well as their families, made money from the activity of selling and buying at the temple, so they didn't like it when Jesus attacked this system.

MOSES

Moses was born in Egypt to Hebrew parents but later was adopted by the Egyptian pharaoh's daughter (Exod 2:1-10). Growing up in Egypt, Moses saw how cruelly the Egyptians treated the Hebrew people. One day Moses killed an Egyptian guard and escaped to the land of Midian, where the LORD told him to go back to Egypt to free the Hebrew people from slavery (Exod 3:1—4:17). He did return to Egypt and warned Egypt's pharaoh that the LORD would send disasters on Egypt unless the pharaoh let the Hebrew people go free. Eventually, Moses led the people out of Egypt and through the Red Sea (Exod 5–15).

Moses was a great leader and a miracle-worker (Exod 15:22-25), but he had many other roles as well. He was the great "law-giver," chosen by the LORD to receive the Ten Commandments and other laws that were to guide the lives and worship of the Israelite people. These laws are described in detail in the books of EXODUS (20–40), LEVITICUS, NUMBERS, and DEUTERONOMY. Moses is also described as a prophet (Deut 34:10), who preached God's words of judgment and promise to the people (Deut 7:12-15).

Though Moses is not called a "priest," the LORD gave to him the directions for building Israel's tabernacle and the rules that were to govern Israel's worship and sacrifices. He also prayed to the LORD on behalf of the whole people (Num 14:11-20) and went to the tabernacle to meet the LORD (Exod 33:7-11).

Moses also decided legal cases, and he appointed judges to help him make decisions on the basis of God's laws (Exod 18:13-26). Moses acted as a military leader when Israel had to battle unfriendly people on their way to the promised land of Canaan (Num 21:21-35).

The LORD did not allow Moses to lead the people of Israel into the promised land because he had disobeyed God before the people (Num 20:1-12; Deut 3:23-29). However, Moses was able to look across the Jordan Valley from Mount Nebo and see the land that was to become the land of Israel (Deut 32:48-52).

The New Testament primarily refers to Moses' role as "law-giver" (Matt 19:7; John 1:17; 2 Cor 3:7-14), but he is also described as an example of faith (Heb 3:2; 11:23-28) and as a prophet (Acts 3:22, 23).

See the chart on the next page for a list of key events and miracles in the life of Moses.

KEY EVENTS IN MOSES' LIFE

EVENTS	SCRIPTURE PASSAGES
Moses is born in Egypt	Exod 2:1-10
Moses kills an Egyptian and escapes to the land of Midian	Exod 2:11-15
Moses marries Zipporah, a Midianite	Exod 2:21, 22
God speaks to Moses from the burning bush	Exod 3:1—4:17
Moses and Aaron confront the king of Egypt and the LORD brings about ten plagues	Exod 5:1—12:30
Moses leads the people of Israel out of Egypt and through the Red Sea	Exod 12:31-42; 13:17—14:31
The LORD makes the bitter waters at Marah drinkable	Exod 15:22-25
The LORD sends bread (manna) from heaven	Exod 16; Num 11:4-9
The LORD gives water from a rock	Exod 17:1-7; Num 20:1-13
Moses receives the Ten Commandments at Mount Sinai	Exod 20:1-17; Deut 5:1-21
Moses receives laws concerning community life matters	Exod 21:1—23:9; Num 30:1-16; 35:9—36:13; Deut 15:1-18; 16:18-20; 17:8-20; 19:1—25:16
Moses receives instructions about the tabernacle and other religious matters	Exod 25:1—31:18; 35:1—40:38; Lev 1—27; Num 19:1-22; 28:1—29:40; Deut 12:1—14:29; 15:19—16:17
The people make an idol in the shape of a calf and Moses breaks the stones with the LORD'S Commandments written on them	Exod 32:1-35; Deut 9:6-29
The LORD gives a second set of commandments	Exod 34:1-9; Deut 10:1-5
Moses' face shines from being in the LORD'S presence on Mount Sinai	Exod 34:29-35
The LORD gives Moses instructions about making the tribe of Levi into priests to serve in the tabernacle	Num 3:5-13; 8:5-26; 18:1-32; Deut 10:8, 9
Korah, Dathan, and Abiram rebel against Moses' leadership	Num 16:1-40
Moses makes a bronze snake to heal the people bitten by poisonous snakes	Num 21:4-9
The LORD refuses to let Moses enter Canaan	Deut 3:23-29; 32:48-52
The LORD gives Moses the most important commandment	Deut 6:1-9
Moses blesses the tribes of Israel	Deut 33:1-29
Moses dies in Moab	Deut 34:1-8

NUMBERS IN THE BIBLE

Certain numbers had special meanings in the ancient world and to the writers of the Bible. This chart gives some key examples. Keep in mind, however, that sometimes these numbers represent actual quantities and are not intended to be understood symbolically.

ONE	**Monotheism, uniqueness, and unity.** "The LORD our God, the LORD is one." *Deut 6:4* "One Lord, one faith, one baptism." *Eph 4:5*
THREE	**Completeness or totality. Many ancient religions considered three a divine number.** Three men visited Abraham at Mamre *Gen 18:1-15* Three annual pilgrimage festivals (Unleavened Bread, Harvest, Ingathering) *Exod 23:14-19* Number of days and nights Jonah was inside the great fish *Jonah 1:17* Number of days between Jesus' death and resurrection *Mark 8:31; 1 Cor 15:4*
FOUR	**Totality of the created world. Most cultures speak of four winds or directions, and divide the year into four seasons.** Number of rivers flowing out of the Garden of Eden *Gen 2:10* Four living creatures of Ezekiel's vision *Ezek 1:4-28 (see also Rev 4:6-8)* Four horses and riders of John's vision *Rev 6:1-8*
SEVEN	**Completeness and perfection. Like three it was considered a sacred number to many cultures in the ancient world.** Number of days in the week based on Creation story *Gen 1:1—2:3* The "seventh" day is a holy day of rest (Sabbath) *Exod 20:8-11* The Israelites were to let the land rest every "seventh" year (sabbatical year) *Exod 23:10, 11* Every fiftieth year (7 X 7 + 1) the Israelites were to celebrate a Year of Jubilee to mark a time of freedom and forgiveness *Lev 25:8-55* Temple furnishings and decorations were often arranged in seven parts *1 Kgs 7:17; Ezek 40:22, 26* Number of times blood is to be sprinkled during sacrificial ceremonies *Lev 4:6, 17; 14:7; Num 19:4* Number of several items mentioned in REVELATION (lampstands, stars, churches, seals, trumpets, bowls) *Rev 6–11; 15; 16* Number of times Jesus said to forgive (77 times) *Matt 18:21, 22*
TEN	**Because ten is the sum of three and seven it sometimes represents complete perfection.** The number of plagues God sent on Egypt *Exod 7:14—12:30* The Ten Commandments *Exod 20:1-17; Deut 5:1-22*
TWELVE	**Also a number of completeness and perfection.** Number of Jacob's sons, and the number of tribes of Israel *Gen 35:23-26; 49:1-28* Number of gates to Jerusalem in Ezekiel's vision *Ezek 48:30-34 (see also Rev 21:11-21)* Number of Jesus' apostles *Matt 10:1-4; Mark 3:14-19; Luke 6:13-16; see also Acts 1:12-26*
FORTY	**A long, but limited period of time.** Number of days it rained during the Great Flood *Gen 7:4, 17* Number of days Moses stayed on Mount Sinai *Exod 24:18* Number of years the Israelites wandered in the desert *Num 14:33, 34; Deut 2:7; 29:5* Number of days Jesus went without eating in the desert *Matt 4:2; Mark 1:12, 13; Luke 4:2* Number of years David and other favored kings ruled *2 Sam 5:4; 1 Kgs 11:41, 42; 2 Chr 24:1*

These two special spring festivals were brought together in the Jewish calendar long before the time of Jesus. Passover was celebrated to remind the people of Israel how God rescued them from slavery in Egypt (Exod 12, 13). It was to be celebrated on the fourteenth day of the first month, Abib (later called Nisan), a month that overlaps March and April on modern calendars. Passover started at sunset. The Feast of Unleavened Bread began the next day, the fifteenth day of the first month, and lasted for seven days (Lev 23:4-8; Num 28:17-25).

During the Passover festival, a lamb was to be killed, roasted, and eaten. The blood of the lamb was a reminder of the blood that the Israelites put on their doorframes before God sent a final plague on Egypt. God's angel of death "passed over" the Israelite homes that were marked by the blood, but the death angel killed the firstborn in the families of Egypt (Exod 12:1-27). The unleavened bread that was to be eaten during Passover and during the seven days of the Feast of Unleavened Bread was a reminder of how quickly the people had to leave Egypt. They did not have time to let the dough for their bread rise, so they made bread without using yeast (leaven). Bread made this way will always be flat, like a cracker.

The Feast of Unleavened Bread also became a time to give thanks to God for the annual harvest of grain, which provided food for all the people. Later, these two feasts were joined and celebrated partly at the temple in Jerusalem and partly in people's homes. Jewish people came from all

Family gathered to celebrate the Passover meal. In Jesus' day, only men had to take part in this ritual pilgrimage festival. On the first day of the festival, a Passover meal was celebrated in which the men reclined around a low table. Today, men and women alike take part in the ritual, called a Seder, which includes foods that have symbolic meanings connected to the story of Exodus.

over the world to be in Jerusalem to take part in these yearly feasts. Here they recalled with thanks what God had done for them in the past and celebrated their life together in the present.

The reports of the celebration of these meals in the time of Jesus includes both the offering and eating of the sacrificial lamb, eating unleavened bread and drinking wine. Children were taught the meaning of the meal as they ate it. Jews throughout the world continue to celebrate these important feasts in much the same manner.

 PURITY (CLEAN AND UNCLEAN)

Ancient Israel defined being pure in three ways: (1) to be free of dirt or pollution; (2) to have no contact with anything that was unfit for a religious person to touch; or (3) to be free of actions that were evil or that hurt others and went against God's commands.

According to the Law of Moses, different things could be clean or unclean (pure or impure). People could become unclean if they had certain kinds of diseases, when they touched a dead body, or when they ate certain foods—like pork or certain kinds of fish. The Law told the people what to avoid so they wouldn't become unclean (see especially Lev 11–18). It also told them how they could become clean again by waiting for a period of time and then being washed and making the right kind of sacrifice.

God's priests also showed the people how to take care of who or what was unclean. Other people who lived in the ancient Near East believed that evil powers or spirits lived in certain kinds of animals and plants. Some of the nations that lived around the Israelites thought other animals, such as pigs, were holy or sacred. The Law of Moses told the Israelites not to eat or touch such animals.

Once a year on the Day of Atonement all of the people were made pure. On this day, an animal was killed and its blood was sprinkled in the Most Holy Place of the tabernacle or temple. This was an offering to God as a sacrifice for the sins of the people. Another animal (a scapegoat) was driven out into the desert and carried Israel's sins away (Lev 16; 23:26-32; Num 29:7-11).

The early Christians understood that the sacrifice that made the people pure and clean was the death of Jesus Christ (Mark 10:45). Jesus' blood was poured out for the forgiveness of sins (Matt 26:28), and it cleanses his people from all sin (1 John 1:7). The death of Jesus, they affirmed, makes it possible for his followers to be with God, and it makes their hearts and minds pure (Heb 10:19-22).

RESURRECTION

When people in ancient Israel died and were buried, it was believed that their souls went down and stayed in the dark underworld called "Sheol" or "Hades." Some Hebrew prophets introduced the idea of someone coming back to life after being dead (Isa 26:19; Ezek 37). This helped the people of Judah who were in exile in Babylon about 600 years before Jesus was born to look forward to the future with hope. The prophet Daniel declared that people will be raised from the dead. The wicked will be punished, but those who have obeyed God will awaken to everlasting life (Dan 12:2, 3).

Other cultures in the ancient world had similar, but not identical, ideas about what happens to people after they die. Many Greeks, for instance, believed in the immortality of the soul, meaning that the soul would continue to exist even after the body died. But resurrection as it is often described in the New Testament is different because a person's whole being, including the body, is raised to life.

The disciples who saw Jesus after he had risen from death believed that God had accepted Jesus' death as a sacrifice for human sins. The Gospels report that the disciples actually saw Jesus after his resurrection (Matt 28; Luke 24; John 20, 21). Paul describes how he met Christ risen from the dead, just as Peter and many others had (1 Cor 15:3-8). Adam's disobedience was the model for all human beings until Christ came. Now all God's people can be sure of life beyond the grave, since Christ continued to obey God even when it led to his being put to death (Phil 2:8). So, he was raised from death (Phil 2:9-11) and became the first of a whole new family of God (1 Cor 15:20-24) who would be raised from death.

Even though Jesus had told his followers that God would raise him from the dead, they did not believe him until he met them as the risen Christ and Lord. They were given his promise that they would always live with him (John 14:19, 20) and that they would be accepted by God (Eph 2:5, 6). The new family of God (Col 1:18) has confidence that sin and death will be completely overcome and that even now they are being changed by God and given new life (2 Cor 3:18; Phil 3:21). The climax will come when Christ comes back again as the one who defeats death and the powers of evil (1 Cor 15:23, 24; 1 Thes 4:14). Christ's people will join with him in ruling over a brand new creation (Rev 20:4).

SATAN

In the Old Testament, Satan (the "Accuser") is described as: (1) a troublemaker who incites King David to count the fighting men of Israel, demonstrating a prideful dependence on military might rather than on God (1 Chr 21); (2) the one who is allowed to cause suffering for Job (Job 1:6—2:7); and (3) the one who accuses God's chosen servant, Joshua the high priest (Zech 3:1, 2). The serpent who convinces Adam and Eve to eat the fruit that God warned them not to eat (Gen 3) is sometimes called Satan, but this name is not used in that story.

In the Greek translation of the Jewish Bible, this enemy of God was called the Devil, from the word *diabolos*, which means "accuser." During the two hundred years before Jesus was born, Satan (the devil) became known more and more as the force of evil that opposed God. In the Bible, the battle between God and Satan is fought in human history and will end when God defeats the powers of evil.

In Jesus' time, the powers of evil were known as the kingdom of Satan. The New Testament describes Jesus as the one who came to turn people "from darkness to light, and from the power of Satan to God" (Acts 26:18). The Gospels describe how Jesus struggled against Satan's temptations (Mark 1:12, 13; Luke 4:1-13) and drove out Satan's demons who harmed human beings (Mark 1:21-28, 32-39; 5:1-13; 7:24-30). Some people accused Jesus of working for Beelzebub, another name for Satan (Mark 3:22-26). But Jesus said that his power to defeat Satan came from God and that his victory over Satan was an example of God's kingdom at work (Luke 11:18-20).

The apostle Paul believed that Satan tried to keep him from preaching the good news about Jesus (2 Cor 12:7; 1 Thes 2:18). He also said that Satan sometimes makes himself look like an "angel of light" in order to trick God's followers (2 Cor 11:14, 15). But Paul was sure that God would crush Satan (Rom 16:20). Revelation 20 describes the final battle between God and Satan, which will end with the devil being thrown into a lake of burning sulfur (Rev 20:10).

SHEPHERDS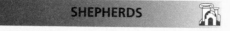

In Jesus' day, shepherds either wandered from place to place living in tents, or lived in villages. Peasant shepherds who lived in a village had the right to let their flocks feed in the pastures near the village. When food supplies got scarce, they would move their herds to higher pastures in the hot summer or to warmer valleys in the winter.

Life was often difficult for shepherds. They spent most of their time outside watching over the herd and often slept near their flock to protect it from robbers and wild animals. At night, they gathered their flocks into places called sheepfolds. These could be stone walls made by the shepherds or natural enclosures like a cave. Shepherds counted their flocks when they came into the fold at night by separating the sheep from the goats with a walking stick. They counted them again in the morning when they left for the pastures.

A flock often included both sheep and goats. Sheep are timid animals that need constant protection. Goats are harder to handle than sheep, because they like to climb up the rocky hillsides. Sheep produce wool for clothing and meat for special meals. Many sheep were also used for sacrifices at the temple in Jerusalem. It is likely that some of the sheep in the fields near Bethlehem at the time of Jesus' birth were intended to be offered as temple sacrifices on one of the important Jewish festivals.

Jesus identified with shepherds, even though many in society looked down on them. Jesus called himself the Good Shepherd who would lay down his life for his sheep (John 10:11-16). The writers of the psalms (Ps 23:1; 100.3) and the prophet Ezekiel pictured God as a shepherd who would save his flock, the Israelite people (Ezek 34:11-16).

SIN

Sin is pictured in GENESIS as beginning with Adam and Eve, who disobeyed God by eating fruit from the tree of the knowledge of good and evil (Gen 2:16, 17; 3:1-6). The Jewish Scriptures, which Christians call the Old Testament, describe sin in a number of ways:

1. Sin is breaking the Law of Moses and failing to live as God intended (Exod 20:20; 32:31-34), or turning one's back on God to follow other gods (Ezek 44:10).

2. Sin is defying God or rebelling against God (Jer 2:22-24, 29-37), with the

result that a right relationship with God is broken.

3. Sins are acts of violence against others (Gen 6:11-13), or ways of secretly hurting or harming others (Ps 64:1-6).

4. Sin occurs when the people do not follow the Law of Moses by failing to offer correct sacrifices. This makes them unfit to come into God's presence (Lev 4, 5; Num 5:1-4).

5. Sinful people are proud of the wrongs they have done (Isa 2:12). The prophets understood this pride to come out of an evil human heart (Jer 17:9-11).

6. Sin is not living up to or reflecting God's glory. Humans are to reflect God's glory, since they were created in God's image (Gen 1:27; Ps 8:3-8). Sinful people do not live by the Law or love others as God desires. This is why Paul says in Romans 3:23 that "all have sinned and fall short of the glory of God."

7. The sin of one person can have consequences for many others. For example, when the head of a family did wrong, all members were considered guilty (Josh 7; see also Exod 20:5). God was expected to punish the wicked, and the final punishment was to be death (Gen 2:17; Exod 21:15-17; Lev 24:10-17).

The New Testament brings a new message of hope. All people are descendants of Adam and are inheritors of sin that leads to death. But Jesus brings new life because he brings forgiveness. This new life includes being raised to life from the dead (1 Cor 15:22, 23). God used Jesus' death to take away the power of sin (Rom 3:9) by having Jesus suffer the guilt for the sins of everyone (1 Cor 15:3; 2 Cor 5:21). He was sacrificed in order to forgive sins (Rom 3:25, 26; Heb 2:17; 9:25-28). Jesus paid the penalty for our sins, and God has made a new covenant with people, which includes eternal life (Rom 6:23). Instead of continuing as slaves to sin, God's new people are now slaves to God (Rom 6:20-22).

SLAVES AND SERVANTS IN THE TIME OF JESUS

The word in the New Testament usually translated as "servant" actually means "slave," and refers to someone who was owned or controlled by someone else, not just a servant hired to do a certain job. Some slaves performed common household tasks. Others, called "managers," supervised the work of lesser servants or managed the master's finances. In the time of Jesus, some people were slaves because they were born to slave parents. Others were captured in war and were forced to become slaves. Some people actually sold themselves as slaves because they could have a higher standard of life as a slave than if they had to keep struggling to find housing or food on their own.

Some slaves were better educated than their masters and served as teachers of their master's children. Slaves of rich masters had all kinds of opportunities that they would never have had on their own. But slaves had no freedom, and their owners could do with them whatever they wanted, including selling them to someone else. After slaves became 30 years old, many would become "freedmen," now employed by the former master. Some slaves earned enough money to buy their own freedom, which would mean that their children could be free also.

Both the Old and New Testaments give regulations for treatment of slaves. Such regulations were not condoning slavery, but were God-given practical ways to deal with a cultural reality. When Paul gives advice to slaves and masters, he does not condone slavery nor does he recommend revolt against the system. Instead, he calls on slaves and masters to show Christian principles in their relationship (Eph 6:5; Col 3:22—4:1).

SPICES AND PERFUMES

In the ancient Near East, most spices were considered to be a valuable luxury (1 Kgs 10:10, 25; Ezek 27:22), especially those that had to be imported by traders and merchants from lands far away. The following chart provides a description of the spices mentioned in Song of Songs 4:13, 14 and lists some other Bible passages where they are mentioned.

SPICE	DESCRIPTION AND USE	SCRIPTURE PASSAGES
Henna	This small tree has light green spear-shaped leaves, thorny branches, and sweet-smelling flowers. Its leaves are dried, crushed, and mixed with warm water to make a dye used for coloring fingernails and toenails. The fragrant flowers of the henna plant were put in small bags and worn by women around the neck.	Song 4:13
Nard	Also known as spikenard, this plant grows in the Himalayan countries of Bhutan, Nepal, and Kashmir. The fragrant root and lower stems were dried and used in a perfumed ointment.	Song 1:12; 4:13; Mark 14:3; John 12:3
Saffron	This probably came from the blue-flowered saffron crocus, which may have grown in Palestine in ancient times. Part of the flower was used to make a yellow dye and for coloring food, clothing, and walls. It was also mixed with oil and used as a cooking spice, and for perfumes and medicines.	Song 4:14
Calamus	This probably refers to a fragrant long-stemmed reed or cane that was imported to Palestine. It was used in making the sweet-smelling anointing oil (Exod 30:23, "cane") used by Israel's holy priests.	Song 4:14; Isa 43:24, Jer 6:20
Cinnamon	Cinnamon comes from the brown inner bark of an evergreen tree. It had to be imported to the Near East from countries as far away as Ceylon and Malaysia. It was used as a cooking spice, perfume fragrance, and as an ingredient in holy oil.	Exod 30:23; Prov 7:17; Song 4:14; Rev 18:13
Incense	This white gummy resin comes from the wood of Boswellia shrubs or trees that grow in India, Somalia, and Arabia. It is uncertain whether these shrubs grew in Palestine. Frankincense resin was pounded into a valuable powder that was burned to make a sweet smell. It was a key ingredient in various ointments and in the holy incense burned by Israel's priests.	Exod 30:34-38; Lev 6:14, 15 Song 4:14; Matt 2:11; Rev 18:13
Myrrh	Some myrrh trees may have grown in Palestine, but most myrrh was imported from Arabia and East Africa. A light-colored sticky resin flows from its branches. After the resin is exposed to the air it hardens and turns brown. Myrrh resin was crushed and used in making expensive perfumes and ointments, including the holy oil for dedication ceremonies (Exod 30:23). Myrrh was also used for embalming the dead (John 19:39).	Esth 2:12; Ps 45:8; Prov 7:17; Song 1:13; 3:6; 4:6, 14; 5:1, 5, 13; Matt 2:11; Mark 15:23
Aloes	Aloes may either refer to the fragrant resin from the tall eaglewood tree that grows in southeast Asia and northern India, or it may refer to the aloe plant, which has thick leaves that form a tight rose shape. Aloe resin has a pleasing smell but it tastes very bitter. It was used for making perfumes, medicines, and for embalming the dead (John 19:39).	Ps 45:8; Prov 7:17; Song 4:14

SON OF MAN

In the Jewish Scriptures, (Old Testament), the expression "Son of Man" often refers simply to a human being. This is clear from EZEKIEL where the LORD's prophet is called "son of man" nearly one hundred times. In this way, the LORD reminded Ezekiel that he was a mere human being, and that he must accept God's power and purpose in the world.

The prophet Daniel also uses the expression, but with a very different meaning. Daniel says he saw in a vision "one like a son of man, coming with the clouds of heaven" (Dan 7:13). Here "son of man" refers to a savior—the person God will choose to rule over all the world and its people. Like this son of man, Jesus comes as God's Anointed One (Messiah).

In the Gospels, Jesus speaks of himself as the Son of Man. Sometimes he uses the term to express his humanity (Matt 8:20) or to emphasize his role as the one who will suffer and die to forgive sins (Mark 8:31; 9:31; 10:45). But this expression is used as well when referring to Jesus' future glory, when God's people will be gathered together and God's kingdom (rule) will be set up (Mark 8:38—9:1). People will see the Son of Man sitting at the right hand of God (Mark 14:62). Also, he will be seen returning to earth with great power and authority (Matt 24:30). It seems clear that in some instances Jesus was using the expression in the same way Daniel was.

People are called to decide and publicly acknowledge who the Son of Man is (Luke 12:8). Those who believe that he was sent by God to renew God's people and to bring all creation under God's control will be part of God's family. They will also be rewarded for what they have done (Matt 16:27, 28).

SYNAGOGUES

Synagogue comes directly from a Greek word that means "gathering." In the broad sense, a "synagogue" was any group of people who met together. Just when the Jewish synagogue meetings began is not certain, but they may have begun after the Babylonians defeated Judah and took many of the Jewish people away in 586 B.C. While in Babylonia, the people could not worship or offer sacrifices to God at the temple in Jerusalem, so they were forced to find different ways to worship.

Later, the Jewish people began moving to other parts of the world, especially to Egypt, Greece, and areas known today as Turkey and southern Russia. They also began meeting together for worship, study, and to keep their group identity. These meetings were called synagogues. In their own land, Jews continued to have these meetings even when Seleucid kings tried to force them to worship Greek gods. One of these kings, Antiochus IV Epiphanes, who ruled Palestine from 175-164 B.C., claimed that he himself was a god, just as Alexander the Great had done years before him. Jewish priests from the family known as the Maccabees led a revolt against the Greek leader. They gained freedom for the Jews and ruled the land, but the actions of the Maccabean leaders later caused divisions among their own people. Some of the people were not content just to go to the temple for worship. They met in homes and public rooms to study the Scriptures and find the real meaning of their lives as God's people.

This was the situation during the lifetime of Jesus (Mark 1:21; 6:2) and the apostles (Acts 1:12-14; 9:2, 20; 13:5). Under Jewish law, a synagogue could be formed only if there were at least ten male heads of families. In locations where there weren't enough Jews to have a synagogue, the meeting places were known as "places of prayer" (Acts 16:13). After the Roman military forces destroyed the Jerusalem temple in A.D. 70, the temple's priests no longer had a place to lead the people in worship of God. With the loss of the temple, synagogues became the most important feature of Jewish worship and community experience throughout the Mediterranean world. The Jewish people continued to meet in homes or public halls, as was the case when Paul was in Ephesus (Acts 19:8-10). It wasn't until the second and third centuries A.D. that houses were remodeled or new meeting places were built to serve as formal settings for worshiping God. These meeting places were also called synagogues. The remains of many have been found in various parts of the land of Israel and throughout the countries that border the Mediterranean Sea.

TEMPLE OFFERINGS

In Jesus' day Jewish people went to worship and to make sacrifices to God at the temple in Jerusalem. Sacrifices required by the Law of Moses included the killing of certain animals and the burning of grains and incense. Some kinds of sacrifices could be made any day of the year, while others were only made on special days like the Day of Atonement. Some of the meat that people offered in the temple was eaten by the priests and Levites who devoted their lives to serving God and making sacrifices for the people of Israel.

In addition to bringing animals and grain to be sacrificed for the forgiveness of sin, the Jewish people also gave vegetables they had grown, valuable items, and money to help with the cost of running the temple and providing for the needs of the priests and Levites. The Law of Moses also stated that the people should give to the LORD one-tenth of what they grew or earned (Lev 27:30-33; Num 18:21-32). This practice was called tithing.

The Jewish people believed that God was present among them in the Most Holy Place in the temple. Offerings were given to God each day in the same way servants might bring gifts or food to their masters. The size of the gift offered was based on who offered the gift. A poor person, for example, was not expected to offer as much as someone who was wealthy.

Some offerings were presented to God in order to confess guilt and to ask for forgiveness of sins (Lev 4:1—6:7; 6:24-30; 7:1-6; 8:14-17; 16:3-22). Other offerings were presented as a way of worshiping God, giving thanks to God, and showing commitment to God (Lev 1–3; 6:8-23; 7:11-34). Compare the praise Jesus had for the poor widow who gave her last two coins (Luke 21:1-4) with the warning he has for people who make a big show of their generosity while neglecting important matters of the Law, such as justice, mercy, and faithfulness (Matt 23:23, 24).

WATER

In the ancient Near East, great civilizations grew up in the areas close to rivers, such as the Nile in Egypt and the Tigris and Euphrates Rivers in Mesopotamia. These rivers provided water for drinking, fishing, transportation, and even for early forms of watering crops. But many areas of the lands described in the Bible were dry or received rain only at certain times of the year. Some ancient peoples survived by wandering from place to place to find water for their herds. Others who settled down to a life of growing grains, fruits, and vegetables had to learn how to store rain water in pits dug in the ground (cisterns), dig wells, or bring water from nearby streams or springs by using water tunnels known as aqueducts. Having enough water meant survival and life, but a lack of water led to crop failure, food shortages, and death.

Water is often at the center of the Bible. In GENESIS, God creates the heavens and the earth by bringing under control the great roaring ocean that surrounded the earth (Gen 1:2). In the creation stories of Israel's Mesopotamian and Canaanite neighbors, creation happened when the waters of chaos, sometimes pictured as a monster, were killed. Hints of this idea can be found in some Old Testament texts in which Israel's God of creation kills or imprisons a water monster known as Leviathan or

Rahab (Job 9:13; Ps 89:8-10; Isa 27:1). Rain is considered a direct blessing from God (Job 5:10; Isa 44:1-4; Joel 2:23). God saves the people of Israel by making the waters of the Red Sea open for them so they can get away from Pharaoh's army (Exod 14), and by giving them water from a rock as they wander in the desert (Exod 17:1-7).

Water is dangerous and a source of fear in many Bible stories. For example, God uses a great flood to wipe out the earth's sinful people (Gen 6–9). A shortage of water causes rival herders to fight with one another (Gen 26:17-22). Those who are suffering or in distress say they feel like they are being drowned in deep water (Ps 69:1, 2; Lam 3:54), and being saved from an enemy is like being pulled out of the waters of death (Ps 18:16). Sometimes the LORD holds back the rain as a punishment when the Israelite people disobey him (Amos 4:6-8; Hag 1:9-11). The people of Israel were severely punished when they openly worshiped the Canaanite gods which were thought to bring rain to fertilize crops (Jer 2:18-28; Hos 5:10; 6:3), and when they forgot that God alone was to be their "spring of living water" (Jer 2:13).

Water was also used in religious ceremonies to make people clean after being healed of certain kinds of diseases (Lev 14, 15), after touching certain kinds of animals that were said to be unclean (Lev 11), or after touching dead bodies (Num 19). If a husband thought his wife had been unfaithful, she was to drink holy water mixed with dust from the floor of the Holy Place and ink from a scroll on which a curse had been written (Num 5:11-31).

In the New Testament, Jesus claims to be a source of life-giving water, like "a spring of water welling up to eternal life" (John 4:10-14). Christian baptism brings together two symbolic meanings for water that echo Old Testament themes. The water of baptism is a symbol of being made ritually clean or cleansed from sin (Matt 3:11; Rom 6:3, 4), and the water of baptism is compared to the waters of the great flood that God used to save Noah and his family (1 Pet 3:20, 21). Baptism waters are a source of both death and life. In the waters of baptism, Christ's followers die (are drowned or buried) with Christ who died to defeat the power of sin, but they also are raised up out of the water to new life (Rom 6:3, 4, 5-7, 8-11).

Water is also important in hope-filled visions of the future. John's vision of a river filled with life-giving water flowing from God's throne in the New Jerusalem (Rev 22:1, 2) is similar to the life-giving stream that flows from the temple in the prophet Ezekiel's vision (Ezek 47:1-12). And both are reminders of the river that God made flow out of the ground to water the beautiful garden of creation (Gen 2:10-14).

THE BEGINNINGS: EVENTS IN PREHISTORY	THE ANCESTORS OF THE ISRAELITES 1900 TO 1700 B.C.	THE ISRAELITES IN EGYPT AND THE WILDERNESS 1700 TO 1250 B.C.
Creation. Adam and Eve in the Garden. Cain and Abel. Noah and the Flood. The Tower of Babel.	Beginning around 1900 B.C. Abraham comes to Palestine. Isaac is born to Abraham. Jacob is born to Isaac. Jacob has twelve sons, who become the ancestors of the twelve tribes of Israel. The most prominent of these sons is Joseph, who becomes advisor to the King of Egypt.	1700-1290 B.C. The descendants of Jacob are enslaved in Egypt. 1290 B.C. Moses leads the Israelites out of Egypt. 1290-1250 B.C. The Israelites wander in the wilderness. During this time Moses receives the Law on Mount Sinai.

In the beginning God created the heavens and the earth.
(Gen 1.1)

The Lord said to Abraham, "Look at the sky and see if you can count the stars. That's how many descendants you will have."
(Gen 15.4)

Moses and Aaron went to the king of Egypt and told him, "The LORD God says, 'Let my people go into the desert, so they can honor me with a celebration there.'"
(Exod 5.1)

ARCHAEOLOGICAL AGES

Archaeologists classify ancient civilizations according to a series of technological "Ages." By naming an Age by the common technology and objects of an ancient civilization, archaeologists describe how advanced that civilization was.

AGE	TECHNOLOGY	APPROXIMATE TIME PERIOD
Stone Age	Making and using stone tools	2,000,000 to 6000 B.C.
Pottery Age (Late Stone Age)	Making and using clay pottery	6000 to 5000 B.C.
Copper Age	Making and using cast copper utensils	5000 to 3000 B.C.
Bronze Age	Making and using bronze (cast copper and tin) tools	3000 to 1200 B.C.
Iron Age	Making and using iron tools	1200 to 300 B.C.

THE CONQUEST AND SETTLEMENT OF CANAAN 1250 TO 1030 B.C.	THE UNITED ISRAELITE KINGDOM 1030 TO 931 B.C.	THE TWO ISRAELITE KINGDOMS 931 TO 687 B.C.		
	KINGS	KINGS JUDAH (SOUTHERN KINGDOM)	PROPHETS	KINGS ISRAEL (NORTHERN KINGDOM)
1250 B.C. Joshua leads the first stage of the invasion of Canaan.	1030-1010 B.C. Saul	931-913 B.C. Rehoboam		931-910 B.C. Jeroboam
	1010-970 B.C. David	913-911 B.C. Abijah		910-909 B.C. Nadab
Israel remains a loose confederation of tribes, and leadership is exercised by heroic figures known as the Judges.	970-931 B.C. Solomon	911-870 B.C. Asa		909-886 B.C. Baasha
				886-885 B.C. Elah
				7 days IN 885 B.C. Zimri
	David said, "A ruler who obeys God and does right is like the sunrise on a cloudless day." (2 Sam 23.4,5)			885-874 B.C. Omri
		870-848 B.C. Jehoshaphat	Elijah	874-853 B.C. Ahab
				853-852 B.C. Ahaziah
The LORD said to Joshua, "Now you must lead Israel across the Jordan River into the land I'm giving to all of you. Wherever you go, I'll give you that land, as I promised Moses." (Josh 1.2)		848-841 B.C. Jehoram		852-841 B.C. Joram
		841 B.C. Ahaziab	Elisha	841-814 B.C. Jehu
		841-835 B.C. Queen Athaliah		
		835-796 B.C. Joash		
				814-798 B.C. Jehoahaz
		796-781 B.C. Amaziah		798-783 B.C. Jehoash
				783-743 B.C. Jeroboam II
		781-740 B.C. Uzziah	Jonah	6 mo. in 743 B.C. Zechariah
			Amos	1 mo. in 743 B.C. Shallum
				743-738 B.C. Menahem
		740-736 B.C. Jotham	Hosea	738-737 B.C. Pekahiah
				737-732 B.C. Pekah
		736-716 B.C. Ahaz	Micah Isaiah	732-723 B.C. Hoshea
				722 B.C. FALL OF SAMARIA
		716-687 B.C. Hezekiah		

THE LAST YEARS OF THE KINGDOM OF JUDAH 687 TO 586 B.C.

KINGS	*PROPHETS*
687-642 B.C. **Manasseh**	
642-640 B.C. **Amon**	
640-609 B.C. **Josiah**	**Zephaniah**
3 MO. IN 609 B.C. **Joahaz**	**Nahum**
609-598 B.C. **Jehoiakim**	**Jeremiah**
3 MO. IN 598 B.C. **Jehoiachin**	**Habakkuk?**
598-587 B.C. **Zedekiah**	**Ezekiel**

JULY 587 OR 586 B.C.
FALL OF JERUSALEM

The Babylonian soldiers . . . carried off the bronze things used for worship at the temple . . . The people of Judah no longer lived in their own country.
(2 Kgs 25.13,14-21)

THE EXILE AND THE RESTORATION 586 TO 443 B.C.

	PROPHETS
586 B.C. The Judeans taken into exile in Babylonia after the fall of Jerusalem.	
539 B.C. Persian rule begins.	
538 B.C. Edict of Cyprus allows Jews to return.	**Haggai** **Zechariah**
520 B.C. Foundations of new temple are laid.	**Obadiah** **Daniel**
445-443 B.C. The walls of Jerusalem are restored.	**Malachi** **Joel?**

Cyrus told the people of his kingdom, "The LORD God will watch over and encourage any of his people who want to go back to Jerusalem and help build the temple."
(Ezra 1.2,3)

A WORD ABOUT DATES

The initials B.C. have traditionally been an abbreviation for "Before Christ." Based on information presented in LUKE, then, Jesus was born at least four years before the years known as A.D. began. (A.D. stands for the Latin phrase "in the year of our Lord.") Christian dating was actually not introduced until A.D. 526 by a monk named Dionysius Exiguus. He was given the job of creating a calendar for the feasts of the church. He fixed the birth of Jesus in the Roman year 754, which was selected as the first year of the Christian era beginning on January 1. Dionysius apparently misjudged Herod's reign by about five years.

The initials B.C.E. (Before the Common Era) and C.E. (in the Common Era) are sometimes used in place of the traditional B.C. and A.D.

All dates in this timeline are approximate.

THE TIME BETWEEN THE TESTAMENTS
333 TO 4 B.C.

333 B.C.
Alexander the Great establishes Greek rule in Palestine.

323-198 B.C.
The Ptolemies, descendants of one of Alexander's generals, who had been given the position of ruler over Egypt, rule Palestine.

198-166 B.C.
The Seleucids, descendants of one of Alexander's generals, who had acquired the rule of Syria, rule Palestine.

166-63 B.C.
Jewish revolt under Judas Maccabeus reestablishes Jewish independence. Judas' family and descendants, the Hasmoneans, rule Palestine.

63 B.C.
The Roman general Pompey takes Jerusalem.

37-4 B.C.
Puppet kings appointed by Rome rule Palestine. One of these is Herod the Great.

"Then the greatest kingdom of all
will be given to the chosen ones of
God Most High. His kingdom will be eternal,
and all others will serve and obey him."
(Dan 7.27)

THE TIME OF THE NEW TESTAMENT
6 B.C. TO A.D. 70

Birth of Jesus.

Ministry of John the Baptist; baptism of Jesus and beginning of his public ministry.

around A.D. 32
Death and resurrection of Jesus.

A.D. 37
Conversion of Paul (Saul of Tarsus).

A.D. 41-65
Ministry of Paul.

A.D. 65
Final imprisonment of Paul.

A.D. 70
Herod's temple destroyed.

Jesus said, "I am the light for the world!
Follow me, and . . . you will have
the light that gives life."
(John 8.12)

Growth of the Roman Empire, 27 B.C to A.D. 180

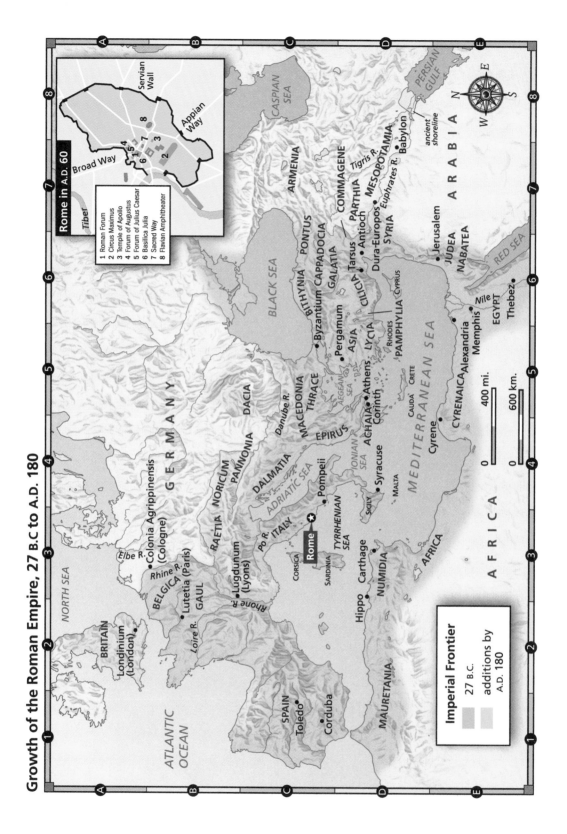

Rome in A.D. 60

1 Roman Forum
2 Circus Maximus
3 Temple of Apollo
4 Forum of Augustus
5 Forum of Julius Caesar
6 Basilica Julia
7 Sacred Way
8 Flavian Amphitheater

Servian Wall
Broad Way
Appian Way
Tiber

CASPIAN SEA

PERSIAN GULF

ARMENIA

COMMAGENE

MESOPOTAMIA

ARABIA

Tigris R.

Babylon

ancient shoreline

PARTHIA

Antioch

Dura-Europos

SYRIA

Euphrates R.

PONTUS

BITHYNIA

CAPPADOCIA

GALATIA

Tarsus

CILICIA

Jerusalem

JUDEA

NABATEA

RED SEA

Byzantium

Pergamum

ASIA

LYCIA

CYPRUS

PAMPHYLIA

RHODES

Nile

BLACK SEA

THRACE

MACEDONIA

AEGEAN SEA

Athens

Corinth

ACHAIA

CRETE

CAUDA

Thebez

Memphis

Alexandria

EGYPT

EPIRUS

Syracuse

IONIAN SEA

MALTA

CYRENAICA

Cyrene

MEDITERRANEAN SEA

Danube R.

DACIA

PANNONIA

NORICUM

RAETIA

GERMANY

DALMATIA

ADRIATIC SEA

Pompeii

Rome

TYRRHENIAN SEA

ITALY

Po R.

SICILY

CORSICA

SARDINIA

Carthage

Hippo

NUMIDIA

AFRICA

MAURETANIA

AFRICA

Colonia Agrippinensis (Cologne)

Elbe R.

Rhine R.

BELGICA

Lutetia (Paris)

Lugdunum (Lyons)

GAUL

Rhone R.

Loire R.

NORTH SEA

BRITAIN

Londinium (London)

ATLANTIC OCEAN

SPAIN

Toledo

Corduba

400 mi.

600 km.

0

0

Imperial Frontier

27 B.C.

additions by A.D. 180

Palestine Under the Herods, 4 B.C to A.D. 44

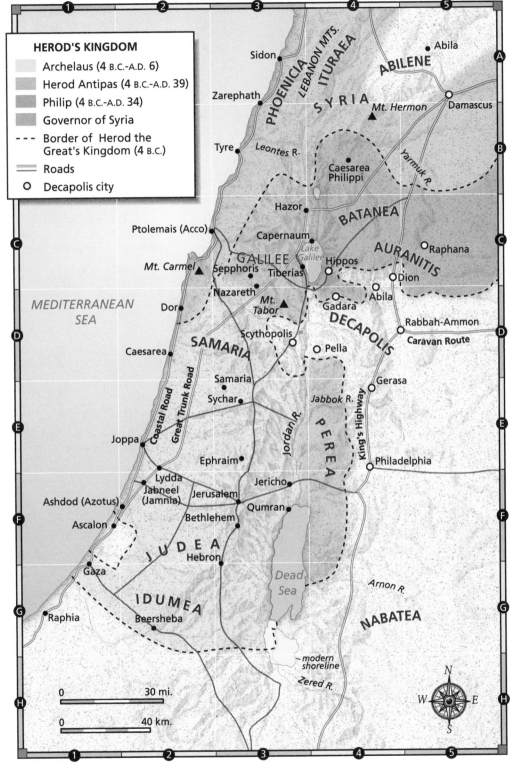

HEROD'S KINGDOM

- Archelaus (4 B.C.-A.D. 6)
- Herod Antipas (4 B.C.-A.D. 39)
- Philip (4 B.C.-A.D. 34)
- Governor of Syria
- - - - Border of Herod the Great's Kingdom (4 B.C.)
- Roads
- ○ Decapolis city

Abila

Sidon

ABILENE

PHOENICIA   LEBANON MTS.   ITURAEA

Zarephath

SYRIA

Mt. Hermon   Damascus

Tyre   Leontes R.

Yarmuk R.

Caesarea Philippi

Hazor   BATANEA

Ptolemais (Acco)   Capernaum   AURANITIS

Lake Galilee   Raphana

Mt. Carmel   Sepphoris   GALILEE   Hippos

Tiberias   Dion

Nazareth   Abila

Dor   Mt. Tabor   Gadara

MEDITERRANEAN SEA   Scythopolis   DECAPOLIS   Rabbah-Ammon

Caesarea   SAMARIA   Pella   Caravan Route

Samaria   Gerasa

Sychar   Jabbok R.

Joppa   Coastal Road   Great Trunk Road   Jordan R.   PEREA   King's Highway

Ephraim   Philadelphia

Lydda   Jericho

Jabneel (Jamnia)   Jerusalem

Ashdod (Azotus)   Bethlehem   Qumran

Ascalon

Gaza   JUDEA   Hebron

Dead Sea   Arnon R.

IDUMEA   NABATEA

Raphia   Beersheba

modern shoreline

Zered R.

0   30 mi.

0   40 km.

N
W   E
S

Palestine in the Time of Jesus, A.D. 6 to 30

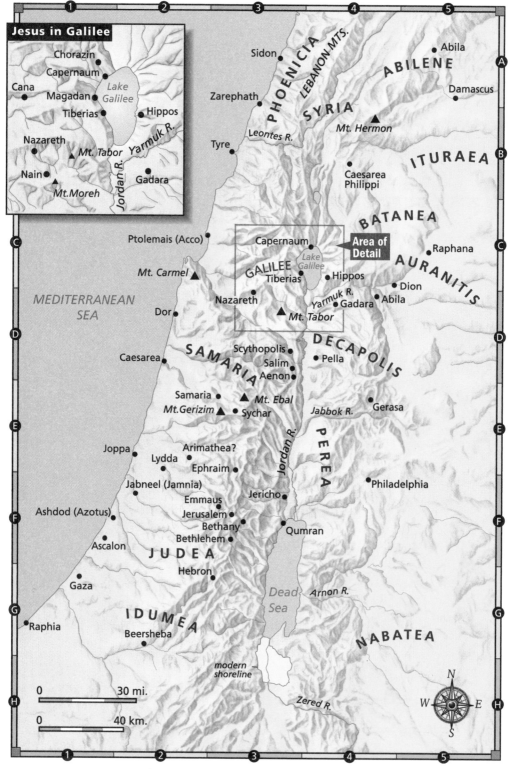

Jesus in Galilee

Chorazin
Capernaum
Cana
Magadan
Tiberias
Hippos
Lake Galilee
Nazareth
Mt. Tabor
Nain
Gadara
Mt. Moreh
Jordan R.
Yarmuk R.

Sidon
PHOENICIA
LEBANON MTS.
Abila
ABILENE
Damascus
Zarephath
SYRIA
Leontes R.
Mt. Hermon
ITURAEA
Tyre
Caesarea Philippi
BATANEA
Ptolemais (Acco)
Capernaum
Area of Detail
Raphana
AURANITIS
Mt. Carmel
GALILEE
Lake Galilee
Hippos
Dion
Tiberias
Abila
MEDITERRANEAN SEA
Nazareth
Yarmuk R.
Gadara
Dor
Mt. Tabor
DECAPOLIS
Scythopolis
Salim
Pella
Caesarea
SAMARIA
Aenon
Samaria
Mt. Ebal
Gerasa
Mt. Gerizim
Sychar
Jabbok R.
Joppa
Arimathea?
PEREA
Lydda
Ephraim
Jabneel (Jamnia)
Jericho
Philadelphia
Emmaus
Jerusalem
Jordan R.
Ashdod (Azotus)
Bethany
Bethlehem
Qumran
Ascalon
JUDEA
Hebron
Dead Sea
Arnon R.
Gaza
IDUMEA
Beersheba
NABATEA
Raphia
modern shoreline
Zered R.

0   30 mi.
0   40 km.

N W E S

Jerusalem in the Time of Jesus, Around A.D. 30

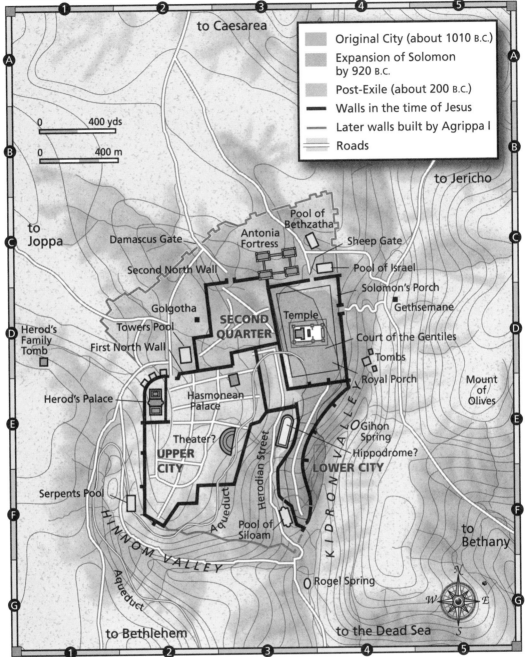

Legend:
- Original City (about 1010 B.C.)
- Expansion of Solomon by 920 B.C.
- Post-Exile (about 200 B.C.)
- Walls in the time of Jesus
- Later walls built by Agrippa I
- Roads

0 — 400 yds
0 — 400 m

to Caesarea
to Jericho
to Joppa
to Bethany
to the Dead Sea
to Bethlehem

Damascus Gate
Antonia Fortress
Pool of Bethzatha
Sheep Gate
Second North Wall
Pool of Israel
Solomon's Porch
Golgotha
Gethsemane
Towers Pool
SECOND QUARTER
Temple
Herod's Family Tomb
First North Wall
Court of the Gentiles
Tombs
Herod's Palace
Hasmonean Palace
Royal Porch
Mount of Olives
Theater?
UPPER CITY
Gihon Spring
Hippodrome?
LOWER CITY
Serpents Pool
Aqueduct
Herodian Street
Pool of Siloam
HINNOM VALLEY
KIDRON VALLEY
Aqueduct
Rogel Spring

CREDITS

Cover top Hebrew inscription on a sarcophagus: Jesus (circa B.C. 100), Erich Lessing/Art Resource, NY. **center, spine, and back cover** Sumerian terracotta tablet from the town of Shurrupak (Pre-Sargonic, 2550 BC) Erich Lessing/Art Resource, NY. **bottom** Private Palace of Cyrus the Great, Pasargadae, Iran. (Archaemenid period), SEF/Art Resource, NY.

12 Illustration by Hal Just, © ABS. **17** Hatigammana Uttarananda, Sri Lanka. "Woman at the Well," from *The Bible through Asian Eyes*, by M. Takenaka and R. O'Grady. **23** Samuel H. Kress Collection, © 1997 Board of Trustees, National Gallery of Art, Washington. **25** Illustration by Hal Just, © ABS. **29** The Saint Louis Art Museum: bequest of Curt Valentin. **34** S.M.A. Fathers. **35** © G. Dagli Orti, Paris. **40** Erich Lessing/Art Resource, NY. **45** Jyoti Sahi, Bangalore, India. "Washing the Feet," from *The Bible through Asian Eyes*, by M. Takenaka and R. O'Grady. **49** © Zev Radovan, Jerusalem. **55** Erich Lessing/Art Resource, NY. **58** Illustration by Gregor Goethals, © ABS. **59** Artist unknown/SuperStock. **61** Illustration by Gregor Goethals, © ABS. **63** Michael Smither, Taranaki, New Zealand, "Doubting Thomas," from *The Bible through Asian Eyes,* by M. Takenaka and R. O'Grady. **77,78** Illustrations by Hal Just, © ABS. **82** Illustration by Laszlo Kubinyi, © ABS. **84,85** Illustrations of scroll, stone tablets, ram's horn, candlesticks by Steve Morrell, © ABS. Illustration of barley by Gregor Goethals, © ABS. Illustration of loaves of bread by Theresa Heidel, (c) ABS. Illustration of priest with scapegoat by Hal Just, © ABS. Illustration of shelter by Kate McKeon, © ABS. **87** Scala/Art Resource, NY. **91** Statuette of the goddess Isis and the child Horus, Egyptian, Late Period (c. 664-332 BC) Louvre, Paris, France/Peter Willi/Bridgeman Art Library. **92** Erich Lessing/Art Resource, NY. **93** Vanni/Art Resource, NY. **98** Erich Lessing/Art Resource, NY. **100** Grec **139** f. 136v The Penitence of David, with David and Nathan, from a psalter, 10th century/Bibliothèque nationale de France/Bridgeman Art Library **101** Woodcut print by Sally Barton Elliott, 1973. **103** Erich Lessing/Art Resource, NY. **105** © North Wind Picture Archives. **110** Illustration by Hal Just, © ABS. **top left photo inset** Collection of the Israel Antiquities Authority, courtesy of the G. Barkay, Ketef Hinnom Expedition. **top right photo inset** Photograph by Bencini Raffaello, Florence, Italy, © American Bible Society Archives. **112,124,127** Illustrations by Hal Just, © ABS. **138-141** Maps by Joe LeMonier, © ABS.